If I
Ever
Get Back
to Georgia,
I'm Gonna
Nail
My Feet
to the
Ground

If I Ever Get Back to Georgia, I'm Gonna Nail My Feet to the Ground

LEWIS GRIZZARD

Published by Random House
Large Print in association with

VILLARD BOOKS
NEW YORK 1990

TO BISHER,
WHO KNEW WHAT HE WAS TALKING
ABOUT AFTER ALL

THIS LARGE PRINT BOOK CARRIES
THE SEAL OF APPROVAL OF N.A.V.H.

Copyright © 1990 by Lewis Grizzard
All rights reserved under International and Pan-American Copyright Conventions.
Published in the United States by Villard Books, a division of Random House, Inc.,
New York, and simultaneously in Canada by Random House of Canada Limited,
Toronto.

Villard Books is a registered trademark of Random House, Inc.

Library of Congress Cataloging-in-Publication Data
Grizzard, Lewis.
If I ever get back to Georgia, I'm gonna nail my feet to the ground /
by Lewis Grizzard.
    p.   cm.
ISBN 0-679-40046-X (lg. print)
1. Chicago Sun-Times—Humor. 2. Newspapers—Humor. I. Title.
PN6162.G786 1990   814'.54—dc20   90-50225

9 8 7 6 5 4 3 2
First Large Print Edition

If I
Ever
Get Back
to **Georgia,**
I'm **Gonna**
Nail
My Feet
to the
Ground

1

Before I became a newspaper *columnist,* which is the job I currently am holding down and will continue to hold as long as I don't get fired, don't say to hell with all of it and open a liquor store, and don't die, I was a newspaper*man.* Newspaper columnists aren't really newspaper-men, or newspaperwomenpersons, as one might think.

Columnists don't have anything to do with the editing of the paper, the way a paper looks, or how the news is displayed. Unless we start stinking it up for a long period of time, we also never get punished; no one ever makes us columnists go out in the cold at four in the morning to deliver the thing to the readers' doorsteps.

I don't think people who deliver the paper get enough credit, quite frankly. I don't care how good the paper is, if the man or woman who is responsible for having it on your lawn—come rain, sleet, snow, or hangover—falters, what difference does it make if four gorillas and an orangutan produce the paper?

(Of course, four gorillas and an orangutan could put out a better newspaper than the ones some people try to shove down the readers' throats. Most gorillas and orangutans I know at least aren't pinko, left-wing communist bed-wetters, which a lot of newspaper people are.)

Newspaper columnists aren't reporters, either. We can simply make things up if we want to. I, for instance, make stuff up all the time. I once made up an interview I had with God. God said, "Tell Jimmy Swaggart he's fired." If I actually had interviewed God, I'm convinced that's one of the things He would have said, along with, "Boy, was the ayatollah surprised when we met him at the Pearly Gates with a bazooka."

I even quoted my dog once. I wrote, "My dog drinks out of the toilet. One day, I said to my dog, 'Why do you go to the toilet on my living room rug?' And my dog said, 'Well, you go in my water bowl.' "

A reporter couldn't have quoted my dog because my dog can't talk. He can barely bark anymore after he ate a wasp's nest one day. You get a couple hundred wasp stings on your vocal chords, and you'll have trouble barking, too. Now, my dog barks in a whisper. He goes, "WHOOF."

I knew a guy who had a dog who actually could talk, however. (Now you have to guess if I'm making this up or not. Being a columnist is great fun.)

He took his dog into a bar one day and said to the bartender, "For a free drink, my dog will talk to you."

It had been a long day, so the bartender said, "What the hell. You got your free drink, now let me hear the dog talk."

The guy says, "Okay, ask him who was the greatest home-run hitter of all time."

The bartender asks the dog, "Okay, dog, who was the greatest home-run hitter of all time?" and the dog responds, "Roof."

So that riles the bartender and he throws the guy and the dog out the door of the bar. The guy and the dog roll out onto the sidewalk and land in the street.

The dog gets up, licks a few asphalt burns, and says to his master, "I still say it was Roof. Hank Aaron had more at bats."

Other things I made up and printed in my column:

* The Beatles caused the Vietnam War.
* Jerry Falwell runs rabbits.
* Bugs Bunny is gay.
* Nobody actually lives in North Dakota.
* Muamar Qaddafi and former major-league baseball pitcher Joaquim Andujar are the same person.
* Eating liver causes shortness of breath, zits, flatfeet, anxiety, and prolonged menstrual periods.
* Richard Nixon was born wearing a suit.
* In a fit of rage, Buffalo Bob once whittled Howdy Doody into a likeness of Pinocchio and bit off his nose.
* Elvis actually *is* dead. Of course, nobody really believed that. I had a letter from a woman in Topeka who said Elvis had appeared at her Tupperware party disguised as a plastic egg carton.

"We weren't really sure it was Him," she wrote, "until he recited the entire dialogue from his movie *Viva Las Vegas.* We all got nekkid and danced around him while he sang 'Down in the Ghetto.' It was a religious experience."

Newspaper reporters, of course, occasionally do make things up, but not all the time. Only in emergencies. Which is why there was that story about the Exxon oil spill in Alaska. It was a slow news day, and an editor in Fairbanks said to his environmental reporter, "We don't have a thing other than another Eskimo eaten by a walrus. Why don't you make up a story about an Exxon oil tanker spilling a couple of billions of gallons of oil in Prince Rupert Sound?"

The reporter said, "Give me thirty minutes," and came back with a story about a drunken tanker captain who put some dingbat at the wheel, who promptly runs into a reef and spills a bunch of oil, which kills a bunch of fish and birds.

The editor and reporter didn't think the story would make it out of Alaska, but suddenly it went worldwide, and it took the entire news staff all night to fill up Prince Rupert Sound with No. 2 ink to make the story look as if it actually happened.

Watergate never really happened either; Woodward and Bernstein and *Washington Post* editor Ben Bradlee made the whole thing up as a joke on Richard Nixon on his birthday.

Woodward, Bernstein, and Bradlee got soused one night at the Sans Souci, and Bradlee said, "Hey, you wanna get one on Nixon?"

Bradlee was Woodward and Bernstein's boss. What were they going to say, "Forget it, Jason, let's have another drink"?

Of course not. That's another thing about reporters: If your editor makes a suggestion, you follow it as gospel.

"So," Bernstein said (Woodward was too drunk to comment), "what did you have in mind?"

"Let's make up a story about Nixon being involved in some sort of cover-up," said Bradley, just before he screamed at the waitress, Nora Ephron, "Hey, bitch. Who do you have to know to get a drink around here, Linda Lovelace?"

Bernstein, who also needed another drink, said to waitress Ephron, "Right, what's the holdup here?"

And waitress Ephron replied, "One day, you'll be sorry you talked that way to me," and dumped a Perrier she was taking to John Tower right on Bernstein's crotch.

Just then, Jack Nicholson walked in with Rob Lowe. The plot thickens.

Anyway, so Bradlee and Woodward and Bernstein concoct this story about a third-rate burglary at National Democratic Headquarters and, as happened in Alaska later, things got out of hand. Bernstein, at least, got punished. He wound up marrying Nora Ephron, who later divorced him, and then later still wrote all about their marriage and divorce, which wound up as a movie called *Heartburn,* starring Jack Nicholson and Meryl Streep.

Even Nicholson couldn't save that dog. The worst two movies in the past five years? I mean, besides all those movies like *Friday the 13th* ad nauseam, where nobody in the cast is over seventeen except Freddie. They are 1. *The Accidental Tourist* and 2. *Heartburn. Amadeus* is third, incidentally, followed closely by *The Last Temptation of Christ.*

And speaking of Rob Lowe, he just goes to show you how even the best reporters often miss a great story.

The Democrats held their 1988 national convention in Atlanta, where I live. The editors at the *Atlanta Journal and Constitution,* where I work, got very excited about the convention coming to town and spent about half the Vietnam War debt covering it. (Notice, I didn't use the normal cliché, "the French War debt." That's because I've never forgiven the French for not letting us fly over their airspace when we wanted to bomb Qaddafi/Andujar or for how they treated President Bush's entourage when he went over to help them celebrate the bicentennial of Bastille Day. Imagine not giving all four thousand members of the entourage VIP treatment.)

I wasn't all that excited about the convention coming to Atlanta myself. Bring a World Series to Atlanta, now you've got a story. Having a World Series in Atlanta would be sort of like holding the Winter Olympics in Miami. Both would be Man-Bites-Dog stories of the highest order.

The problem with spending all that money and effort covering the convention was that everybody knew what was going to happen before it happened. Let's say the entire country already knew San Francisco was going to beat Denver in the Super Bowl. How many reporters would show up for the game?

Everybody knew Dukakis was going to get the nomination. Everybody knew Jesse Jackson would make speeches that sounded great unless you actually listened to what he was saying. And that is exactly what happened. But with hundreds of newspeople in town, nobody got the big story. The Rob Lowe story.

It's too much fun not to do over again.

Rob Lowe is the actor. Actually, I think I should make that "actor." The kid looks good, which I assume is how he got into the movies. As an actor, he couldn't carry Bill Frawley's derby hat.

For some reason I am yet to determine, Rob Lowe came to the Democratic Convention in Atlanta. Maybe he had a thing for Kitty Dukakis.

See what you can get away with if you're a columnist?

I write, "Maybe he had a thing for Kitty Duka-kis," and you read it and tell somebody, "You know what Lewis Grizzard wrote in his latest book?"

And they say, "You mean the one called *If I Ever Get Back to Georgia, I'm Gonna Nail My Feet to the Ground,* that costs $19.95 and everybody in the country should go out and buy immediately?"

And you say, "That's the one. He wrote, 'Maybe Rob Lowe had a thing for Kitty Duka-kis'!"

Your friend tells the story a couple of more times, and one day you pick up *USA Today* and there's a story saying, "ROB LOWE DENIES HAVING KINKY SEX WITH KITTY DU-KAKIS IN DEMOCRATIC LOVE NEST." Rumormongering is another fun thing about being a columnist.

But back to the convention. Rob Lowe shows

up with a guy who was referred to as a "traveling companion." They hit an Atlanta joint called Club Rio across the street from the convention site. There they meet these two girls, and Rob and his pal take them back to their hotel suite and set up a video camera. They invite the two girls to perform a little lesbian thing and they record the performance, quite a smashing one (a *lot* better than *Amadeus*), according to those who later saw the videotape.

What transpired afterward was the big news. One of the girls on the tape was only sixteen. A minor. Only six years out of the fifth grade. She later allegedly tried to blackmail Rob Lowe because if she goes to the cops, Rob gets hit with all sorts of nasty things such as contributing to the delinquency of a minor, making child pornography, and having sex in the Bible Belt.

Then, the sixteen-year-old's mom sees the tape, and she sues Rob Lowe. At this writing, nothing involving the incident has been settled, but do you see what I mean? How does Rob Lowe getting a sixteen-year-old and her buddy to get naked and do it to one another on a video camera in a hotel room compare with Lloyd Bentsen's acceptance speech as far as reader interest goes? No comparison. Rob and the lesbian stuff wins hands down over Lloyd and his recommendations for the economy. But Lloyd was front-page news.

It took six months for the Rob Lowe story to break.

I realize at this point that I have strayed far off the original path I had intended for this, the opening chapter, but I wanted to throw in some stuff about celebrities and sex to get you this far.

My theory is that if somebody goes into a bookstore and starts browsing through a book, whether or not they buy it probably depends on how they enjoy the first few pages. You can't stand around in a bookstore and read an entire book and then put it back on the shelf, thereby actually *stealing* the book, unless, of course, it is *very* short, which is why most writers make their books so long. Tolstoy, for instance, was so concerned about somebody doing that to *War and Peace* that he wrote one of the longest books in the history of books.

So I'm going for the sensational and the prurient early, figuring the browser might say, "Hey, this is pretty exciting stuff. I'd better buy this book so I don't miss what else is in it."

I'm not saying there isn't going to be any more juicy information here. (I'll make up some if I have to—remember, I'm a columnist.) But now let us go ahead with the book's main thesis.

This is going to be about newspapers, because since I was eight I've been in love with them, and because people have the damnedest ideas about newspapers and a great deal of fascination with them, as well.

How could you be literate and not be fascinated with newspapers? Every day of most people's lives, a newspaper sneaks in there at some point. They are delivered right to our homes, just like pizza, only pizza is more expensive. There's another connection, too: Newspapers and pizza can both give you heartburn.

I love newspapers because they are a constant in my life. No matter what happened to me the night before, I know there will be a newspaper on my lawn the next morning. It's my little friend.

I get up. I put on the coffee. I go outside and get my little friend. Then, I read it and drink my coffee.

Everybody has a different method of reading their newspaper, I suppose. Mine is another constant in my life. I always read the paper—any paper—the same way: I glance at the front page first. If no war has been declared, no tidal wave is expected to hit my neighborhood, and no announcement that cigarettes really don't cause cancer, or other such astounding news, I then go directly to the sports section.

I read everything in the sports section that isn't about hockey, soccer, and hunting. I've said for years, if the deer had guns, too, then, and only then, would hunting really be a sport.

I go back to the front page after I finish reading sports. I read very few news stories with foreign datelines because I basically don't care about what's going on in South Yemen. I should, but I don't. I think I'm a fairly normal reader, and the fairly normal reader usually wants to read about what's going on in his or her hometown. No matter how the jet airplane has shrunk the world, it's still difficult for somebody in Meridian, Miss., or Minot, N.D., to care what's doing four or five thousand miles away in some place covered with sand, unless they know somebody there.

I quote a colleague of mine who, during a discussion concerning what emphasis should be put on international stories, said, "I don't give a damn what happened last night in Outer Mongolia. I just want to know who cut who down at Slick's Lounge."

People were always getting cut (southern for "knifed") at Slick's in Atlanta. And shot, too. Two guys got into an argument about who was the better wrestler, Vern Gange or Argentina Rocca, and one guy pulled a gun and shot at the other guy. He missed and hit an innocent by-stander in the knee, instead.

I happened to know the emergency room doctor that treated the victim.

When he asked the patient what happened, the patient replied, "Man, I was just sittin' there drinkin' a Schlitz and some fool shot my ass in the knee."

If something really interesting or odd happened in a foreign country, I will read that, however.

There was a story about a British Airways jet recently. The windshield in the cockpit blew out at 23,000 feet and it sucked the pilot out. Luckily, another crew member grabbed his feet and held on to him until the copilot could land a half-hour later.

That's even better than a guy getting knifed in the stomach at Slick's for saying Richard Petty couldn't have carried Fireball Roberts's lug wrench.

I usually get through most of the "A" section in a paper fairly quickly, stopping only to read good political gossip, and the latest on where the killer bees are now located and how long it will take them to get to my house.

Then, I read the editorial pages. I rarely read the unsigned editorials that come under the newspaper masthead. They are usually about something happening in South Yemen.

I enjoy the readers' letters, however, especially the ones from members of the National Rifle Association who say if we outlaw the sales of AK-47's, the favorite weapon of drug dealers and drive-by murderers, they may also eventually lose their hunting guns and that they are actually doing the deer a favor by shooting them. If we ever do take away the AK-47's from drug dealers, I think we ought to give them to the deer.

I also enjoy editorial columns on the op-ed page. I'm always amazed how angry readers get at columnists. If Carl Rowan or William Safire or Richard Reeves writes an opinion, it's his prerogative. I might say to myself, "Carl Rowan must have drunk some bad buttermilk when he wrote this," or "What on earth was William Safire trying to say?" But I don't ever get mad at them and call down to the paper and threaten to cancel my subscription. Disagreeing with a columnist is a lot of fun. A good columnist will stir debate and reaction.

After the editorial page, I read the feature section of the paper which has names like "Lifestyle" and "People" and "Arts and Leisure." That section usually has the comics, the TV and movie listings, and a lot of stuff women enjoy reading, like Dear Abby and stories about how women will soon take over the entire world and tell all the men to get up and go cook their own breakfasts and "Don't let me hear any pots or pans rattling."

News for and about women is big in those sections. "News you can use" is a new catch phrase in the industry, which means running a lot of stories about why you should eat oat bran and how to make your house safe from radon gas.

I do the Jumble every morning. That's where you unscramble four words in order to figure out the answer to a puzzle.

Okay, in ten seconds, what is this word: "Tigura"?

Time's up. "Guitar." It took me an hour one morning to get that. I only glance at the business section because I don't understand much about business.

Reading my morning paper is, quite often, the highlight of my day. I'm always a little sad when I finish. To put off finishing the paper as long as I can, I even read stories about art exhibits. If I'm really desperate, I'll even read Scheinwood on bridge. And I don't know the first thing about bridge. I just don't want it to be over.

I fell in love with newspapers when I was eight because they took me to every minor league and major league baseball game. They taught me about Duke Snider and Senor Al Lopez, the manager of the Chicago White Sox. I could sit in Moreland, Georgia, and read about Mantle's three home runs for the Yankees. There were a lot of people in the rural South who didn't think there really was a New York City. Nobody knew anybody who had actually been there. But I'd been there, in my sports page box score where the Tigers' Yankee Killer, Frank Lary, had beaten the Yanks again before 40,000 in Yankee Stadium.

I'd also been to Wrigley Field in Chicago and Tiger Stadium in Detroit and Crosley Field in Cincinnati and Connie Mack Stadium in Philadelphia.

I can go on all day about this, so here are "25 More Reasons I Love Newspapers Besides All the Stuff I've Already Talked About":

1. They ain't heavy, except on Sunday.
2. The Far Side.
3. Mike Royko's column out of Chicago.
4. You don't have to look at the ads if you won't want to. It's hard to escape television commercials no matter how fast your remote control finger is.
5. Editorial cartoons.

6. They are brief about the weather: "Today: Cloudy with a high near 75." Television weather lasts longer than some thunderstorms.
7. Baseball box scores that can tell you exactly what twenty-three guys did in a two-and-a-half-hour period in about three inches of agate type.
8. Peanuts.
9. B.C.
10. Adult movie ads. I once saw one called "Thar She Blows."
11. Occasionally I have the pleasant surprise of finding humorous writing on the editorial page.
12. The personal ads. They keep me up on what's kinky.
13. As I read my paper, I often fantasize about owning my own newspaper. Its slogan would be "Born to Raise Hell."
14. They don't play any loud rock music.
15. The fact there's a crossword puzzle in every day in case I ever decide to take up doing the crossword puzzle.
16. If you read a newspaper every day, there will be very few topics you can't talk about.

17. The Wizard of Id.

18. College football and basketball odds.

19. Those "People" columns where they tell you what's doing with Prince Charles and Lady Di and Elizabeth Taylor.

20. You can serve your dog leftover steak bones on a newspaper.

21. You can be going through your grandmother's attic and find a paper from 1939 and have a lot of fun reading it. You will want to say, "Watch out for Hitler."

22. Newspapers make great starters for fireplace fires.

23. Automobile dealers can't do their own commercials.

24. Newspapers are the only romance in my life that hasn't eventually picked up and left me.

25. If you really think about it, newspapers are one of the last great bargains. Most daily newspapers cost a quarter. What else can you get for a quarter that tells you how various wars and famines are going, how much money you lost in the stock market or betting on a ball game, what new thing will kill you according to researchers, how many people got killed

in the latest soccer riot, how many people are going to have AIDS by the year
2015, what Congress did, how bad the
president is doing, what the weather is
going to be like, not to mention informing
you of the day and month and year it is?

What really gets me is, after all the service
newspapers give people, most people don't
really *like* newspapers. Perhaps it's the old
messenger-who-brings-the-bad-news thing. A
newspaper tells you the ozone layer is going to
disappear in twenty years and you're going to be
fried alive, and you get mad at the newspaper.

Readers are always asking, "Why don't you
print more good news?" The answer is simple:
There's not any.

If there were any good news, we'd print it.
Let's say I was interviewing God again, and He
said, "Tell everybody we're going to throw out
the Sixth Commandment on Judgment Day."

You recall the Sixth Commandment. Moses
tried to get God to forget it in the first place, but
God didn't know at the time that the Playboy
Channel would come along on cable and make
everybody want to commit adultery.

So now God realizes "Thou shalt not commit
adultery" isn't really an operative thought any-

more, and He tells me He's going to overlook it for everybody born since 1945, except for Jimmy Swaggart, of course. God would have forgiven him for simply committing adultery, but he couldn't forgive him for selecting that sweat hog he found in a New Orleans motel room as his adultery-ette.

Anyway, if that story broke, it would indeed be good news and newspapers would carry it, front page, top story.

The New York *Daily News* would say:

"GOD ON SEX: 'LIVE IT UP'"

The New York Post would say:

"I WANT YOUR BODY"

The New York Times would say, in a headline size much more dignified than that of the *Daily News* and *Post:*

"GOD GRANTS FORGIVENESS FOR ADULTERY FOR THOSE BORN AFTER 1945."

Followed by these subheads, in descending type size:

"SUPREME BEING INDICATES SIXTH COMMANDMENT PASSÉ"

"PLAYBOY'S HEFNER
ELATED AT NEWS"

"POPE STARTLED,
CANCELS TRIP"

"THOUSANDS CELEBRATE
IN TIMES SQUARE"

"WADE BOGGS GOES 5-FOR-5
IN BOSOX ROMP OVER YANKS"

So this is to be a book about newspapers, written by a man who has been both a newspaperman and a newspaper columnist, and that makes me an expert on just about everything about newspapers except how to sell advertising, how to crank the delivery trucks, and why the accounting department always questions my expense accounts. This is also going to be a book about how and why I got into the newspaper business and where it has taken me. Not all of it will be pretty. I'll have to deal with my days as sports editor of the Chicago *Sun-Times,* for instance. This was the worst period of my life. I was dragged to court by one of my sportswriters, divorced by my second wife, once sat next to a man who had a rooster on his head on a Chicago Transit bus, and had to help push a friend's car, which had a dead battery, eight blocks through the snow, quite a shock to my southern-born hatred of cold weather.

To work your tail off getting a paper out, and then be handed a first edition, which always felt warm to me somehow, like it had just been taken out of the oven, was a joy. It was instant reward. I would never have been happy in a business where it took more than forty-five minutes to see the results of my labor.

And after I got into the business, I met a thousand characters who loved newspapers as I did and didn't really give a damn they were getting paid so poorly.

There were so many other rewards. Like knowing we got the news first and it was our job to tell everybody else. It's an awesome responsibility, but it's also good for the ego. I always felt a little superior to civilians.

I got my first newspaper job when I was ten. I didn't get paid, but I did get to see my name above an article for the first time, and it was a thrill the likes of which I have not often known again.

That makes thirty-four years in the profession. I mentioned earlier that, one day, I might quit all this and open a liquor store, but I won't.

In the immortal words of Frank Hyland, a friend and colleague, "Wouldn't it be hell to have to go out and get a real job?"

It would.

2

If it hadn't been for my Uncle Grover, who married my mother's sister, Aunt Jessie, I could have wound up in any number of careers other than newspapering. The fact I give my Uncle Grover credit for getting me started toward the profession I chose is a little strange when I tell you Uncle Grover, oddly enough, was illiterate.

Uncle Grover had grown up hard and poor and had gone to work in a cotton mill in Carroll County, Georgia, when he was ten, and he never really escaped.

He married my Aunt Jessie in the thirties and moved to the next county and tiny Moreland, Georgia, in the early fifties. They had four chil-

dren by this time, and both worked in the Moreland Knitting Mill, which produced women's hosiery. Aunt Jessie sat at a sewing machine ten
hours a day for a pittance and Uncle Grover was
in charge of keeping whatever machinery there
is in a knitting mill in running order. Uncle Grover
may not have been able to read or write, but he
could take apart most any machine and put it
back together again with all of the parts in the
same position as they were when he started.
This is a gift.

People came to my Uncle Grover from all over
the county to have him work on their tractors,
trucks, automobiles, and power lawn mowers,
which is another story. I'm not sure when power
lawn mowers were invented, but one didn't appear in Moreland until the late 1950s. Boyce
Kilgore ordered one from Sears and Roebuck. It
had a rope crank to it and an adjustable blade
(it went up and down). You still had to push it,
like the mowers of old, but the engine made a
nice sound and it cut more evenly than the pow-
erless mowers and Boyce said it made cutting
the grass a real pleasure.

He shouldn't have said that, because everybody took him literally and began offering him
the opportunity to cut lawns all over town.

He also inherited the grass-cutting job at both the Methodist and Baptist churches, not to mention both parsonages.

Boyce finally admitted to Loot Starkins he was, and I quote him, "goddamn tired of cutting every goddamn blade of goddamn grass in this goddamn town," and Loot said, "Hell, Boyce, that's what you get for thinking you're better than everybody else and going out and buying yourself a power lawn mower."

What all that has to do with my Uncle Grover is beyond me, except that Boyce's power lawn mower did quit running one day, and Uncle Grover offered to fix it for him, but Boyce said, "Goddamnit, Grover, you put one hand on that goddamn power lawn mower and your ass is mine."

Boyce never did have his power mower repaired until three or four others had popped up around town, and he could pass on his heavy grass-cutting duties to somebody else.

Uncle Grover's mechanical sense actually came close to making him rich. I know very little about machines, so I can't be specific here, but Uncle Grover tinkered around with one of the machines at the hosiery mill and altered it so it would do approximately twice the work it was doing before in half the time.

Before you knew it, all sorts of big business-
men and slick-talking lawyers descended upon
Uncle Grover. And this confused him greatly.
He'd had so little in his life, and now he was
getting offers of thousands of dollars for the
rights to his invention.

It was unfortunate that Uncle Grover was illiterate, because what eventually happened was
he sold the rights to his invention to a big cotton
man from Memphis for a check for twenty-five
thousand dollars. Memphis went on to make
millions from Uncle Grover's genius.

But Uncle Grover did take some of his money
and spent it on two things he wanted all his adult
life—a new Pontiac and a trip to the Kentucky
Derby. Nobody, not even Aunt Jessie, knew
Uncle Grover cared anything for thoroughbred
racing, but it turned out that he did, and he and
Aunt Jessie drove the new Pontiac to Louisville
for the Derby.

Uncle Grover never would say if he won any
money betting at the Derby, but did tell everybody about the motel he and Aunt Jessie stayed
in outside Chattanooga that had a bed that
would vibrate if you put a quarter in the slot on
the night table and about how smoothly the Pontiac ran.

After he returned from the Derby, Uncle

Grover went back to the knitting mill and resumed his duties, making sure the machines he invented that made the guy in Memphis filthy rich operated properly. Uncle Grover and Aunt Jessie never moved out of the house they were living in before the twenty-five big ones, and Uncle Grover was still driving the '54 Pontiac when he died in the late sixties.

Now, how Uncle Grover had a part in starting me toward journalism:

My parents separated when I was six, and my mother and I moved in with her parents in More- land. My grandparents lived next door to Uncle Grover and Aunt Jessie.

My grandfather was still able to farm twelve acres back then, and certain agricultural chores were placed upon me even at my tender age.

I was in charge of gathering the eggs from the henhouse in the morning, rain or shine. That wouldn't have been such a difficult task had it not been for the fact my grandfather's rooster, Garland, didn't like me. The minute I would set foot in the henhouse, Garland would charge at me. Six-year-old boys aren't that much bigger than a rooster. I had to gather the eggs while defending myself from a crazed rooster with my legs, my hands being occupied with the eggs, of course.

"Get back, you goddamn rooster!" I screamed out one morning, unaware that my grandmother, a foot-washing Baptist, was in earshot. After a fifteen-minute sermon, based on the Commandment that says, "Thou shalt not take the Lord's name in vain," my grandmother cut a switch off a small tree and thrashed me severely.

"When you say your prayers tonight," she scolded me, "you must ask God to forgive you for what I heard you say in the henhouse."

That night I prayed, "I'm sorry I said what I did in the henhouse, and would you please kill that goddamn rooster for me?"

Garland, however, was the Methuselah of roosters. I forget the exact year he died, but he outlived all the hens and two of my dogs.

The henhouse experience was enough to sour me against agriculture, but there were other things that made me even more certain I wanted no part of any career that had to do with dirt and attack roosters.

I had to pull corn one Saturday morning. There I was, relaxing with a bowl of Rice Krispies, when my grandfather said, "I need you to help me pull corn this morning."

Corn doesn't want to be pulled. It's more stubborn than a rooster protecting his harem. Ears of corn grow on the cornstalks, and the idea is to separate the ears from the stalks. Mr. T. probably wouldn't have any trouble pulling corn, because he can lift a Roto-Rooter van. But not me. I was a small, thin boy and my hands developed blisters and my grandfather said things like, "You'll never make a good farmer if you don't learn how to pull corn."

"If he thinks I'm going to be a farmer," I said to myself, "he is sadly mistaken, e-i-e-i-o."

I won't go into all the stuff about shelling butter beans and digging up potatoes and planting tomatoes and going out, as they said in those days, to pick a mess of turnip greens. Simply know that as I hurried toward an age that included double figures, I was certain agriculture wasn't in my future.

Some might tell a youngster that he doesn't have to pick a career until he's older, but that's wrong. The earlier you decide what you are going to do in life, the bigger head start you get in pursuit of same.

My father had been a soldier, but I didn't want to be a soldier. All that marching. My mother was a schoolteacher, but I didn't want any part of that, either. Imagine having to go to school every day for your entire life.

I toyed with the idea of driving a train for a

while. The Crescent Limited ran through Moreland between Atlanta and New Orleans on the
Atlanta and West Point Railroad, and it seemed
all the guy who drove the train had to do was sit
there and blow the horn. I mean, you didn't have
to learn a lot about steering.

After that, I considered opening a truck stop.
The only businesses Moreland had was the knit-
ting mill, Cureton and Cole's store, Bohannon's
Service Station, Johnson's Service Station and
Grocery Store, the Our House beer joint, and
Steve Smith's truck stop.

A boy could learn a lot in a place like Steve
Smith's truck stop. Steve was sweet on my
mother, I think, and before she remarried (another guy), she would take me down to Steve's
for a cheeseburger. We'd sit in one of the
booths, and I'd eat while Steve and my mother
would talk.

Among the wonders I saw at Steve's was a
pinball machine that truckers would pour dime
after dime into. I didn't know it at the time, but
Steve paid off on the pinball machines. Let's say
you aligned three balls, you won twenty free
games. Steve paid a dime for each free game.
The more dimes you put into the machine, the
more free games you would win. Legend had it
a man driving for Yellow Freight scored two

thousand free games one night and won two hundred dollars. That legend brought truckers in by the droves, and Steve was just sitting there talking to my mother getting rich while truckers fed his pinball machine because of the two-thousand-free-game rumor. Advertising, false or otherwise, pays.

There was also one of those beer signs in Steve's where the little strands of color danced across the sign.

"How does that work?" I asked Steve one night.

"It's magic, kid," he said, and went back to talking to my mother.

I went to the rest room one night at Steve's and noticed a strange machine on the wall. There was a place to put a quarter for what was described on the machine as a "Ribbed French-Tickler—Drive Her Wild."

My mother wouldn't allow me near the pinball machines, but here was my chance to do a little gambling on my own. I happened to have a quarter, which I put in the slot. Lo and behold, I won. I received a small package and immediately opened it. There was a balloon inside. I filled it with air, tied a knot on the end, and walked out with it.

"Look, Mom," I said. "I put a quarter in the machine and got this balloon."

"Gimme that," said Steve, trying to take my balloon away. He ordered the waitress to bring me another Coke. In addition to the balloon, I also got a Coke out of the deal, so I figured the quarter had been well invested.

After the urge to open a truck stop when I grew up passed, I even had a brief flirtation with the idea of becoming a minister. My grandmother was always talking about her sister's boy, Arnold, who "made a preacher."

I wondered, how hard could it be being a preacher? You figure there's Wednesday night prayer meeting, then the Sunday service. Throw in a few weddings and funerals here and there, and that's about it. Also, somebody would always be trying to get you over to their house to eat, and nobody serves anything bad to eat to preachers. Plus, you'd never have to cut your own grass.

Only a few days into my thoughts of become a minister, however, an older cousin explained to me a minister wasn't allowed to do all the things I was looking forward to doing when I became an adult. Namely, drinking, smoking, cussing whenever you wanted to, and, since by that time I had learned what the balloon in the machine at Steve's truck stop was all about, I figured preachers likely would be denied that little pearl, too. I got off the minister thing in a hurry.

At this point, we finally have arrived at where this chapter was headed. I tend to run on now and then, but that is called "expanding a theme," which really is nothing more than vamping, which is nothing more than stalling, for which I apologize. But it has always been one of my weaknesses. I showed up at all three of my marriages late and, as a writer, I am notorious for putting off projects for as long as I possibly can. I should have written this book, for instance, five or six years ago, but I stalled, hoping someone else would do one of those unauthorized biographies of me and include all this, so I could stall around on something else.

I'm doing it again.

As I said, Uncle Grover couldn't read. But each day when he and Aunt Jessie left the mill to drive home for lunch, a quarter-mile away, they would stop by the post office, which was next to the knitting mill. There they would stop to pick up their mailed morning edition of the *Atlanta Constitution* and bring it home with them at lunch. Atlanta was a lot farther from Moreland back then than it is now.

When I was ten, it was at least five thousand miles to Atlanta, because I knew my chances of ever getting there were quite slim. Today, it's thirty-five minutes by interstate. My grandmother's yard looks a lot smaller to me when I see it now, too, so you know what time does to a lot of things. Shrinks them.

By the time I was ten, my brain was well on its way to being consumed by baseball. A lot of boys are like that, of course, but I may have gone to extremes heretofore unachieved. I never actually ate a baseball, or any other piece of baseball equipment, but I did sleep with the baseball my grandfather gave me for my birthday, and probably the only reason I didn't eat it was I knew my grandfather certainly was not a man of means and might have had a difficult time replacing it with any sense of dispatch.

There was a marvelous baseball team in Atlanta when I was ten. They were the Atlanta Crackers. For years, I thought they were named the Crackers because they had to do with, well, crackers.

Later, I would learn that the term came from the fact Georgians were bad to carry around whips in the days of Jim Crow and slavery. And whips go "crack," and, thus, the name of the ball team. But at ten, in 1956, my world was an almost totally isolated one, and I finally decided the name had something to do with saltines, but I didn't have time to figure out exactly why or how.

How I came to fall in love with the Atlanta Crackers, I just remembered, should have come earlier, but remember my admissions about stalling.

Remember the part about Uncle Grover getting the twenty-five big ones for diddling with the machine at the knitting mill and how he bought a new Pontiac and took Jessie to the Kentucky Derby?

Well, that's not all he did. He also bought the first television set in Moreland. When word got out, people came from as far away as Grantville, Luthersville, and Corinth to get a glimpse of Uncle Grover's and Aunt Jessie's amazing box. It had about an eight-inch screen, if I recall correctly, and you had to sit real close if you wanted to see any detail, such as whether or not someone on the screen actually had a head. The adults would watch John Cameron Swayze on the national news and Vernon Niles, who claimed to be his second cousin from Corinth, would always say, "If that's John Cameron's head, I've seen better hair on fatback."

Even my grandmother became interested in television once she witnessed *TV Ranch,* a musical show that came on an Atlanta station each day at noon.

TV Ranch featured Boots and Woody Woodall singing country music as well as a comedian named Horsehair Buggfuzz, who probably said a lot of funny things, but I can't remember any of them.

What my grandmother enjoyed most about *TV Ranch* was the closing number, which featured Boots and Woody in the day's "song of inspiration."

This was your basic hymn, like "Rock of Ages," "Precious Memories," "When the Roll is Called Up Yonder (I'll Be There)," or "Shall We Gather at the River?" But every now and then, they'd sing a comedy-hymn Horsehair Buggfuzz wrote, like "When the Lord Calls Me Home, I Hope Mildred Haines Ain't on the Party Line, 'Cause He'll Never Get Through If She Is."

The second most endearing thing to me about Uncle Grover and Aunt Jessie's television was *Lucky 11 Theatre,* which featured a western movie each afternoon at five.

Johnny Mack Brown would walk into a crowded saloon and say, at the top of his lungs, "I'll have a milk!" which always seemed to me to be inviting trouble.

In the first place, if it was milk he wanted, why did he go into a saloon? I would spend a great amount of time in saloons later in my life, and I don't remember anybody ever walking in and ordering a glass of milk, although I did know an old trombone player once who drank scotch and milk. After a few drinks, he'd play air trombone, which I like to think of as spiritual father to the air guitar.

Why didn't Johnny Mack Brown hit a convenience store if he wanted milk? Oh, there weren't any convenience stores in the Old West. There were all those cows, though. If Johnny Mack had wanted milk so badly, he could simply have pulled one off of the range somewhere and self-served himself all the milk he wanted.

But no. Johnny Mack Brown had to walk into a crowded saloon where there were always ornery galoots.

As soon as he'd order the milk, the piano player would stop playing, the dance-hall girls would stop dancing, and a cowboy in a black hat at the bar would say, "Give 'im a shot of red-eye, Sam." (All bartenders in old western movies were named Sam.) "He needs a little hair on his chest."

Johnny Mack Brown, who had been a famous football player at the University of Alabama, would say something akin to, "If it's all the same to you, padnuh, I think I'll just stick to my milk."

It *never* was the same to the guy in the black

hat, and a fight would always ensue in which thousands of dollars of damage would be done to the saloon. Nobody had insurance back then, either, is my guess.

All western movies also ended with the grandfather of the automobile chase scene. The star, whether he be Johnny Mack Brown, Hoot Gibson, Lash LaRue, the Durango Kid, Roy Rogers, Gene Autry, Gunther Toody (Forget him. He wasn't a cowboy. I just tossed him in to see if you were paying attention.), Tom Mix, Bob Steele, Wild Bill Elliott, *ad cowboyseam,* would chase down the bad guy in the last moments of the movie and jump off his horse, taking the bad guy off his.

They would then tumble down a hill like a couple of tumbling tumbleweeds, and once they had stopped tumbling, would get up and fight. The Johnny Mack Browns would always win.

There was also the question of the six-shooter that would shoot 408 rounds of ammunition without needing to be reloaded, but there weren't any Siskels and Eberts in those days to point out such obvious flaws in such films, which is what people who think they are better than everybody else call movies.

Okay, so we got through a headless John Cameron Swayze, Horsehair Buggfuzz, and

Lucky 11 Theatre. Let us continue. The Atlanta Crackers, powers of the Class AA Southern Association, often had their games broadcast on television from their home field, hallowed be its name, Ponce de Leon Park, which Atlantans pronounced "Pontz dee Lee-ahn," as in "Pontz dee Lee-ahn Russell," the singer.

I could sit in my aunt and uncle's house and watch my beloved Crackers, nearly all of whom I still remember.

There was Bob Montag (known affectionately as "Der Tag") Corky Valentine, Poochie Hartsfield, Sammy Meeks, Earl Hersh, Ben Downs, Jack Daniel, not to mention Buck Riddle, a great first baseman. I have spent many hours in recent years with Buck, and I beg him for stories of the Southern Association, the games they played, the women they loved, the whiskey they drank, and the trains they rode.

The Southern Association in those days included the Crackers, the Birmingham Barons, the Mobile Bears, the New Orleans Pelicans, the Little Rock Travelers, the Memphis Chicks, the Nashville Vols, and the Chattanooga Lookouts, whowererunbyamannamedJoeEngelwhoonce tradedashortstopforaturkey.

I eventually would make it to Ponce de Leon Park to see the Crackers in person—and to eat a marvelous ice-cream treat they had there known as a vanilla custard—but television gave me enough to make me want to know and see even more.

The left-field fence at Poncey went as far as left center; then there was an open area that led to a terrace where there grew a magnificent magnolia tree. What a tree. A Cracker center fielder named Country Brown had become a legend by going, yea unto the base of the magnolia tree, to haul in fly balls.

There was a row of signs that was the right-field barrier. Above it sat a high bank that led up to the Seaboard Air Line Railroad, where the northbound Silver Comet, bound for Washington and New York, would pass sometime around the bottom of the first inning.

The Crackers were known as the Yankees of the Minors. I eventually would read somewhere that they had the most league championships of any minor-league franchise in the country, and I just thought of some more names:

Bob Thorpe, Bob Sadowski, Buddy Bates, the manager, Beans Hadley, the groundskeeper, Ken McKenzie, Don Nottebart, Ray Moore, the TV announcer, and Hank (the Prank) Morgan who did the radio play-by-play, recreating the road games by tape.

It was the television that summoned me first to the Crackers, but it was that copy of the *Constitution* Aunt Jessie and Uncle Grover brought home each day at noon that sustained my interest and affection. And one day, when I was reading of a Cracker sweep of a doubleheader in faraway Little Rock, it finally occurred to me:

The guy who wrote the story I was reading got to go to all the Cracker games, home and away, and ride trains, and actually got paid for doing it. What a revelation! My life set its course at that very moment.

I would be a sportswriter! Wasn't I sitting in my aunt's living room with my grandmother as she watched *TV Ranch,* and didn't I arise and declare, "Mama Willie! I've decided I want to be a sportswriter!"

And did she say, "Hush, Boots and Woody are about to sing 'Beulah Land,' " or did she say, "So that means you're not going to make a preacher?," or did she ask, "What's a sportswriter?"

I honestly can't remember, but from that day I had but one ambition, and that was to be the guy who covered the Atlanta Crackers, home and away, rode trains, and got paid for it.

There was something about that newspaper. Something that said to me it knew everything that was happening in the whole world but would kindly share it with me.

I cannot describe the anticipation I felt during the summers as I waited for Uncle Grover to drive into his driveway in the Pontiac with that paper.

I would begin my daily paper watch about eleven-thirty. It would seem a lifetime until a few minutes from noon when I would see Uncle Grover's Pontiac heading down the street.

Aunt Jessie usually held the paper, while Uncle Grover drove the car. She would never make it into her house with the paper, however. I would meet her as she stepped out of the car, and she would hand over that precious folding of newsprint.

I must mention *The Atlanta Journal* here, as well. The *Constitution* and the *Journal* were both owned by the Cox family of Ohio. The *Journal* was the afternoon paper.

My friend Bob Entrekin's father took the *Journal,* which I always read when I went to visit my friend.

I didn't understand how newspapers worked at that point, and I thoroughly enjoyed the *Journal* because it had all the stories and box scores from night games that the early edition of the *Constitution* didn't have.

What I didn't know was the early edition of the *Constitution* closed before night games were finished, but the *Journal* didn't close until the next moning.

I also became quite found of the *Journal* because the sports section included sports editor Furman Bisher's column. It was funny. It was biting. It was a daily treasure. I made up my mind that when I became a sportswriter, I would write like Furman Bisher, and if it ever came down to a choice, I would rather work for the *Journal* than for the *Constitution.* You have to work out the details of your career early.

The odd thing is, now that I look back, after making my decision as to what to do with my life, it really wasn't that difficult achieving it. Maybe it's because I was just lucky. Maybe it's because my decision was just so *right.* I don't really know. I do know that most everything that has happened to me afterward in the newspaper business has felt natural and that must mean something.

My first sportswriting job came when I was ten. Moreland and the surrounding hamlets had no organized Little League program, as they did in the county seat of Newnan, where the well-to-do, not to mention the pretty-well-to-do, all lived.

Out in the county, we were not-well-to-do-by-any-means.

What happened when I was ten was that the Baptist churches in the county decided to start a baseball league for boys. I was a Methodist at the time, but I showed up at the very next Baptist baptismal and was immersed in the name of the Lord, as well as in the name of a nicely turned double play or a line drive in the gap between left and center.

I was a pitcher. When our coach asked me, "What position do you play?" I simply said, "I am a pitcher," and that was that.

It also occurred to me it would be a fine thing to have the results of our league printed in the local weekly, the *Newnan Times Herald,* which always carried all sorts of news about the fancy-ass Newnan Little League, where all the teams actually had uniforms. They also got a new baseball for every game.

For the first time in my life, I attempted a phone deal. I called the editor of the paper and told him of my desire that he run results of my baseball league.

The *Times-Herald* did run bits of news from the outlying areas, normally in a column under a thrilling heading that read, "News from the

Moreland Community," which would be followed by something along the lines of the following:

*Mr. and Mrs. Hoke Flournoy were the guests
of Mr. and Mrs. Lon Garpe at their lovely
double-wide home, located in the Bide-A-
Wee Trailer park, Sunday afternoon. Iced tea
was served and a watermelon was cut.*

*Miss Jeanine Potts visited her mother, El-
vira Potts, this weekend. Jeanine is currently
a student at the Kut 'N' Kurl beauty school in
Macon. Jeanine said Macon is a nice place
to visit, but she was having troubles meeting
fellow Christians.*

*Hardy Mixon and his wife, Flora, have re-
turned home after their vacation to Panama
City, Florida. Hardy said he enjoyed the air
conditioning in the motel, the Sun 'N' Surf,
but that Flora made him turn it down because it made her feet cold.*

*Narkin Gaines caught a possum last week
and promptly ate it.*

*Brother Sims, the Baptist preacher,
brought us a lovely message Sunday morning at the worship hour concerning the coveting of thy neighbor's ass.*

As it turned out, it wasn't that difficult a proposition talking the paper's editor into carrying the results of our games.

"You get 'em to us by Tuesday," he said, "and we'll have 'em in the paper on Thursday."

I had my very first sportswriting job. And the very first week, I ran into my very first journalism ethics problem. In Moreland's opener, I happened to no-hit Macedonia Baptist in a 14–0 rout in which Dudley Stamps hit three home runs.

We hosted the opening tilt ("tilt" being one of the first sportswriting clichés I ever learned). For some reason, "tilt" can be used as a replacement for "game," "contest," or "showdown." At the field behind the Moreland school, which had no fences, Dudley hit three shots into the patch of kudzu in deep left, and by the time they found the balls, he was already back on the bench pulling on a bottle of Birley's orange drink.

I had results of other league games phoned in to me, but there wasn't much there in the Arnco-Sargent vs. Corinth, well, tilt. They had to end the game after four innings, with Corinth ahead, 11–7, when various cows from a pasture that bordered the ballfield broke through a barbed-wire fence and into the outfield, which they left unfit for further play.

In the Grantville–Mills Chapel engagement (I was learning more clichés by the moment), the only thing that happened that was the slightest bit interesting was that a stray dog had wandered onto the field, chased down a ball that got through the Grantville defense, and tried to run away with it. The dog was finally caught by the Grantville shortstop, who would become the league's fastest man and most prolific scorer, but by that time, the dog had gnawed several of the stitches off.

Since that was the only ball anybody had, they had to finish the game with it, and by the end of the sixth inning, it resembled a rotten peach more than a baseball. The game ended in a 8–8 tie, and Jake Bradbury, who owned the dog, was told to keep it penned during future games.

Clearly, my no-hitter was the big news, but should the lead of my first sports story feature my own exploits?

Later, I would learn journalism ethics were nebulous, to say the least, so I followed my developing nose for news and went with the following:

Brilliant Moreland right-hander Lewis Grizzard, in his first start in organized baseball, baffled the visiting Macedonia Baptist nine

Saturday afternoon with a no-hitter. Dudley Stamps, in a lesser role, had three home runs in the 14–0 romp.

Uncle Grover and Aunt Jessie also took the weekly *Times-Herald.* When they brought it home at Thursday noon, I opened it even before the *Constitution.* Besides, the Cracker game had been on television the night before, so I'd seen little Ernie Oravetz lead the Chattanooga Lookouts to an easy 9–4 victory.

I will never forget gazing upon my name appearing in a newspaper for the first time. In fact, my name appeared in the newspaper for the first time *three times.*

The headline read:

"MORELAND'S LEWIS GRIZZARD NO-HITS MACEDONIA 14–0"

Then came my byline:

By LEWIS GRIZZARD

Then came the lead of my story, "Brilliant Moreland right-hander Lewis Grizzard . . ."

I had also mentioned my heroic exploits to the lady who wrote the column about who had iced tea and watermelon with whom, in hopes she might also make mention of my no-hit game. But she said she ran out of space because there was so much to tell about the Women's Bible class taking a trip to an all-night gospel singing in Grantville that featured LeRoy Abernathy and Shorty Bradford (known as "the Happy Two"), as well as the Sunshine Boys, the Blackman Brothers Quartet, and a little blind girl who sang "Just as I Am." There wasn't a dry eye in the house after that lineup.

Despite that, I still broke into organized baseball and sportswriting in a big way, and I would wonder afterward if there was a possibility I might play for the Crackers when I grew up and also cover the games and get paid by the *Constitution.*

My dream of pitching professionally, however, came to an abrupt end my senior year in high school. They bused those of us out in the county to Newnan High School.

It was my final game as a Newnan High baseball player. We were playing mighty Griffin. We led 3–2 in the bottom of the sixth when I faced the Griffin catcher, who, with two outs and the bases loaded, looked about twenty-five years old.

I had whiffed the Griffin catcher in two previous plate appearances with slow curveballs.

Now I worked the count to two balls, two strikes. My coach called time and came to the mound.

"Grizzard," he said, "don't throw this guy another one of those slow curveballs. He's seen too many of them already."

What did he know? The slow curve was my out pitch. The slow curve to me was what a piano had been to Mozart, a rifle to Davey Crockett, a tank to George Patton.

The Griffin catcher dug in, and I delivered that tantalizing dipsy-do of mine.

Are you familiar with the term "hanging curveball"? Mine not only hung, it actually stopped directly over the plate and waited for the Griffin catcher to hit it.

After the game, which we had lost 6–3, I asked my left fielder, "Did you have any chance to catch that ball the Griffin catcher hit?"

He said, "No, but I did manage to get a brief glance at it as it was leaving the planet."

So, no offers of a professional contract or a college baseball scholarship were forthcoming, but I still had my dream of being a sportswriter. At least you didn't sweat as much up in the press box as you did down on the field actually playing the game.

My journalism career stalled for a time after I got too old to play ball for the Baptists and report on my heroics on the mound for Moreland.

I was quite frustrated by this, especially during my first two years in high school where they tried to teach me such things as algebra.

Why should I have to take algebra? I asked myself. How on earth will I ever use it as a sportswriter? Did Red Smith have to go study algebra? I should be taking courses on word-smithing and how to turn in an expense account after a road trip to Little Rock.

They tried to teach me biology, too, but I resisted. When it came time to dissect a dead frog, I refused on the basis that I might throw up during the procedure and that since I had no interest whatsoever in becoming a doctor, a veterinarian, or frogologist, I should be allowed to go to the library and read some Victor Hugo.

I was lying about reading Victor Hugo, in case you couldn't tell. What I really wanted to do, since it was September, was to go get the *Constitution* they kept in the library and read the sports papers to brush up on my clichés.

My biology teacher thought about my proposal for a second and then issued the command, "Cut."

As I made my initial incision into Mr. Dead Frog, fighting back the gag reflex, the thought occurred to me, How does the school get its hands on all these croaked croakers? There was probably no place you can order them from, or was there? I made myself a mental note to check the phone book when I got home to see if there was somebody in the business of selling dead frogs to schools for tenth-graders to mutilate.

What if there *was* no such place? Then how did the school get their frogs? Does the biology teacher call up the chemistry teacher and one of the assistant football coaches late in the summer and say, "Hey, guys, it's almost time for school, how about helping me go out and get some frogs?" Then do they go out to a pond somewhere, sneak up on a bunch of frogs, catch them, and put them in a sack? And if they do that, how do they kill them? Or do they put them into jars of formaldehyde while they're still alive?

Just then, my biology teacher walked behind and asked, "How's it going?"

"I'm on my way to the stomach right now," I answered. "By the way, how did you get your hands on all these dead frogs?"

The question obviously made my biology teacher uncomfortable. He stammered around with an answer for a couple of seconds and then said, "Keep cutting."

Hmmmmm. So, there *was* something fishy (we also had to cut up a perch one day) going on here after all.

There were two things I noticed about myself at that point.

One, I obviously was a budding animal-rights activist and, two, I just as obviously had what every newspaperperson should have—the proverbial "nose for news."

I also discovered something else about my nose. It didn't like smelling formaldehyde and dead frogs. Before I finished my dissection, I did have to be excused while I went to the boys' room and threw up. I also swore to myself I'd never eat frog legs, which brought up another question: What do they do with the rest of the frog when they take off his legs for frying?

I was a deep thinker as a young man.

Anyway, algebra, biology, chemistry, geometry, and such were quite unappealing to me during my formative years. I did like some history, especially the part about George Washington slipping out his window at night during rainstorms in order to rendezvous with one of his slave girls and subsequently catching a cold and dying.

You didn't know about that? It was in all the papers.

That was when I realized something else about myself: I really like famous people being involved in scandals, which is an explanation of why I thought the Rob Lowe thing was the best story to come out of the 1988 Democratic Convention.

I did pay a great deal of attention in English class, however. I was learning my craft there. I probably—no, I *was*—the best diagramer of sentences in the history of Newnan High School. I didn't care how long or how complex the sentence, if it could be diagramed, I could diagram it in a matter of seconds.

I originally thought this rare ability might get me some girls, but it didn't.

I was fascinated by grammar. I thrilled at the term "antecedent." I was Mr. Appositive. And how could anybody be interested in delving into the innards of a dead frog when there were onomatopoeia, hyperbole, similies, and metaphors to be studied?

And English literature. I dived deeply into the satirical writings of H. H. Munro (the biting "Saki"). And Thurber's visit to the bank. And "Quoth the raven" and "Me and my Anabelle Lee." I even enjoyed Shakespeare and wondered what he would have written if he had covered Don Larsen's perfect game for the

Yankees in the '56 World Series. (I probably ought to take a stab at his lead, but to be quite honest, I have forgotten most of what I knew about Shakespeare, and since he was English, he wouldn't have known very much about baseball in the first place. Plus, if he happened to be working for the sports section of *The New York Times,* they'd probably have him off somewhere covering a yacht race anyway.)

I read Thoreau and Emerson and Hawthorne and Whitman and Frost and Sandburg. They weren't that bad to be as old as they were. I also discovered the humor of such writers as S. J. Perelman and Henry Wodehouse. O. Henry was a newspaperman, I learned, and "The Ransom of Red Chief" was my favorite of his works. He played a major role formulating my own style as a columnist. Poor O. Henry had to come up with all those stories on a daily basis. That's a lot to make up, but I decided if O. Henry could do it, so could I. That's where I got the inspiration to, when I became a columnist, make up a lot of stuff and never let facts get in the way of a good column.

There were several of my high school teachers who influenced me and inspired me. One of them wasn't my biology teacher, of course. I have no idea whatever happened to him, but I hope he was eventually arrested for doing something like trying to dissect his neighbor's cat.

Richard Smith, an English teacher, should be mentioned first. The man loved words and writing as much as I did. One day in the tenth grade, I asked him why my talent with diagraming sentences with such speed and accuracy wasn't getting me any girls. He answered, "I don't know."

This also helped me later in life, because, if you work for a newspaper, people think you know more than they do and they're always asking you questions like, "Why the hell didn't Rob Lowe look at the girl's driver's license before he started videotaping her lesbian sex acts?"

I was able to answer, "I don't know," and not feel guilty about it. Actually, however, I do have an answer to that question, but it didn't come to me until I'd been asked it a hundred times.

The answer comes from a scene in the movie *One Flew Over the Cuckoo's Nest.* Jack Nicholson, playing the part of a mental patient who had more common sense than his doctor, was being interviewed by a psychiatrist, who brings up the fact Nicholson's character had an arrest record that included having sex with an underage female.

Nicholson's excuse for committing such an act was something like, "Doc, when you're this close to [a part of the female anatomy], you don't go asking for no driver's license."

Richard Smith did more for me than what I just mentioned, of course. He knew of my interest in writing, and one day I asked him another question:

"Do you think when I grow up I can make a living writing?"

He answered, "A meager one, perhaps, but it beats selling shoes, which is what Norman [the Monk] Montgomery is going to wind up doing."

The Monk *was* stupid. In fact, he was the only member of my senior class not to graduate on time, which brings up another of my teachers who impressed me, the late Miss Maryella Camp, who taught senior English.

Miss Maryella was an elderly lady. She was quite southern and called everybody "shugars." She also could recite *The Canterbury Tales* in the original auld English, and brought the Bard alive for me in her classes. Come to think of it, I probably should have asked Miss Maryella, such an expert on Shakespeare, what his lead might have been if he had covered Don Larsen's perfect game for the Yankees in the '56 World Series. She might have had some idea that I could have used on the previous page where I, instead, copped out.

What Miss Maryella did for me that was most important, however, was to teach me that the best way to deal with stupidity is by the use of humor.

Miss Maryella's best line had to do with the Monk, as a matter of fact. She was also senior-class sponsor and called us all together as graduation neared.

"Shugahs," she began, "only one member of the class is not going to be able to graduate—Norman Montgomery." At this point, the Monk uttered a "god-dammit" under his breath, only the Monk was so stupid he uttered under his breath the way most people screamed, and Miss Maryella heard him. She immediately replied, "Don't blame Him, shugah, He's not the one who failed Senior English."

It would also be a terrible oversight if I didn't mention Mrs. Sarah Jane Skinner here. I mentioned the fact my career as a journalism practitioner stalled for a time. I picked it up again in the eleventh grade, however. It was eleventh-graders who produced the school newspaper, *Tiger Tracks,* which ran every Thursday as a part of the *Newnan Times-Herald.*

If an eleventh-grader wanted to have something to do with the school newspaper, all he or she had to do was go see Mrs. Skinner, who taught a class in journalism and was, quite naturally, the school newspaper's sponsor.

The first day I was in the eleventh grade, I went to Mrs. Skinner and said if she didn't let me be sports editor of *Tiger Tracks,* I was going to write a book one day about my newspaper career, and in the part where I told about how I got started, I was going to write about her as a cruel person who didn't know a well-written obituary from a dissected dead frog.

That didn't seem to get her attention, so I told her if I didn't get the job as sports editor, I was going to kill myself and leave a note saying she was responsible.

She sent me to the principal's office for being disrespectful to a member of the faculty, but she did give me the job of sports editor. As a result, please notice I am a man of my word and mention her here in favorable terms.

Mrs. Skinner was (and still is, I might add, sticking with favorable) a dark, attractive lady whom students called "Gypsy Woman" behind her back. There was always some discussion as to who was the better looking, Mrs. Skinner or Miss Fleming, the algebra teacher.

I always held out for Mrs. Skinner, on the

basis of anybody who would teach algebra for a living would eventually grow old and ugly. I don't know if Miss Fleming grew old and ugly, and I'm sorry to have to mention her in such a light, but she should have known better than to send me to the board to work out algebra formulas in front of the entire class when my interest in her subject was too small to be represented by any mathematical term.

I didn't last very long as sports editor of *Tiger Tracks.* Newnan High had a terrible football team my junior year. (I didn't play because I weighed only 130 pounds at the time and was afraid of the Monk, who played linebacker.) In my first column ever, I questioned the ability of the head coach and suggested he get out of coaching and be made assistant biology teacher.

Realizing the controversy this might lead to, I wrote a phony column that brought Mrs. Skinner's approval. Then I suggested that I be the one to take all the *Tiger Tracks* copy down to the *Times Herald.* She agreed and, when I got to the *Times Herald,* I exchanged columns.

When the column appeared, the football coach threatened to make me do blocking drills against the Monk. (It would have been an even more severe punishment if he made me attempt to have an intelligent conversation with him.) Mrs. Skinner was aghast at what I had done, and the principal, Mr. Evans, said if I ever, *ever* got near *Tiger Tracks* again, he would personally flog me with a piece of the cafeteria's Wednesday "mystery meat" (I always figured it was horse or dog).

Controversial Tiger Tracks sports editor Lewis Grizzard was relieved of that position today after a column critizing the Newnan High head football coach.

Said principal A. P. Evans, "Never in my thirty-five years in education have I run across a student with such obvious disdain for authority. His column was filled with lies and hateful innuendos, and he has brought harm to our head coach and shame upon himself and the school."

Mrs. Sarah Jane Skinner, school newspaper sponsor and journalism teacher, said, "I was shocked to learn that Lewis had substituted another column for the one I approved. I will not, and cannot, tolerate such deceit.

"There is no place in journalism for such, and I will devote the rest of my year to cramming that fact down Lewis's throat."

Coach Albright's only response was,

"After the Monk gets through with him [Griz-zard], I'm going to kick the little piss-ant all over Coweta County."

Okay, so that never actually appeared in print, but it's *sort* of what did happen. What *exactly* did happen was they took away my job and my title and called my mother, who said to me, "I certainly didn't raise you this way."

Fortunately, Coach Albright was told he couldn't kick the little piss-ant all over Coweta County because I might get seriously injured during the process, and although I did, in fact, deserve to be seriously injured, it might not look good with the Board of Education, and he already was on thin ice with them for producing such a rotten football team.

I might have, indeed, been a little piss-ant back then, but at least I was a clever little piss-ant. Camilla Stevens was social editor of *Tiger Tracks.* What the social editor did was keep up with who was going steady with whom and that sort of thing. One day I said to Camilla, a good friend, "Let me write your column this week."

Camilla had a big date with Dudley Stamps coming up on Saturday night and figured she needed the extra time to spend on her hair, so she granted my request.

I figured I was safe here, because no mem-

bers of the faculty knew beans about who was
going steady with whom and that sort of thing,
so I could get away with a lot.

The lead in the column I wrote for Camilla
went, "What's this? Filbert Fowler and Phyllis
Dalyrimple seen holding hands on their way to
study hall? Tell me, guys and gals, is this the
start of something big?"

Here was the deal. Filbert Fowler, a Presbyte-
rian minister's son, was afraid of girls because
his father had warned him that any interest in
the flesh would stunt his growth and send him
straight to hell. Phyllis Dalyrimple, on the other
hand, was known to be the loosest girl in school
and was rumored to have taken on the entire
tenth-grade boys' shop class in the back of
Scooter Williams's '54 Chevy.

To link Filbert Fowler with Phyllis Dalyrimple
was maybe the funniest thing my school readers
had ever heard of. I had some other gems, too:

"Can't mention names, but a certain quarterback is said to have his eye on a certain tenth-
grader who sits in the second chair of the first
row in fifth period home economics class. . . ."

The quarterback obviously was Phil Manderson, the best-looking boy in school, and as soon
as everybody checked out who sat in the second chair of the first row in fifth-period Home Ec

class and discovered it was Linda (the Haint) Cunningham, they broke up.

The Haint not only was ugly, she was scary. The word was, she could spook an entire Holiday Inn by herself. The Haint had ratty hair, was cross-eyed (when she faced southward, her left eye looked toward Galveston and her right toward Miami), and had zits that could have won prizes for both size and color. Her feet, placed end-to-end, would have stretched from the library halfway to the audiovisual room.

The only people who were not amused by my linkage of the quarterback and the Haint were the quarterback and Camilla Stevens. (The Haint didn't read the school paper, or anything else for that matter, because of a large zit that sat on the end of her nose and blocked out her eyes when she looked down to read something.) The quarterback, young Mr. Manderson, was not used to being held up to public ridicule. He quickly tracked down Camilla, whom he thought to be the source of his troubles, and said, "If you weren't a girl, I'd make you bleed in numerous places."

Camilla ratted on me, of course, and told quarterback Manderson who was really to blame for linking him with the Haint. He tracked me down in the hall between second and third

period and said, "When school's out this afternoon, I'm going to kill you."

At sixteen, I was about to have to deal with the
first of many irate readers to come.

I did a lot of thinking as I waited to be killed
when school was out. Should I offer Phil Manderson money not to kill me? Should I ask for
asylum in the principal's office? Should I move
to Wyoming?

I decided the best path was to go ahead and
confront Phil Manderson and attempt to reason
with him. That failing, I would take one punch, hit
the deck, and pretend to remain unconscious—
if I wasn't actually unconscious—until he got
bored with me and left.

He tracked me down in the parking lot about
eight seconds after the three-thirty bell rang.

"Trying to get away?" he said to me.

"Listen, Manderson," I began, beginning the
try-to-reason-with-him part of my plan, "at least
I spelled your name correctly."

He didn't seem impressed with that fact.

"Hey, I was just having a little fun," I went on.
"It was a joke. Where's your sense of humor,
man?"

He hit me in the stomach. I didn't have to
pretend to fall down. I really did fall down because he hit me in the stomach. But I did continue to remain fallen down.

"Get up!" he ordered.

I didn't move. My eyes were closed tightly.

"Are you okay?" he finally asked. I could sense he was beginning to think he had killed me.

Still no response.

"Hey, Monk," he called to Norman Montgomery. "I think I've killed this son of a bitch."

"Let's see," said Monk, kicking me in the ribs. More pain, but still I remained still.

"I believe you *have* killed the son of a bitch," said Monk, adding, "Let's go. We'll be late for practice."

"Do you think I'll get in any trouble if I really did kill him?" Manderson asked the Monk.

"They might make you sit out a couple of games, but that's about it," said the Monk.

When I was certain they had gone, I got up off the ground, got into my car, and drove home. I was in a great deal of pain, but I knew I had acted correctly. To have attempted to fight back would have resulted in getting hurt even more. Plus, I sensed I had brought at least a smidgen of guilt into Phil Manderson's life, and I was pleased with that.

As far as Filbert Fowler and Phyllis Dalyrimple were concerned, they actually did get together before the school year was out. Against his father's protests, Filbert wound up marrying Phyllis when they were twenty, and both had a long career in porno movies. Filbert produced them, while Phyllis played various starring roles.

Camilla got over being mad at me eventually, and she now gives me credit for launching her own career in journalism. She later made it to New York, changed her name to Liz Smith, and became a premier gossip columnist.

I had no more opportunities to practice my craft the rest of my high school days. Oh, I wrote a sonnet here and there, did a Chemistry essay entitled "Halogens: Friend or Foe?" and wrote a magnificent paper on President Chester A. Arthur, but that was it.

I did, however, have the opportunity to learn something that would benefit me greatly as a professional journalist. I learned to type.

My basketball coach, Mr. Sheets, taught typing. I've seen enough newspaper movies by now (Bogart's *Deadline USA* and Jack Webb's *30* to name a couple), to know you had to be able to type if you wanted to write for a newspaper. Writing things out longhand becomes painful after a time (during the last eight or nine pages of my Chester A. Arthur tome, I developed severe hand cramps), and I didn't have a particularly attractive handwriting style in the first place.

Mr. Sheets would not allow the two-finger

hunt-and-peck system, so I learned the technique where you put the fingers of your left hand on *asdf* and the fingers on your right hand on *jkl;* and went from there. It was surprisingly easy.

The first thing I could type fast without making an error was: "Now is the time for all good men to come to the aid of their country." (I didn't make a mistake just now, nearly thirty years later, either.)

I also learned to compose on a typewriter. A lot of people learn to type so they can get a job typing what other people have written down longhand. *I* learned to type so I could sit before my typewriter in Sulphur Dell, where the Nashville Vols played, and compose:

By LEWIS GRIZZARD
Atlanta Journal Staff Writer

NASHVILLE, TENN—First baseman Buck Riddle picked the Atlanta Crackers off the canvas here Saturday night with a three-run homer in the top of the 9th inning that hatched a come-from-behind 6–4 Atlanta Cracker victory.

Of course, Mr. Sheets did insist that I copy a few things on the typewriter and not make any mistakes. He'd give tests in that. I did okay, but

I've never been the neatest of typers. And, just as I figured it would, it worked out that if you write for a newspaper, you can be as messy as you want to be with your typing. When you make a mistake while writing your story, you can simply crossover the mistake with a bunch of *x*'s.

In those days, when you were on the road, you would send your stories back to the newspaper by Western Union, and Western Union sent back every word in all caps, no matter how you typed it. That meant you could type your entire story in lower case, since it would still be sent back in all caps. That saved a lot of time and energy, too.

By the end of the year, I had composing on a classroom typewriter locked, and my mother found out my Aunt Emily, on my father's side, had a typewriter that had belonged to her late husband, my Uncle Frank. She called Aunt Emily and asked if I could have it.

Aunt Emily agreed, as long as we would come over to her house to pick it up. I was reluctant to go, because my Aunt Emily was a little strange. She talked quite fast and had once been a fortune-teller—or witch, I forget which— and I was afraid she would put some sort of hex or curse on me.

Also, Aunt Emily's daughter, Cousin Helen,

was much younger than I was, but the last time I had seen her, she had kicked me on the shin.

"Aunt Emily is giving you Uncle Frank's typewriter, and you should be grateful enough to at least go ride over with me to pick it up," said my mother.

"But what if Helen kicks me in the shin?" I asked.

"You're afraid of a nine-year-old girl?" my mother asked back.

I didn't say anything else and, somewhat ashamed, got into the car. When we arrived at Aunt Emily's she suggested Helen take me outside to see their new horse. I had no interest whatsoever in seeing a horse, but my mother cut me one of those looks that said, "Get out there with Helen and see that horse. *Now.*"

We were looking at the horse, Helen and I, when she snuck behind me and poured a bucket of water she'd found in the stall all over my head. It didn't just stay on my head, of course; it dripped down on the rest of me.

I attempted to catch Helen and feed her to the horse, but she ran inside and said, "Mama, make Lewis stop chasing me!" Great, I thought. Not only is my mother going to get mad at me, but here's where Aunt Emily gives out the curse.

I did explain why I was chasing Helen, of

course, and the fact I was drenched in water from head to foot gave my story a great deal of credibility.

"You shouldn't pour water on your cousin," Aunt Emily said to Helen.

"Oh, he'll dry out," said my mother, thinking, I'm sure, What am I raising here? A young man who can't deal with a nine-year-old girl cousin?

Many years later, when I got divorced for the third time, my mother said, "Your troubles with women may have started with your Cousin Helen."

I wondered to myself if I had been able to get even with Helen, which I never did, would my marital record perhaps be a brighter one?

I did get Uncle Frank's typewriter that day, however, and practiced writing sports stories. I even practiced what I would write if the time came when I had to compose my first professional column:

Hello, world, for the first time, subjectively.

I thought it was low-key, yet obviously written by a man who had stored up a lot of things he wanted to say.

I don't remember the first line of the first professional column I ever wrote—which would appear years later on the sports page of the *Daily News* in Athens, Georgia, but I know it wasn't what I had practiced on my Uncle Frank's typewriter during high school. Still, I did get around to using the line—right here—which is why my advice to young people who want to be writers is:

1. First learn to type
2. Practice writing
3. Never turn your back on your cousin in a horse stable.

3

Before my newspaper career actually began (like all other careers, a writing career actually begins when you begin getting paid), I spent one morning as a salesman and three months working at a bank. These vocations didn't last longer because I couldn't sell anything and because the only way I could have found working at a bank interesting would have been if they allowed me to handle some of the money. Unfortunately, I never saw even one roll of pennies.

How all this came about is how a lot of things come about. I was in love. King Edward renounced his throne because he was in love. I suppose that was Steve Garvey's excuse, too. So why not me?

I was in love with Paula. I fell for her madly in the eighth grade, dated her exclusively throughout high school, and would eventually marry her.

Love in the sixties was quite different from love in the nineties.

We didn't have such things in the sixties as recreational pregnancies or Kim Basinger and Prince. All we did was drive around the Dairy Queen or go to the drive-in and grind our lips together while Rock Hudson was wooing Doris Day. We know all about Rock now, but did you hear the rumor about Doris Day once making it with Wilt Chamberlain?

My friend Ronnie Jenkins said he read about it in one of those newspapers they sell at the grocery checkout counter. Ronnie was in the grocery store buying wienies. We still had wienie roasts in those days. (There's a Rock Hudson line in there somewhere, but tempt me not, evil Muse.)

Paula. She was lovely, tall, and blond, and she

wanted to be a model. She decided college would be a complete waste of her time, so upon graduation she took a job in Atlanta at a bank and enrolled in one of those modeling schools where they teach you to walk that way.

I had been accepted at the University of Georgia, where I would study journalism, beginning in the fall. What to do with the three summer months after my high school graduation, that was the key question.

After giving it about eleven seconds of thought, I decided to go to Atlanta myself and seek summer employment, thus allowing me to be near my beloved Paula, who, for the first time in her life, would not be near her mother. This had possibilities I had heretofore never dreamed of. Remember, this was 1964. I still had the unused condom I had bought at Steve Smith's truck stop in 1959.

My friend Ronnie Jenkins also had found work in an Atlanta bank. The idea was for me to find a job, for Ronnie and me to get an apartment near the apartment Paula and her friend had taken, and for the rest to be the great summer of '64, especially if we could find somebody of age to buy beer for us.

Ronnie found a one-bedroom apartment in a duplex on Atlanta's Sixth Street, which was just showing the signs of becoming a slum. Paula's place was not far away, perhaps the distance a mugger could make in ten minutes if he was the subject of hot pursuit.

I began an ardent search for the job. My first stop, obviously, was at the *Atlanta Journal and Constitution.* After college, it was my intention to go to work for one of the papers.

I realized I wasn't going to be hired to cover baseball for the summer, but I reasoned that when I told whoever I'd have to talk to of my future intentions, that person would realize it might be wise to go ahead and hire me for the summer so a lot of orientation wouldn't be necessary when I returned four years later with my journalism degree and the knowledge that would include, such as knowing who invented movable type, Johannes Gutenberg.

The paper was located at 10 Forsyth Street, next door to Union Station, which served the L & N Railroad. A few passenger trains still stopped and departed there, the most notable, the Georgian, ran from Atlanta to St. Louis. We are talking the fourth quarter of pre-Amtrak passenger trains, and Union Station had that forgotten-but-not-gone look to it.

I asked the security guard at the paper to direct me to the personnel department. I caught an elevator to the third floor. There was a lady at a desk.

I said, "Hello. My name is Lewis Grizzard, and I'll be majoring in journalism at Georgia this fall. I'd like to see about a summer job here, since I'm going to be pursuing a newspaper career upon my graduation."

The woman at the desk looked at me as if perhaps I had a booger peering out of one of my nostrils. Finally, she spoke. "We don't have any summer jobs," she said.

And that's all she said. I wished she had said more, because I was already nervous enough, and now, with one small statement, uttered in somewhat of a you've-got-to-be-nuts tone of voice, I really had no place to go with the conversation.

"So," I finally stammered, "let me see if I have this straight. You don't have any summer jobs. Am I correct?"

"That's what I said," said the woman.

I looked down at the floor, which is a great place to look when you're dead, you know you're dead, and all you want at that point is to think of a way to exit gracefully.

I must admit I was rather shocked at the coldness the woman had shown me. You spend your entire childhood dreaming of a newspaper career, and then you can't get past a personnel secretary when you apply for your first job.

I recall vividly what I said to the woman as I left. I said, "Well, thank you for your time," which wasn't exactly a graceful way to leave. As a matter of fact, it was a rather puny way to leave.

Later, I wished I had said, "Okay, you win round one, but I'll be back in four years and we'll see who wins round two."

Why is it you never think of clever things like that to say until it's too late? I don't have an answer, but the question reminds me of a story that has nothing to do with me or the newspaper business, but does have to do with wishing.

Two guys from Detroit are driving through rural South Carolina at the precise speed limit in a new Cadillac. A deputy sheriff, parked in the bushes, spots the car, sees the Michigan license plate on the Cadillac, and figures, "They got to be doing something wrong."

He pulls the car over, and walks over to the driver's side.

The window is still up, so the deputy sheriff takes out his nightstick and taps three times on the glass. The driver, quite smugly, pushes the power window button.

Zuuuuuu. The window comes down.

The sheriff immediately begins to beat the driver upon his head and shoulders with his nightstick.

"What are you doing?" screams the driver. "I wasn't speeding."

The deputy, having administered what he considered an appropriate amount of blows, replies:

"Let me tell you something. The next time you are driving through South Carolina and a law-enforcement officer pulls you over, you have your window down and your driver's license in your hand ready to be inspected. Do you understand?"

"I certainly do, Officer, sir," said the driver, as his head continued to swell.

The deputy then walked around to the passenger's side. The window there was still closed.

Tap, tap, tap, went the deputy's nightstick, on the window.

Zuuuuu went the window as it came down.

As soon as there was a big enough opening, the deputy began to beat the passenger with his nightstick.

"What's wrong with you, man?" asked the passenger, knots beginning to appear on him as well.

"I'm just making your wish come true," said the deputy.

"What wish?"

"Let me tell you something," said the deputy, "I know and you know that when y'all get about three miles down the road, you're going to turn to your friend then and say, 'I wish that son-of-a-bitch had hit *me* with that stick!'"

As I stepped back on the elevator and pushed the button to take me back to the streets—defeated in my first attempt to begin my real newspaper career—it occurred to me that what I should do is find out where the *Journal* sports department was located, go there, find Furman Bisher Himself, and share my career intentions with him. On the way down in the elevator, I played Fantasy Interview:

"Mr. Bisher?"

"Yes?"

"Mr. Bisher, sir, my name is Lewis Grizzard. I'm going to attend the University of Georgia in the fall, and I intend to major in journalism, learn everything there is to know about it, and then return here after graduation to work for you.

"I admit that at the present time I have no earthly idea who invented movable type, but you can bet your butt I'll know in four years.

"But what I was wondering, sir, is that since

I am obviously a bright and promising young man, is there any way you could give me a summer job?"

"You've been to see personnel?" Mr. Bisher would reply.

"Yes, sir, but I couldn't get past the secretary."

"I know her, the old bat. She wouldn't know a bright and promising young man from a Shetland pony. My boy, you have come to the right place. I happen to need—just for the summer—somebody to travel all over the world with me to take notes, make certain I have enough typing paper and fresh ribbons for my typewriter.

"There will, of course, be a great deal of travel involved. We'll be going to the U.S. Open golf tournament, Wimbledon, to the All-Star baseball game and other such places. When can you come aboard?"

Just then, the elevator door opened onto the ground floor. I walked out, found a security guard, and asked him where the *Journal* sports department was located.

"Go to the fourth floor," he said, "take a right off the elevator. First door on your right."

I got back on the elevator and pushed *4.* I got off the elevator, took a right, and walked into the first door on my right.

The room was small. There were maybe ten desks crammed together. All the desks had manual typewriters sitting on top of them. All of them also had immense amounts of such items as unopened mail, brown typing paper, ashtrays filled with cigarette butts, an occasional empty doughnut box, black telephones, empty coffee cups, and on one desk I spotted a box of Mueller's spaghetti sticks. I made a mental note to ask one of my future journalism professors the significance of such a find.

There was also a horseshoe-shaped desk in the room, with chairs on the two outside rims. Inside the horseshoe sat another chair. On the desk was a glass pot filled with what appeared to be glue. The desk seemed to be the central focus of the room. Something important went on at that desk, I concluded.

Behind the horseshoe desk sat a teletype machine that spit out words at an astounding rate. I walked over to the machine. It was typing the current major-league baseball standings. I had no idea as to where the source of this machine was located, but the sound of it gave out both a sense of urgency and energy. This, I reasoned, was the background music for the practice of big-time sports journalism. Against that sound, it seemed to me, a man could put zest in the words he typed. That sound likely was what set Furman Bisher into his mood to crank out his poetry.

To my left, I saw a glass-enclosed office. The door to it was closed. On the door it said, FURMAN BISHER, SPORTS EDITOR.

This was Furman Bisher's office! I looked through the glass. There was a desk, just as cluttered as the ones outside. An obviously elderly manual typewriter sat on a table near the desk. The Oval Office in the White House could not have impressed me any more.

This was it. This was where Furman Bisher wrote. All those columns of his I'd read since childhood came out of this hallowed place. Bisher on riding the train to Little Rock with the Atlanta Crackers. Bisher on Bobby Dodd, the legendary Georgia Tech football coach. Bisher from the World Series. Bisher from the Kentucky Derby. Bisher from the Masters.

I was looking at where Michelangelo mixed his paints, where Edison conceived the light bulb, where Alexander the Great plotted his battles, where Irving Berlin beat out the first notes of "White Christmas."

I knew I would work in this place one day. Sometimes you just know, the way you know you won't like liver even if you've never tried it.

It wasn't going to be this summer. The idea of talking to a man of Furman Bisher's stature and having him be so awed by my only credentials— the fact I was Lewis Grizzard, the future journalism student—that he would give me a summer job as his caddie, suddenly seemed a bit ridiculous.

But at least I had been to this room. I had heard the sound of the teletype and seen my first glue pot. And I had noticed a certain order to all the mess. This is what I thought a sports department at a large newspaper would look and feel and sound like, and one day I would be in the middle of it. I had seen my dream, I had stood in it, listened to it, and, by God, it would come true.

I swore to devote myself to that end. It didn't matter what it would take. I would do it.

Just before I left the room, I said something to it. Out loud. "I'll be back," I said. Profound, no. But filled with determination.

I returned to the elevator and pushed the button for the ground floor again. I hadn't accomplished what I had wanted to accomplish, a summer job, but being in that place had stoked the fire in my belly.

I had to walk back past Union Station to get to my car. There was a newspaper box in front of the station. "Aha, the classified ads," I said to myself.

I put a dime in the box, took out a copy of the *Journal,* fresh from next door. I walked into the station. It was a death wish inside, dark and lifeless. A wino was asleep on one of the benches in the waiting room. He, like everything else in the place, was covered with grime. But at least it was quiet, save the wino's occasional snore. And I had spotted a pay phone. So I pulled away the front section of the paper, put it down on one of the filthy benches, and sat on it.

I went directly to the classifieds and began to read under the "Help Wanted" section. Amid all the small type was a display ad that stopped me.

"Do you like people?" asked the ad. "Would you like to make as much as $125 per week in the exciting field of sales?"

How did they know this was just what I was looking for? I *loved* people. I could hang out with people the rest of my life and never get tired of it. And $125 a week? I looked back at the ad to make certain it hadn't said "month" instead of "week." It did say "week."

Classes at Georgia didn't start until the middle of September. I counted up the weeks and figured I could make nearly eighteen hundred dollars in that period, getting rich in the exciting field of sales just by liking people.

I called the number given in the ad. A woman answered. I introduced myself and explained I was the man the ad was looking for.

"First," said the woman, "I need to ask you a few questions."

"Go ahead," I shot back, my confidence at eye level.

"Do you like people?"

"Do I like people? I *love* people. People to me are, well, what it's all about. I mean, you give me some people, and I'll like them right away. I don't even care what kind of people they are. As long as I know they're people, you can bet I'm going to like them. What's the next question?"

"Could you come by this afternoon?"

I had the job. No question. Eighteen hundred big ones. The first thing I would do would be to buy Paula one of those Evening in Paris perfume sets, the one that also came with the powder.

The woman gave me the address of the office. I said I could be there in half an hour.

Driving to my interview, a question came to mind. Ever notice that when everything is really going great for you, annoying questions come to mind?

There you are, having just finished a term

paper, and you think, This is a great term paper. Then a question pops into your mind. "I wonder if the teacher is going to count off for spelling?"

You have a date with a great-looking girl. You're standing outside her door, awaiting her arrival, and a question pops into your mind. "Do I have a booger?"

The plane is about to take off for Cancun. You feel great. Then, a question pops into your mind. "Are Eastern's mechanics still unhappy?"

The question as I drove to the interview was, "What will they want me to sell in the exciting field of sales?"

That hadn't occurred to me before. They could want me to sell any number of things. My mind raced. Vacuum cleaners? Boats? Shoes?

I had an older cousin who worked in a shoe store once. He said you got to look up a lot of woman's dresses, but it was tough on your back.

What if they wanted me to sell jewelry or soap or flower seeds or salt? This salt salesman came into the store back in Moreland once and convinced Miles Perkins, the owner, to buy six hundred boxes of salt.

Loot Starkins walked into the store next day, saw all that salt, and said to Miles, "You must sell an awful lot of salt."

"Naw," said Miles, "but there was a fellow come by here yesterday could flat sell the hell out of it."

What if I couldn't sell whatever it was they wanted me to sell? I could like people and want to make as much as $125 a week in the exciting field of sales, but what if I couldn't convince anybody to buy whatever it was I was selling?

Would they still pay you in that case?

"Well, Lewis," the boss would say, "how many boxes of salt did you sell today?"

"Actually, sir," I would say, "not a one."

"But did you like the people you met?"

"Loved 'em."

"Fine, then, here's your week's check for as much as a hundred twenty-five dollars."

But that didn't sound realistic to me, and I noticed I was beginning to perspire. With my confidence level having sunk all the way to my thighs, I drove into the parking lot of a six-story building, got out of my car, and went inside.

I entered the elevator, went to the fourth floor, as the woman on the phone had instructed me to do (I made a mental note to point out how I had followed instructions well), and looked for an office marked 452.

I found 452. The name of the company wasn't on the door. Just 452.

Do you knock first? How did I know? I'd never interviewed for a job before. Did you knock or did you simply open the door, walk in, and state your business? Why hadn't they covered some of this in high school? What the hell was I supposed to do with two years of algebra and general science at this particular moment?

I decided simply to open the door, walk in, and state my business. The door was locked.

I knocked on the door. Nothing. I knocked harder. Still nothing. My underarms were a rice paddy. So I banged on the window with my fist.

Suddenly, the door swung open, and there stood a man. He had a thin mustache and was wearing a black suit that was very shiny. He looked like a cross between Zorro and a salt salesman.

"Don't let it be salt," I said to myself. I couldn't even sell a box to Miles Perkins back home. He still had three hundred boxes left.

"Come in, kid," said Zorro. I noticed his shoes weren't shined, and one of the collars on his white shirt was frayed. When he began talking to me, he talked out of the side of his mouth because on the other side there dangled an unfiltered cigarette, the ashes of which defied all laws of gravity. The cigarette, I could see, was a Chesterfield.

Then it hit me. Used cars! I'd seen used-car salesmen before. They wore shiny suits, their collars were frayed, they talked out of one side of their mouth, and they smoked Chesterfields out of the other.

I knew about used-car salesmen. They'd sell a clunker to their own mother and didn't love the Lord. What if I spent the summer selling used cars and showed up on the campus of the University of Georgia with no morals and unshined shoes?

I looked around the office. I didn't see the woman I had talked to on the phone. As a matter of fact, all that was in the office was the desk, one chair, one phone, and a lot of cigarette ashes on the floor.

"I spoke with the lady on the phone earlier," I began. I noticed my voice went up on the "earlier," and I had made my statement in nearly the form of a question.

I had noticed that about myself and about others before. Whenever one isn't sure about one's self, one tends to raise the level of one's voice when one comes to the last word of one's statements in the form of near-questions. But I don't know why.

"What's your name, kid?" asked Zorro.

"One," I replied, "No, no, it's not. I'm sorry, I was thinking about something else. My name is

Lewis. Lewis Grizzard, and I like people and I would also like to make as much as a hundred twenty-five dollars a week in the exciting field of sales. But I wouldn't cheat my mother."

The man looked puzzled.

"I mean," I quickly added, "My mother already has a car and it runs well, so I don't think she'll be looking for another one anytime soon."

"You okay, kid?"

I could tell I was blowing it. What if I didn't get this job and had to go back home to Moreland and not live with Ronnie in his apartment that was near Paula? What if I and my already-aging condom had to go back home together? The summer of '64. The summer from hell.

"Look, kid," said the man, as the ashes finally fell off his cigarette and onto his shoes, "I got a warehouse full of encyclopedias I need to move. I'm hiring four guys to help me. I got three. You meet me here at seven each morning. We drive out in a van and I drop each of you off in a neighborhood with a sales kit. You work the neighborhood. I pick you back up at five. You move the books, I pay you a commission. No sales, no money. You want the job or not?"

"This ad said I could make as much as a hundred twenty-five dollars a week," I said. "Is this true?"

"Could be. More books you move, the more

money you make. I ain't no fortune-teller. I don't know how much money you can make. It all depends on you. Now, I'm busy. Be here at seven in the morning."

"You don't want me to fill out an application or something?" I asked. "I have a high school diploma, and I was active in sports and clubs."

"Kid," the man said, and I could see he was becoming annoyed, "I don't care if you didn't make it through kindergarten. Either you'll sell the books, or you won't. You sell 'em, fine. You don't, that's fine, too. I'll find somebody who can. Be here at seven."

I walked out of the office. My first thought was, What happened to the woman with whom I had talked on the phone? She seemed pleasant enough.

And why hadn't Zorro asked me anything about how much I liked people? It wouldn't have been in the ad if it hadn't been important.

He hadn't asked anything about my references, either. I was going to put down my high school principal, my senior English teacher, and my basketball coach.

And what about all those times teachers had warned us, "Foul this up and it could go on your permanent record"?

I hadn't fouled up one thing in high school. As

far as I know, I had a completely unblemished permanent record. But this guy hadn't asked me, "Is there anything on your permanent record I should know about before we sign a contract?"

I never even chewed gum in high school. I didn't want it on my permanent record. I never smoked in the boys' bathroom like Ronnie Jenkins did. What was going on here? Disillusionment had replaced all my confidence.

Just then, a woman walked out of the elevator and came toward me. "Excuse me," I said. I introduced myself and continued, "Were you the one I talked to on the phone a little while ago? I was the one who liked people. Remember?"

The woman looked at me for a second. It was not a nice look.

"I'm Margie," she said. "I answer the phone for Dipstick in there and go out for beer. He couldn't make a living selling used cars because he was too big a creep even for that, so now it's encyclopedias. What else would you like to know?"

"Can I really expect to make as much as a hundred twenty-five dollars a week in the exciting field of encyclopedia sales?" I asked.

"Wear loose-fitting shoes and don't get too

close to the door so you don't get your nose broke when they slam the door in your face," said Margie, as she turned and walked into room 452, slamming the door in my face.

I went back to Ronnie's apartment and told him I had a job.

"Doing what?" he asked.

"I'm not sure," I had to say, "but can I borrow your Weejuns to wear to work in the morning? Mine aren't broken in yet."

Dipstick's (Zorro's) name turned out to be Howard Barnes. He was one mean son of a bitch in the afternoon. At seven in the morning, he was Hitler with a hangover.

The next day at 7:00 A.M., four budding encyclopedia salesmen stood in front of Hitler. Two of the guys looked older than I was. They were probably in their early thirties. One continuously sniffed on a Vick's inhaler. Another one wore a short-sleeved shirt and had a tattoo of a rather sinister-looking snake on his left forearm. I didn't know much about the exciting field of sales at that point, but I did know having a tattoo of a snake on your arm probably wouldn't help in winning the confidence of a potential customer.

The other guy looked to be about my age, or a year or two older. He was quite skinny, and his hair was in a state of complete anarchy. It looked like a clump of palm trees just after a hurricane hit.

The tiny office was hot and filled with Chesterfield smoke. Howard sat behind his desk and looked us over, much as a person would look over a plate of fried rat.

"I'll be surprised if this goddamn group can sell one goddamn encyclopedia," Harold began.

His eyes stopped at Kudzu Head.

"What'n hell's *your* name?" he asked the kid.

"Larry," the kid answered.

"What the hell kind of hair is that, Larry?" Howard asked in a manner that made it quite clear he didn't like the name Larry or anybody named Larry.

"Just my hair," said Larry.

"I've seen better-looking hair than that on fatback," Howard sneered, despite the fact Larry bore no resemblance to John Cameron Swayze.

"Awright," he said next, "everybody downstairs and into the van."

I entered the exciting field of sales for the first and last time at approximately 8:30 A.M. in Pinewood Hills, a subdivision in suburban Atlanta. I was wearing the only suit I owned, a blue one. I wore a red-and-white striped tie and a white shirt, oxford cloth with button-down collars, neither one of which was frayed, and Ronnie's loose-fitting Weejuns.

I carried my sales kit, which was nothing more than a folded poster that showed a picture of Howard's encyclopedias, and about a dozen order blanks.

Howard had given us precious little instruction. In fact, upon letting me out of the van at the entrance to Pinewood Hills subdivision, all he had said was, "I'll meet you back here at five."

There I stood.

Pinewood Hills looked to be an upper-middle-class neighborhood. The houses didn't appear to be over five or six years old. They were mostly ranch, with covered garages sitting on half-acre lots. The lawns were neat. I noticed swing sets in a few of the backyards. My keen sales instincts said to me that meant there were children to go with them, and what better educational tool was there than a set of encyclopedias?

I opened my poster. There were fourteen volumes in each set of encyclopedias, according to the picture. A set cost $189.99. The deal was, you could pay 10 percent down and pay the rest upon delivery of the encyclopedias. If you paid up front, however, you would receive 10 percent off. Howard said we could take checks. "The piss-ants probably don't have that much cash laying around the house," he had explained.

I decided to work from right to left. I'd start at the first house on the right, then cross over to the first house on my left. A salesman needs a plan.

A plan. I hadn't thought of that. I was a salesman without a sales pitch. You didn't just walk up to a body's front door and say, "Want to buy a set of encyclopedias?"

That certainly hadn't worked for the guy who sold toothbrushes on the sidewalk. People would walk by, and he would ask, "Want to buy a toothbrush?"

He never sold a one. But then he got a plan. He made some cookies and put dog do-do in them. When people would walk by, he would say, "How about a free cookie?"

People would bite into the cookie and then spit it out. "This cookie," they would exclaim, "tastes like dog do-do!" At which point the salesman would say, "That's what it's made out of. Want to buy a toothbrush?"

I decided to go with the old "I'm-working-my-way-through-college" routine. I would knock on a door, and when someone opened it, I would say:

"Hello. My name is Lewis Grizzard, and I am

working my way through college. I'm selling encyclopedias, and I was wondering if perhaps you
would be interested in buying a set."

The person at the door would say, "Well,
Timmy's about to start school, and maybe a set
of encyclopedias would really be a help to him.
Won't you come on in? Would you like some
coffee before we start?"

I would say, "Yes, please, Cream only. What
a nice house you have, Mrs. . . . ."

"Carpenter. Mrs. Carpenter. How about a
doughnut with your coffee?"

"That would be nice, Mrs. Carpenter," I would
say, and that would be all there was to it. Just
that, I'd have my first sale on my way to earning
as much as $125 per week.

Nobody came to the door at the first house.
At the second, a small child answered.

I asked, "Is your mother home?"

The small child turned around and screamed,
"Mommy! There's a man at the door!"

And Mommy screamed back, "What does he
want?"

The kid said to me, "What do you want?"

"I'm selling encyclopedias."

The kid turned around and screamed again,
"He's selling plysopdias!"

And Mommy screamed back, "Tell him we
don't want any."

"We don't want any," the kid said to me, and slammed the door in my face.

At the third house, a woman came to the door with curlers in her hair. She wore a bathrobe and a pair of fuzzy slippers.

Having been married to three women who were devoted to wearing curlers in their hair and fuzzy shoes on their feet, I have, over the years, put a great deal of thought into this uniquely female getup. My conclusions—remember that I am still concluding, which happens a lot when a man considers various behavioral patterns of women—is that they put curlers in their hair not to curl their hair but to pick up radio stations without having to turn on a radio.

My scientific knowledge is somewhat limited, but I know my ex-wives often had enough metal in their hair to pick up radio stations as far away as Del Rio, Texas. When they picked up rock stations, you actually could see their curlers moving to the raucous beat of the music. Thus, the term "hair-raising music."

Their curlers were the early runners to the Walkman, and I have further concluded that one of the reasons women say strange things while their hair is up in curlers is they are trying to think at the same time radio waves are bombarding their brains. This causes such utterances as, "You don't love me and it's fifty-five on the

Southside" and "Why don't we ever talk anymore? Hi, I'm Casey Kasem."

As for fuzzy shoes, that's simple. Women
wear fuzzy shoes to keep their feet warm.
Women's feet are always cold. It's a simple fact
of nature, or a quirk of anatomy. Women's feet
are always cold, their bladders are the size of a
White Acre pea, and they can hear whispers at
three hundred paces if they figure the whisper
involves another woman or a piece of gossip.
(And, yes, I realize this entire parenthetical exercise is overtly sexist in nature. Recall, however,
the time frame in which I am currently writing is
1964, before sexism was invented by a group of
women wearing hair curlers and receiving some
liberal talk-show blather from public radio.)

I started my sales pitch. The woman interrupted me and said, with an accompanying
snarl, "I don't care who you are and what you're
selling!"

The force of the door slamming to in my face
must have jolted Richter scales. There is nothing quite as belittling, I was beginning to understand, as a door being slammed in your face. It
said volumes, which could be condensed down
to such few words as: "Get the hell away from
me, you creep."

I lasted in the exciting field of sales until

eleven that morning. I didn't sell a single set of encyclopedias. I was allowed in only two houses.

In one, a small poodle dog kept yapping throughout my entire sales pitch. When I finally had finished giving it, the would-be customer, a lady in her sixties, said, "Sorry, but Mr. Binghampton and I don't read very much."

At the second house, before I even introduced myself and stated my purpose, a lady said, "Come on in, the set's in the den."

She thought I was the television repairman she had called. Do television repairman wear ties on house calls? I wondered. When I told the woman I wasn't the television repairman but a salesman of encyclopedias, she said, "I don't want any encyclopedias. I want my television fixed. Do you know anything about televisions?"

I said that I didn't.

She showed me the door.

I walked out of the subdivision and found a bus stop. When the bus came, I left my sales kit on the sidewalk, got on the bus, and retired.

I would often wonder later what ever became of Howard Barnes.

Many years later, there would appear on television sets across the country a left-handed guitar player/singer/yodeler named Slim Whitman.

He would have a pencil-thin mustache and would appear somewhat shiftless. All I'm saying is if Slim Whitman doesn't look like an ex-used car/encyclopedia salesman, a 1957 Plymouth will start on the first try on a cold morning in February.

*   *   *

The morning after my early retirement from sales, jobless again, I drove back to downtown Atlanta, parked at Union Station again, and got into banking in a matter of hours. I headed down Marietta Street and came to the First National Bank. Why not? I walked inside and located the personnel department.

"I'm Lewis Grizzard," I said, leaving out the part about my future in journalism, "and I was wondering if you have any job openings."

A woman, pleasant for a change, handed me an application. I filled it out, gave it back to her, and then she said, "I must ask you to take our standard test."

Test? That concerned me. What sort of test would I have to take? A test about banking? All I really knew about banking was, the pens were always missing when you went into a bank to cash a check or fill out a deposit slip.

Although most banks went to the trouble of attaching their pens to their desks with little chains, the pens still were always missing, which concerned me greatly. How can an institution be trusted to watch over my money when it couldn't even keep people from stealing its pens in broad daylight?

The woman handed me the test and directed me to a small room. Inside the room was one chair and one desk.

"Complete the test and bring it back to me," said the woman.

I went into the room and sat down in the chair. Then I realized I didn't have a pen. There wasn't one on the desk, either. I was certain someone had stolen it.

I walked back outside and asked the woman, "Do you have a pen?"

"I've got one here somewhere," she said, beginning a search of the top of her desk. Failing there, she began to pull out desk drawers. She didn't find a pen there, either. Finally, she went to her purse. No pen.

"Let me ask Mr. Gleegenhammer, the personnel director, if he has one," she said.

A few minutes later, the woman returned with a pen.

"It's the only one Mr. Gleegenhammer has," she informed me. "Be certain to return it when you're finished with your test."

I thought to myself, If I really wanted to make

a lot of money in my life, what I would do is sell pens to banks.

Instantly recalling my previous experience in the exciting field of sales, however, I took the pen and went to work on the test.

It was a pretty easy test. On the left side of the test, I found a number. Let's say the number was 314. On the right, I found five numbers. Let's say they were, 11, 478, 6, 925, 314, and 9. The idea was to circle the number in the right series of numbers that was the same as the one on the left.

My test score was perfect. Why had I wasted my time studying algebra? I could have aced the test with the mathematical knowledge I received playing with my counting blocks when I was four.

"You did quite well on your test," the woman said. (You mean people come in here who *don't?*) "Mr. Gleegenhammer will see you now."

"Give me my pen back," said Mr. Gleegenhammer as soon as I had sat down in the chair in front of his desk. The next thing he said was, "We currently have an opening in our loan-payment department. It pays sixty dollars a week."

"Hmm," I said to myself. "Banking apparently doesn't pay as well as the exciting field of sales." But banking also didn't involve hoofing it around some neighborhood getting doors slammed in your face.

"I'll take it," I told Mr. Gleegenhammer.

"Fine," he replied, "Report to the loan-payment department in the morning at eight and see Mr. Killingsworth."

I thought about asking, "What will I be doing in the loan-payment department?" but it wouldn't have mattered. It was obviously inside work with no heavy lifting involved, and if that idiot test was an example of the mental prowess it would take to work in the loan-payment department, I figured by eight-thirty the next morning I'd be able to perform any task put before me. I might even make vice president. Mr. Gleegenhammer hadn't asked if I had wanted temporary or permanent employment, so I hadn't volunteered such information. A couple of weeks before classes started at Georgia, I'd simply announce I had been thinking it over, that banking just wasn't my pot of glue, and that I had decided to go to college and study journalism. What could they do to me? Put something bad on my permanent record? Ronnie Jenkins had been caught smoking in the boys' bathroom about a thousand times, and that fact had been put on *his* permanent record, but Ronnie had got a job at a bank, too, so banks apparently had very little interest in permanent records.

I'll get my duties in the loan-payment department over in a hurry: Customers who borrowed money from the First National Bank of Atlanta—and I would find there were many such people—received loan-payment books, made up of computer cards.

You know these cards. Do not fold, staple, or mutilate these cards. There is a reason the bank doesn't want you to do that. I'll get to why later.

Each loan-payment card had the amount of the monthly installment printed on it. The idea was for customers to send in their loan-payment cards with a check for the exact amount shown on the card. Me and a guy named Harvey, who had zits and a beard made up of three hairs, would open the envelopes with the cards and checks inside them. We would put the checks into one pile and the cards in the other. We would make several stacks, called "runs," of checks and cards.

We would then add each stack of checks on an adding machine. We would do the same with the cards. In a perfect world, the total of the checks would be the exact total of the cards.

But this is an imperfect world, and that is what

made working in the loan-payment department of the First National Bank of Atlanta a frustrating experience.

Dingbat customers, whom I came to hate, would have a payment of, say, $19.99 per month. And they would say to themselves, "I'll make it easy for Lewis and Harvey down at the bank and make my check out for an even twenty."

So I would add the stack of checks, and it would be one cent more than the total of the corresponding cards, and it would take me hours to go back through the stack and find the check and card that didn't match.

After finally getting a balance of checks and cards, I then had to carry all the cards to a machine on another floor. The machine, which was the first computer I ever saw (and not much of one, I suppose, compared to those of today) would add the total of the cards again, serving as a backup for the total Harvey and I had got earlier on the adding machine.

Why we didn't put the cards in the computer in the first place is something I never found out. I asked Mr. Killingsworth, a sour little man, about it one day, and he explained, "I don't know."

Anyway, now we come to do not fold, staple,

or mutilate your loan-payment card. If a card had a staple in it, the card with the staple would upset the computer, which would begin eating all the cards. If the card was folded or otherwise mutilated, it would also upset the computer, which would begin eating all the cards. What I would be left with was a lot of loan-payment cards torn to shreds, which meant I had to go back upstairs and punch out new cards, which was a helluva lot of trouble.

I had a couple of other jobs before this one. I sacked groceries for one dollar an hour. I worked with one of those companies that put up shell homes—"a dollar and a deed is all you need." I scraped paint off windows and helped two guys named Marcus and Willie dig up stumps in the yards. I got five dollars a day for that.

None of those jobs was very much fun, but I never came to hate them the way I came to hate my job at the First National Bank, dealing with dingbats and chewed-up loan-payment cards.

On top of everything I've mentioned so far, there was the matter of the organization chart, which was on the wall in the loan-payment department for everybody to see.

Mr. Killingsworth was on top of the chart. Next

came his assistants, and so on. On the very bottom of the chart was my name alongside Harvey's. It's one thing to know you are scum and dirt and whale dung, but it is quite another to have to look at it and have others see it on a big chart—every single day.

What retained my sanity for me, of course, was the fact that come September, I was gone. I would tell Mr. Killingsworth what he could do with his checks and stapled payment cards and I would be out of there, leaving the others to torment and doom.

What else helped was that life outside the office was wonderful. Ronnie and I hadn't been mugged in the neighborhood, Paula and I had graduated into another level of romance. And we had found a place to buy beer where they didn't check your ID.

And I would soon be the recipient of an incredible break. From the bad start at the newspaper, from my three hours as a walking encyclopedia salesman, from dingbats who would round off their checks and staple them to their loan-payment cards. I would meet a man, and he would put in motion how I got from the summer of '64 to the spring of '77, where this adventure is ultimately headed.

"Balls," cried the queen. "If I had 'em I'd be king."

—An old expression regarding courage.

4

I hadn't had the guts to try to see Furman Bisher again that summer. After the episode of viewing his office—the Throne Room—I decided it would not be wise to show up there with no education and no experience. He'd probably just say, "Come back to see me in four years" or, worse, "Get out of my office, kid."

But I was sitting in the apartment one night watching the television Ronnie's parents had given him for graduation. It had a screen the size of a pocket watch. If you strained your eyes, you occasionally could make out a human form.

The CBS affiliate six o'clock news came on. More on the civil-rights movement and Goldwater.

Following the news and the weather came sports, and the familiar face and voice of Ed Thelinius, the station sports director, who also broadcast the radio play-by-play of University of Georgia football games.

I didn't really want a career in sports broadcasting, but it occurred to me as I watched Ed Thelinius that maybe I could sit down with him and tell him of my plans and he could give me some help. I was hoping his help would be: "Next time I run into Furman Bisher, I'll mention your name," or "Want to do my show tonight?"

With trembling hands, during my morning break the next day at the bank, I cold-called Ed Thelinius at his television station. It took some guts.

Ed Thelinius, or at least his voice, had become legendary in Georgia. He never got rattled like some football announcers and made the mistake of screaming into the microphone such phrases as "We score!" or "Would you look at that son of a bitch run!" which some announcer said once if I am to believe a radio blooper record I heard.

Thelinius was extremely low-key. He would have handled the explosion of the *Hindenberg* like this:

"Here comes the *Hindenberg.* There goes the *Hindenberg.*"

Thelinius did have his pet sayings, of course. Most sportscasters do. Red Barber said, when Bobby Thompson hit the home run to beat the Dodgers in the pennant play-offs in 1951, "Well, I'll be a suck-egg mule."

I suppose I should explain that statement. Red Barber came from the South, and southerners are taken to referring to animals to explain the current state of our emotions. "I'll be a suck-egg mule" was Red Barber's southern way of saying, "Blow me down and call me Shorty," or "I'm not believing this, sports fans."

Southerners, attempting to explain great joy, might say, "I'm happy as a pig in slop." They might express their exhaustion by saying, "I feel like I've been rode hard and put up wet."

Come to think of it, southerners use animals to explain just about anything, such as the answer to "Where's John Earl?" The answer there is, "He went to the woods to take a crap, and the bears ate him."

I suppose I should also explain the term "suck-egg mule." Certain animals are taken to performing the dastardly act of getting into the henhouse and partaking of the eggs. Dogs are particularly bad to do such a thing, thus the phrases "You dirty ol' egg-sucking dog" and "Lassie sucked eggs," which I saw written on a rest-room wall once in Tupelo, Mississippi.

I really didn't know mules would also suck eggs, but if Red Barber referred to himself as he did in 1951, I figure he had personal knowledge of such a quirk in the personality of this particular animal. I have never witnessed a chicken play the piano, but a friend said he did at a county fair. You simply must take somebody's word on occasion.

Ed Thelinius. When Georgia went into its huddle in those days, five players would line up abreast, and then five more would move into the same formation behind them. The quarterback would then face his teammates and call the play.

Whenever Georgia huddled, Thelinius would say to his audience, "Tarkenton talks to his two rows of five."

What he was most noted for, however, was what he said before each opening kickoff. Very few college football games were televised in those days, so Thelinius attempted to give the listener some sort of orientation as to which team was defending which goal.

He would do that by saying, "Imagine your radio as the field in front of me. Georgia will be

moving up on the dial, while Auburn will be moving down."

Clever. Of course, that led to a lot of takeoffs,
such as one that went, "Imagine your radio as
the field as I see it. The red marks will be
Georgia and the black will be Auburn. The dial
will be the football."

This was before the digital radio. In fact, this
was before a lot of things, such as instant re-
play, the Copper Bowl, SAT requirements, and
the ACLU filing a lawsuit because somebody
said a prayer before the game.

Getting Ed Thelinius on the phone that day
was surprisingly easy. The station operator answered, I asked for "Mr. Thelinius," she rang his
line, and he picked up.

"Thelinius," he said.

That's one thing you learn in journalism
school. The proper way for a journalist of any
kind to answer the phone is by saying his or her
last name. It sounds official. Big-time official, like
a guy carrying a clipboard with a pencil tied
to it.

"Mr. Thelinius," I began, noticing once more
my greeting was offered with my voice getting
higher on the "inius" and a question mark on the
end of it. I'm seventeen years old, and I'm talking to a legend. What would you expect?

After the "Mr. Thelinius," I said, "My name is Lewis Grizzard, and I work in the loan-payment department of the First National Bank, but I'm not going to be here much longer, although please don't mention that to anybody who works here because I neglected to mention I'd be leaving after the summer to attend the University of Georgia. . . ."

With that out of my dry mouth, I suddenly thought, Why am I telling Ed Thelinius I'm a liar? I want to gain this man's trust, and in the first thirty seconds I've told him I lie like a dog? (Again, the animal reference.)

But I pressed on, hoping he would forget about my opening statement. "I intend to major in journalism, sir, and I eventually would like to have a career in sportswriting. I realize you are not a sportswriter but a sports*caster,* but I still feel any advice and help you could give me would be quite worthwhile. I was wondering if there might be some time for me to come over to the station and speak with you. It shouldn't take long. I'm merely interested in learning how to become as great as Furman Bisher."

To my utter amazement, Ed Thelinius responded to me by saying, "Why don't you come over right now?"

Right now? You mean at this instant? You

mean, I have asked the Homecoming Queen for sex and she has responded, "Okay, how about right now?"

"I'll be there in fifteen minutes," I said.

I hung up the phone, went to Mr. Killingsworth's office, and told him I felt like I had been rode hard and put up wet and wanted the rest of the afternoon off.

He said, "I'll have to dock your pay."

"Go ahead, banker breath, I'm going to talk to Ed Thelinius," is what I wanted to say. What actually came out of my mouth was a somewhat defiant, "Okay."

I drove to the studios of WAGA-TV, I told the receptionist I had an appointment with Ed Thelinius. She offered no argument, which was refreshing, phoned Thelinius, and said to him, "There's someone here to see you."

There were a couple of heartbeats there when another one of those questions-that-always-come-up-when-things-are-going-great came up, as in, "What if he has forgotten about me since we talked?"

It could happen, couldn't it? Ed Thelinius was a busy, important man. The fact he had made an appointment with a seventeen-year-old kid could have slipped his mind. Or, he simply could have changed his mind, as in, "What's a busy, important man like me doing making an appointment with a kid from a bank?"

I could almost hear the receptionist's next words: "I'm sorry, but Mr. Thelinius has decided you are too insignificant for him to waste his time on."

But no. The receptionist's next words were, "Go through the door on the left. Mr. Thelinius's office is the third one on the right."

I would learn later that radio and television people often have two voices. They have one for when the red light is on and another for when it's off. Drive-time disc jockeys and local television sportscasters come to mind first. When they're speaking into a microphone, their voices drop a couple of octaves, and what comes out is something between Edward R. Murrow and Pat Summerall. In normal conversations, however, they often sound like a cross between Gomer Pyle and Phil Rizzuto talking about the Money Store.

But Ed Thelinius wasn't like that. When he said to me, "It's very nice to meet you," he could have been saying, "Tarkenton talks to his two rows of five." The same resonance was there. Ed Thelinius, I would come to realize, could say,

"Pass the salt," and make it sound like Georgia has just beaten Auburn to win the Southeastern Conference football championship.

We sat there having our little chat. I was nervous, and it occurred to me I'd been nervous a lot that summer. If this was what graduating from high school and leaving home was all about, I would be a nervous wreck and given to episodes of drooling by the time I was thirty.

I told Ed Thelinius of my plans for the future, and he mentioned something about the fact newspapers didn't pay their employees very much, and I said I didn't really care as long as I could get into the ball games for free.

And then, with no warning whatsoever, Ed Thelinius suddenly said to me, "How would you like to work on my Georgia football crew this fall?"

Two miracles in one day. First he had said, "Why don't you come over right now," which would have done me for years in the miracle department. An hour later he's saying to me, "How would you like to work for my Georgia football crew this fall?" If I had known about Red Barber saying, "I'll be a suck-egg mule" at the time, that might have been my reply.

Instead, I handled the situation with my usual aplomb. I jumped in Ed Thelinius's lap, put my arms around him, kissed him square on the mouth and said, "Thank you, thank you, thank you, can I go outside and wash your car?"

Not really. As a matter of fact, a quarter-century and some change later, I don't remember my exact reply. I know I was stunned. Beyond belief. Casey Stengel had just asked me how I'd like to play for the Yankees. Elvis wanted to know if I'd sing backup for him at Vegas.

I probably muttered something like, "I certainly would, Mr. Thelinius, sir." Doesn't matter. Here was the deal:

Play-by-play sportscasters use "spotters," one for each team. The spotters sit on either side of the announcer with a board in front of them. The board, to keep this simple, has the names of each of the players, and, in Thelinius's case, their measurements, their class, and their hometowns.

The spotter's job is to point at the name of the ball carrier, to point at the name of the tackler, to point at the name of someone who has delivered a good block, and to keep the announcer abreast of injuries and substitutions, so the announcer can say something like, "Zawicki is out with a broken neck, and Wojohowitz, the six-one, two-hundred-twenty pound sophomore from Goat City, is in to replace him."

Ed Thelinius had a regular to spot Georgia. What he needed was someone to spot the opposition, and that, by God, was going to be me.

There was even money involved. That hadn't even occurred to me.

"I'll pay you ten dollars a game and pick up all your expenses on the road," Mr. Thelinius, sir, said.

We would work out the details later, he explained, such as where and when to meet him when we left for Tuscaloosa on September 8, for Georgia's opening game against Alabama.

Now, get this picture: I'm seventeen years old. Since nearly the time I learned to dress myself until now, I've wanted a job in sports. I haven't been out of high school two months and already I have one. So it only paid ten dollars a game and travel expenses. It was not only an actual, honest-to-God paying job in sports, but a job with the legendary Ed Thelinius broadcasting big-time college football.

I cried when I got back into my car. I cried and I hollered out loud, and this is what they must have felt like in Times Square when the Japs surrendered.

I said a prayer, too. I thanked God for what had just happened and promised to cut down on my coveting and promised never to make a graven image.

I felt touched by some force that handed out winning lottery tickets.

I always drove down Piedmont Avenue on my way back to the apartment from work. Each afternoon, at the corner of Piedmont and Ponce de Leon, a retarded black man stood selling the street edition of the afternoon *Journal,* the one that included Furman Bisher's column and West Coast baseball scores.

Most afternoons, I would stop and buy a paper from this man. Newspapers cost a dime back then. This day, I felt I needed to come up with a quick good deed to show my appreciation for what had just happened to me. I thought of the man with the newspapers.

I drove over to the corner of Piedmont and Ponce de Leon. There stood the man, as usual, with an armload of papers. I stopped, got out of my car, and said to the man, "I want to buy all of your newspapers."

He didn't understand me. He handed me one paper and held out his hand for a dime.

I said it again. "I want to buy all your papers."

"All?" he asked back.

"All," I said.

I bought 'em all. I'm not certain how many there were. I'll guess thirty. That came to three dollars. I threw in another dollar for a tip. The man looked as if he were going to cry.

I drove back to the apartment and told Ronnie what had happened to me. Then I called Paula, and she came over. We drank a lot of beer that night.

* * *

What Ed Thelinius did for me was give me my Start. You've got to have a Start. Later in life, people would ask me, "How did you get your Start?"

I would answer, "Well, when I was a small boy . . ." and if they were still listening an hour later, I would tell them about Ed Thelinius.

One of life's great dilemmas is, you can't get a job if you have no experience, and you can't get experience without a job. God creates things like that, I think, to build our character and teach us frustration. He also uses such things as busy signals that last for hours, long lines at airport check-in counters, golf's horrid shank, wet newspapers on your lawn in the morning, bicycles that you have to put together on Christmas Eve, holding penalties, Congress, lukewarm morning coffee from room service, dead car batteries, and staples in loan-payment cards.

I worked for two years on Ed Thelinius's Georgia broadcasting crew. I was there the first

time the Bulldogs' soon-to-be-very-successful
head coach Vince Dooley stood on a Georgia
sideline.

Tuscaloosa, 1964. Alabama's Joe Namath
passed Georgia silly. But the very next season,
Georgia would upset Alabama, which went on
to another national championship, 18–17 in
Athens.

When Georgia scored its winning touchdown,
our broadcast booth went a little crazy. John
Withers, who spotted Georgia, stood up, turned
red in the face, and waved his arms around. I
banged on the table and nearly fell out of my
chair. Thelinius said, "Touchdown, Georgia,"
clearly and without emotion. Then he looked at
Withers and me and frowned. No cheering in the
press box. That's in the Bible someplace.

What Ed Thelinius also did for me was give
me access to that hallowed place, the press
box. To get into a press box, where they served
free lunch, somebody had to give you a press
pass. Holding a press pass is terrific for your
ego. It means you're not trash anymore. You are
an official person with a purpose. It might be as
small a purpose as handing out the free
lunches, but at least you are there.

Press passes at sporting events usually are
little pieces of cardboard with a string attached

to them. It usually says on a press pass *Display
At All Times.*

There are several ways to display a press
pass at all times. One, which I favored, is to tie
your press pass to one of your belt loops. Another method is to tie the string around one of
the buttons of your shirt. I even saw a man put
the string of his press pass around his neck.
This man had a very small neck.

Like most everything else, however, there are
some built-in press-box negatives. The first is
losing your press pass, which is worse than fum-
bling on your own two-yard line. It is worse than
losing your rental-car contract, your plane ticket,
your dog, or your pen.

So you fumble on your own two. You can still
get a big bonus when you sign with the pros.
And so you lose your rental-car contract. Somebody's got a copy of it somewhere. You can buy
another plane ticket, your dog will usually find
his way home, and there's always somebody
who has an extra pen you can borrow.

What makes losing your press pass so bad is,
in order to get another one, you have to deal
with press-box security guards, all of whom
begin each day hoping for the opportunity to
shoot somebody. Not many people know this,
but each press-box security guard is put through
rigorous training, conducted by former members

of the Nazi SS. There are several rules press-box security guards learn. Among them are:

* Never be pleasant. If Hitler hadn't been such a nice guy, he might not have lost the war.
* Be suspicious at all times. No matter what anybody says happened to his press pass, under no circumstances allow him into the press box to obtain another one.
* This goes for everybody, seventeen-year-old spotters to Howard Cosell.
* If you're in this business long enough, you may one day have the opportunity to shoot somebody.

I can give you a personal example of what happens when you lose your press pass and have to deal with a press-box security guard.

It was maybe twelve years ago. I was in Jacksonville, Florida, for the annual Georgia-Florida football game in the Gator Bowl. The traffic, as usual, was awful, and I reached the elevator that goes to the press box a minute or two after kickoff.

A female security guard in a green outfit, and packing a large black pistol, stood between me and the press-box elevator. I looked into my briefcase for my press-box pass. It was gone.

Breaking into a geyser of sweat, I dumped everything out of my briefcase on the ground. Still no press pass. The game is now five minutes old.

Here is my dilemma: I absolutely must get to the press box. That is because it's my job. However, I am a veteran dealing with press-box security guards, so I know somebody—probably me—must die if I am to get to my working station.

I decided to attempt to deal with the female security guard from a position of logic.

I said, "I'm Lewis Grizzard of the *Atlanta Constitution,* and I seem to have misplaced my press pass. You must see, however, that here I stand with a briefcase and a typewriter and am not just some nut trying to get into the press box. If you would like, I can show you my press card, my driver's license, and give you my mother's home telephone number to prove I am who I say I am.

"What I propose is that you allow me to go upstairs and obtain another press pass. I will then come back down the elevator—even though the first quarter will be over by then—and allow you to punch my press pass so you will know you haven't committed a breach of Gator Bowl security."

First she unbuckled the top of her holster. She rested her right hand lightly on the butt of her gun. Then she said, "I don't care who you are. You ain't getting on that elevator without no pass."

I tried to keep a clear head, and assessed my options.

One was, I could just get back into my car, go back to the hotel, and watch the game on television. When it was over, I could write a story based on what I had seen on TV and make up some quotes for various coaches and players. Various coaches and players at college football games never say anything interesting anyway, and anybody could make up, "Well, we just got took to the woodshed today."

That, of course, was the easiest and safest way out of my situation. The other option, quite a dangerous one, would be to see if I could gain access to the press-box elevator by force.

I sized up the female security guard. I probably outweighed her by forty pounds and had much the longer reach. I didn't think if it came down to sheer strength, she could keep me from entering.

There was one other consideration, of course. The gun.

If she had had the opportunity to shoot somebody before, perhaps she wouldn't be so quick to shoot me. But what if she was new to the job? What if she'd been through all that rigorous training and still hadn't had one single opportunity to shoot at a living person? What if her trigger finger had developed a powerful itch? What if she had arisen that morning and said to herself, "I'm going to be guarding the Gator Bowl press box today, and the first sumbitch that crosses me is going to get a lead sandwich"?

What I decided was I absolutely had to get inside the press box. Danger is my dateline. So here's what I said to the security guard:

"Ma'am, after thinking all this over, I need to ask you a question that is very important to both of us. I have looked you over, and I do not believe you could physically keep me out of the elevator if I stormed it the next time it comes down. There is, however, the matter of your weapon, or perhaps you refer to it as your 'heater' [trying to get familiar here]. I must know whether or not, if I did decide to force my way onto the elevator, you would shoot me."

She thought for a moment and then answered, "Well I wouldn't try to kill you, but I'd wang you real bad." ("wang," as in "wing," as in, "Shucks, Roy. All he did was wang me.")

I must admit the fact the security guard had

said she wouldn't shoot to kill did convince me to stampede the elevator—but only for a second. Then I thought about all the places a person could be wanged, so I tossed out any ideas about storming past.

I finally did get in, however, about four minutes into the second quarter. I was standing by the elevator, and a photographer friend walked out on his way back to Atlanta with first-half photos.

He went back up the elevator, told officials of my problem, and brought me back a press pass.

As I walked past the security guard toward the elevator, my press pass tied to one of my belt loops, I think I caught a glimpse of a twitch in her trigger finger. "Have a nice day, Marshal Earp," I said a second before the elevator door closed and I was out of range.

There is yet another disaster that can arise in regard to a press pass. It begins when you call the sports information office at, say, the University of Tennessee, and ask for a press pass for Saturday's game against Auburn. Often, one makes such a request too late in the week for the press pass to be mailed.

This is when you hear the words, "You can pick up your press pass at the press gate."

That sounds simple enough, but it's not. I

have no statistics to back this up, but I would be willing to wager a large sum of money that at least 50 percent of the time somebody goes to a press gate to pick up his or her press pass, it's going to be a large hassle.

People who sit in the booths at press dates are a lot like security guards, except they don't wear guns. I believe they usually are packing a knife or hand grenade, however.

Here's a typical conversation between somebody—say, me—trying to pick up his press pass at the press gate thirty minutes before kickoff.

"Hello. Do you have a pass for Lewis Grizzard of the *Atlanta Journal*?"

"What was 'at name?"

"Grizzard."

"Spell it."

"G-r-i-z-z-a-r-d."

"And where did you say you're from?"

"Atlanta. I am from the *Atlanta Journal.*"

This is followed by a long silence while the press-gate person goes through about a thousand envelopes, looking for one with your name on it.

I have often thought that press-gate persons know fully well where your press-box pass is, but they pretend they can't find it because they enjoy doing such things as putting live cats in Laundromat dryers.

"Ain't got no pass for nobody named 'Grizzono.'"

"It's not 'Grizzono.' It's 'Grizzard.'"

"Don't have 'at, either."

"I'm sure it's there somewhere. The sports-information office told me Thursday there would be a pass left here in my name."

"Ain't here."

"Well, could you phone up to the press box and ask for somebody in the sports-information department? They could tell you it's okay to let me in."

"Ain't got no phone."

It is at this point you wish you had gone to law school or opened a liquor store.

Despair. Anger. Frustration. Then, "What did you say your name was again?"

"Grizzard."

"Well, why didn't you say so? Here's your pass."

Press-gate people not only put cats in Laundromat dryers, they also probably have sex with pigs and made motorboat sounds in their soup as children.

One final interesting note about press passes. Until the more enlightened times came, you could always find the following statement written on a press-box pass: *No women allowed in the press box.*

I didn't think much about that the first time I saw it written on a press-box pass. It made sense to me, I suppose. You get a bunch of women in the press box and how are you going to get any work done with them saying, "I'm cold. When is this going to be over?"

Later, of course, women certainly would gain access to press boxes, even to locker rooms. Thinking turnabout is fair play, I once tried to get into the women's locker room at the West Side Tennis Club in Forest Hills, New York, at the U.S. Open, to see if I could get a glimpse of Chris Evert naked. The security guard threatened to shoot me if I took another step.

My Start. I traveled with Thelinius and his crew to famed football arenas around the country, even to Ann Arbor, Michigan, where Georgia upset the Wolverines in 1965. Withers went crazy. I turned over coffee on my spotter board. Thelinius said, ". . . And Georgia wins."

I actually met Furman Bisher one night at Dudley Field on the campus of Vanderbilt in Nashville. He was nice to me and said, "Come see me when you graduate."

I could tell he was thinking, What a bright, promising young man. I wish he had come to see me last summer, I had an opening for somebody to take notes and keep me in typing paper and fresh ribbons.

I also met Wade Saye, sports editor of the *Athens Banner-Herald,* in Georgia's Sanford Stadium before the 1964 game against Clemson. Wade Saye would give me my first paying newspaper job.

Many interesting and bizarre things would happen to me in the coming years, like the time I got blitzed with Bear Bryant in the Eastern Airlines Ionosphere Room at the Atlanta Airport. I was also ringside when Muhammad Ali returned to boxing after losing his license because he didn't want to go to Vietnam. His comeback began at the old Atlanta City Auditorium, and Ali went three rounds with Jerry Quarry. Five feet above me, in the second round, Ali landed a jab, and Quarry's blood splattered down on my typewriter.

But it all goes back to Thelinius. I never did get around to asking why on earth he spoke with me for fifteen minutes and invited me on his crew. I don't guess I ever got around to thanking him, either. Not in person at least. I did write a column about him when he died.

When the National Football League expanded into Atlanta in 1966, Ed left Georgia and went to work with CBS, doing Falcon telecasts. A couple of years later, however, CBS decided to cut back on its announcing staff, and the Turk, in the parlance of pro football, came to visit Thelinius and gave him his walking papers.

He also lost his job as sports director of WAGA-TV. His hair was turning gray, and television only wants to keep fresh faces on the screen.

I never did know just how many wives Thelinius had. Several, I know that. The last time I saw him, he was working as sports director for a small AM country music station in Atlanta. He had a young woman in his office whom he introduced as his "fiancée."

He was dead a month or so later. There were rumors of his heavy drinking. You had to search through the papers to find his obituary.

So I wrote one of those lest-we-forget columns about Ed, wrote what he did for me, and wrote what a fine man he was. Two weeks later, I got a letter from one of his ex-wives. It was mean.

Ed and I would share, as it turned out, more than a broadcast booth.

5

If I had said to my mother, "I don't think I'll go to college," at some point during the years I lived at her house, she would have killed me.

Maybe she wouldn't have killed me, but she would have inflicted severe neck and head injuries upon me.

My mother was like a lot of Baby-Boom parents. As soon as I reached the age where I could understand the basics of the English language, she began saying to me, "I want you to have it better than I did." Translated, that meant, "If you ever say, 'I don't think I'll go to college,' I am going to inflict serious neck and head injuries upon you."

My mother grew up red-clay poor, on her father's precious-few acres in Heard County, Georgia, the only one of 159 Georgia counties that didn't have one inch of railroad tracks.

My mother—and I have my grandmother's

word on this—actually did walk three miles to school barefoot. It rarely snowed in Heard County, Georgia, which is the only thing that saved me from a complete guilt trip when my mother put the "I walked three miles, etc." line on me when I complained I didn't have a Thunderbird.

There were five children in my mother's family. The eldest, Uncle Johnny, also walked three miles to school barefoot and later became a doctor. I wish I could say he became a podiatrist but I can't. Well, I could, but I'd be lying. My mother, the third child, was the only other member of the family to get a degree.

My mother graduated from Martha Berry College in Rome, Georgia. Berry offered students from poor backgrounds one choice: Come here and wash dishes, clean toilets, work on our farm, and we'll give you an education. My mother, in other words, was never a member of a college sorority.

She finished Martha Berry in the thirties with a degree in education. Then she married my father, then World War II broke out, I was born in '46, Daddy went back to Korea in 1950, came back from his second war a complete mess, and left my mother when I was six and she was forty-one.

We left Fort Benning, Georgia, my father's

last station, and moved in with my mother's parents in a tiny little house in Moreland. My grandparents moved there from Heard County in the forties when the few red-clay acres would no longer provide.

My grandmother went to work in a local hospital as a maternity nurse, my grandfather got a job as janitor at the Moreland Elementary School.

Mother had never used her degree. Marriage and a child and life as a military wife had stripped her of an opportunity to do so. But it's 1953, she doesn't have a dime, her husband has split, and no child of hers is going to walk to school barefoot. So my mother got a job teaching first grade in Senoia, Georgia, another small town near Moreland.

Her first year of teaching, she was paid $120 a month. A month. And one day, I would blow the opportunity to make as much as $125 a *week* selling encyclopedias for Howard (aka Dipstick and Zorro) Barnes.

Senoia was six miles from Moreland. Mother needed a car. She bought a 1948 Chevrolet. Its body was the color of an orange Dreamsicle. The top was blue. The stuffing was coming out of the front-seat upholstery. It was hard to crank on cold mornings, and it burned oil.

Mother taught one year at Senoia, and then

she got a break, which she certainly deserved at this point in her life. The first-grade job came open at Moreland Elementary. Mother applied for the position and got it.

The Moreland School was maybe a quarter-mile from my grandparents' house. Most mornings, I walked to school. When I asked my mother if I could go barefoot, she said, "No. You might step on a rusty nail and get lockjaw."

Ever think about all the warnings your parents gave you growing up? Could stepping on a rusty nail really give you lockjaw and cause you to die because you couldn't open your mouth to eat? What a horrible way to die.

Remember "Never drink milk with fish, it'll make you sick"? How about, "No, you can't have a BB gun, you'll put your eye out"?

Today, parents are concerned about their children joining a religious cult or becoming a drug dealer. When I was growing up, they were worried about us putting an eye out.

It wasn't just BB guns. We were also told, "Stop running with that sharp stick. You might fall down and put your eye out." And, "Did you hear what happened to the little boy in Hogansville? He drank some milk with his fish and got sick and was running with a sharp stick and fell down and put his eye out."

My mother would teach first grade at Moreland School for twenty years before the illness that killed her forced her to take an early retirement with a pittance of a pension for her disability.

My mother's background had taught her frugality. I'm convinced my mother could have solved the federal deficit problem. She simply would have said to the government, "Okay, turn all your money over to me and give me the list of what you owe." She would have had us out of the hole shortly.

I cannot remember my mother ever spending a dime on herself for something she didn't desperately need. When the old '48 finally gave out in 1955, she did buy a new car, a green Chevrolet. When the salesman said, "I can put a radio in for another twenty dollars," my mother said, "We already have a radio at home."

I can never remember her buying more than five dollars worth of gas at a time, either. She would pull up to the pump and say each time, "Five, please." I think she was afraid if she filled up the tank and died, she would have wasted money on whatever gas remained in her car.

Mother began saving for my college education with the first paycheck she ever earned. She bought bonds. She put cash in shoe boxes and hid them in the back of her closet.

Having enough money to send me to college

when the time came consumed my mother. Besides the bonds and the shoe-box cash, she kept a coin bank, bought day-old bread, sat in the dark to save on the electric bill, never had her hair done, quit smoking, and never put more than a dollar in the collection plate at church. She used some simple logic for not tithing the Biblical tenth: "If the Lord wanted me to tithe that much, he wouldn't have made college so expensive."

Mother had no problems with my intention to study journalism. She wouldn't have cared if I had studied chicken proctology at the School of Agriculture, just as long as I was enrolled.

As a matter of fact, my mother did have something to do with my interest in putting words on paper. My mother was on constant grammar patrol when I was growing up.

Going to school with children from poor, rural backgrounds, as I did, I often fell in with a bad-grammar crowd.

What follows is a glossary of the way a lot of words were mispronounced around me constantly:

  "His'n" (his)
  "Her'n" (hers)
  "Their'n" (theirs)

"That there'n" (That one)
"You got air asack? (Do you have a sack?)
"I ain't got nairn." (No, I'm afraid I don't)

Mother also disliked another common grammatical error of the times. Many of my friends would say, in referring to their parents, "Daddy, he went to town last night"; or "Mamma, she went with him, and they didn't bring us air a thang."

"There is no reason to say, 'Daddy, he,' " my mother would remind me. " 'Daddy' is identification enough."

"Ain't," of course, was a hanging offense. You never got away with double negatives or the popular answer to "Have you done your homework?" "Yes, I done done it."

My mother did allow, however, certain words and phrases common to southern speech that might not be able to stand a harsh review, in the strictest sense, of whether or not they were proper.

My mother, for instance, had no problem with the use of the term "fixing" in place of "going to" or "it is my intention to," as in "I'm fixing to do my homework." I still say "fixing," and anybody who doesn't like it can stay in Boston and freeze.

My mother also had no problem with certain southern expletives, such as:

Hot-aw-mighty (God Almighty)
Dang-nab-it (Of all the rotten luck)
Dad-gum-it (Same as above)
Shut yo' mouth. (You're kidding me—and please note it's not "Hush yo' mouth," which a lot of people from up North think.)
Lawd, have mercy. (About the same as "Shut yo' mouth.")
I'll be a suck-egg mule. (See previous chapter for explanation.)

My mother would not abide, however, any form of swearing.

I never would have used the following words and phrases in this book if my mother were still alive, because it might have broken her heart. But she's gone now, and I suppose I can offer up such examples of common southern curse words:

Shee-yet far (Southerners can probably say "shit" better than anybody else. We give it the ol' two syllable, "shee-yet," which strings it out a bit and gives it more ambience, if words can have ambience. "Shee-yet far" is southern for "shit fire," which means something between

"Oh, my God" and "Look out, Knute, she's headin' for the brier patch.")

Sumbitch. Southern, of course, for "son of a bitch." However, when people from the North try to say "sumbitch," it doesn't come out exactly right. Jackie Gleason tried to say it a million times in the immortal *Smokey and the Bandit* movies, but he never did pull it off.

I don't think southerners actually say "sumbitch." It's more "suhbitch," as in "That suhbitch can flat play a cello," which I'm not certain has ever been said in the South, but I like to throw in such classy allusions like that to prove we've got more class than Yankees often give us credit for.)

Got-damn (You know)

Ice (We don't say "ass" like other people do. I can't decide exactly how we say "ass," but "ice" comes rather close, as in "Shee-yet far, Randy, if that got-damn suhbitch don't watch his ice, somebody's goin' to break that cello right over his got-damn head.")

The term "ice" also brings up another interesting story about my mother. In the middle sixties the county schools of Georgia were integrated, and my mother wound up with a first-grade class made up mostly of black first-graders.

I almost forgot that "nigger" was taboo in my mother's house, too. In fact, my mother was the only person I knew who *didn't* say "nigger." She was the first person to explain to me that it was a derogatory term.

In those days, however, there were only three substitutes available for "nigger," all three of which are frowned upon by today's blacks and African-Americans.

The three substitutes were "colored," "knee-grow," and "nig-gra."

My mother never indicated to me which of the three substitutes she preferred, but thinking back, I'd think she preferred "knee-grow."

Although there remains the National Association for the Advancement of Colored People," "colored" brings to mind such phrases as "Colored seat from Rear," a command one might have read on a bus or train in the fifties.

And people who used "nig-gra" always seemed to say that word with noticeable disdain. But "knee-grow," I think, was an effort on the part of some white people, like my mother, to also say, "The times they are a-changin', so let's get on with the program."

What concerned my mother (her students referred to her as "Miz Christine") most about the grammar of many of her black first-graders was their use of "axe" for "ask."

She attacked it this way:

She said, "Students, can you say 'assss-ssss'?"

First-graders thought getting to say "assss-ssss" at school was a riot.

After running through "assssssss" several times, my mother would say, "Now, can you make the 'k' sound?" which, I suppose, is "kuh." Then Mother would say, "Put the two together: 'assssssss-kuh.' "

Her methods might be attacked today as a manifestation of racial insensitivity. Blacks have every right to pronounce "ask" as "axe" if they want to, but a person who had been on constant grammar patrol for all those years must be given some forgiveness if her methods reeked of any sort of bias.

I made excellent grades throughout school. Again, if I hadn't, my mother would have inflicted both a verbal and physical beating upon me. My constant fear was, "What if my mother saves up all that money for my college and I can't get in because I made a 'C' in ancient history?" I hated ancient history because I didn't give a shee-yet when Rome was sacked, nor who won the Punic Wars. But because I didn't want to disappoint my mother, I studied and paid a fair amount of attention in class and made an "A" in ancient history anyway.

I applied to only one school, the University of Georgia. My high school counselor, one Mr. "Cheeks" Chandler, as he was affectionately known, told me Georgia's journalism school was one of the best in the country, right up there with the journalism schools at the University of Missouri and Northwestern.

I remember the day the letter came. It said on the front of the envelope, "This is your official University of Georgia acceptance."

I gave Mr. Killingsworth my notice at the bank the middle of August. I went into his office and said, "Mr. Killingsworth, I have decided a career in banking is not for me. This is my two-week notice."

He gazed up at the organizational chart to make certain I was still at the bottom of it, so, I suppose, he could handle this with a so-who-cares attitude. He didn't say, "Who cares?", but I could see it on his face. What he did say was, "Good luck, now get back to work."

I actually was happy with his reaction. I was afraid I was going to have to explain I was leaving his employ to attend the University of Georgia in the fall and he would get suspicious and say, "Hey, you knew all along you were taking this job on a temporary basis, didn't you? You misled me and the bank, and I'm going to see to it you never work in this town again." How did I know that he wasn't Furman Bisher's good friend or neighbor and could say to Bisher, "Let me warn you about this little creep named Grizzard who misled me and the bank"?

The first of September, I packed my things at Ronnie's apartment, assured Paula I wouldn't be interested in any of the college girls I met, and went back home to Moreland. Three days later, my stepfather would drive me to Athens and help me unload my clothes and notebooks and portable typewriter and Sears radio, which is all I owned at the time, into my room in freshman dorm at Reed Hall.

Mama had paid for my first quarter. It was perhaps a two-hundred-dollar lick, counting books. She also gave me two hundred dollars cash from some hidden shoe box somewhere for other expenses.

She hugged me when I left home and said, "I've looked forward to this day for a long time. I know you will do well and don't drink."

I would do well.

One out of two's not bad.

Before classes began, there was the matter of Georgia's opening 1964 football game against Alabama in Tuscaloosa.

Ed Thelinius wouldn't fly. There was a reason

for that. He was frightened to. Freshman were not allowed to have cars at Georgia, so I caught a pre-dawn bus from Athens to Atlanta on the Saturday of Georgia's opener, to be played under the lights at Alabama's Denny Stadium. ("Under the lights" is another sports cliché. It won't be long before I'll get into a lengthy discussion about sports clichés, all of which I had memorized by 1964.)

Thelinius picked me up in his car at the bus station in Atlanta. John Withers, the Georgia spotter, sat in the front. I sat in the back for the ride to Tuscaloosa and didn't say very much.

Georgia's football program had fallen into scandal and hard times. A *Saturday Evening Post* article had claimed former Georgia coach Wally Butts had conspired with Alabama's Bear Bryant to fix the 1962 Georgia-Alabama game in Alabama's favor. Butts and Bryant would win their libel suit against the *Post* later, but when the season opened in 1964, Georgia had had three straight miserable seasons, and the fix scandal still hadn't been resolved.

What the school had done after the 1963 season was to clean the athletic department house and move Joel Eaves of Auburn in as athletic director. Eaves then shocked the state by hiring a thirty-one-year-old assistant coach at Auburn,

Vince Dooley, as the new Georgia head football coach. The alumni wanted a name. They got Vince Who?

Thelinius's broadcast crew consisted of six people. Besides himself and Withers and me, Jim Koger kept statistics, L. H. Christian of WRFC in Athens was the engineer, and a legendary pioneer of radio sportscasting, Bill Munday, provided what we know today as "color."

Munday may be mentioned in the same breath as other sportscasting giants of the Golden Age of Sports and Atwater-Kent radios. The story went that once he was going to do the Harvard-Yale game back in the thirties on nationwide radio. The night before the game, he was having dinner with Harvard officials. At one point, Munday, a Georgia alumnus and son of the South, was asked, "Mr. Munday, who will you be pulling for tomorrow? Yale or Fair Harvard?" Munday thought for a moment, then replied, "Neither one. You're both a bunch of damn Yankees, and I wish there was a way you both could lose."

We took our seats in the visitors' radio booth in the Denny Stadium press box. Thelinius was in the middle. To his extreme left was Koger, who lived in Athens and did Georgia basketball play-by-play.

Withers sat at his near left. I was on his near right. Munday sat next to me on the right. I think he'd had a few pre-game drinks. L. H. Christian was behind us, engineering the broadcast.

Georgia kicked off. On Alabama's first play from scrimmage, Georgia defensive tackle George Patton threw Joe Namath for a loss.

"George Patton throws Namath for a loss," said Thelinius into his microphone.

"Jawja's ready! Jawja's ready!" screamed Munday into his.

I was terrified. In the first place, I was supposed to watch the action on the field through a pair of binoculars Thelinius had provided me. But I had neglected to focus them on the field before the game began. All I saw during the kickoff was white blurs, Georgia, and crimson blurs, Alabama. I had no idea who ran back the kickoff for Alabama, but Thelinius familiarized himself with the players before each broadcast, so he was able to say "Richard Thurgood, a two-hundred-twelve-pound junior from Talladega, Alabama, brings it back to the Crimson Tide twenty-eight."

By the second quarter, I had finally focused my binoculars and actually was able to be of some assistance to the announcer.

As it turned out, Jawja was *not* ready. Namath routed the Dawgs, 31–3.

What else I remember about the evening of my press-box debut is it took four hours to get from Tuscaloosa to Birmingham, thirty miles away, in all the traffic. We got back to Atlanta at six the next morning. Thelinius dropped me at the bus station. I got back to Athens at noon. That's the bad news.

The good news is that Jim Koger rode back with us, and as we sat in traffic in Tuscaloosa, he got out of the car and went inside a package store and bought some beer and gave me one. This was going to be even better than I had thought.

I should note here that Jim Koger eventually left the Georgia crew and involved himself in a number of other ventures, which included a stint (another sports cliché) as a television sportscaster in Columbus, Georgia. After that, he ran the Columbus minor-league baseball franchise and may have been the first person to think of having parachutists jump out of airplanes and land on an athletic field before some sort of contest.

I'm not certain what-all he did after that, except that the last time I saw him, approximately twenty years after the night in Tuscaloosa when he gave me a beer, he informed me he was a born-again Christian and that the End was near.

What I want to say here is that if Jim Koger is

still feeling guilty about giving a seventeen-year-old a beer in 1964, he shouldn't be. I would have found a way to get my own beer. And as far as the End is concerned, I really don't think God will count off for drinking beer. Tequila shooters, maybe. But not beer.

I got off to a terrible start when classes began. The first really bad thing that happened to me at Georgia was that I was told upon registering for fall-quarter classes that I was eligible to take part in the Honors Program.

That sounded impressive. I had been a member of the Beta Club in high school, and being eligible for the Honors Program in college seemed to indicate to me I was just as smart as I thought I was.

I registered for three 5-hour courses. All freshman journalism students were required to take Introduction to Journalism. Besides that, I also registered for the honors version of Psychology 101 and Math 105.

There were only six of us in Honors Psych 101. The first day of class, the instructor, whose suit was too small for him, gave us a list of books we must buy for his course. Three of the four books, the instructor had written. I smelled a laboratory rat.

The second day of class, the instructor, who

wore the same ill-fitting suit he had worn the first day, gave his first lecture.

I didn't understand anything he was saying. And he said it all too fast, so I panicked.

I looked around at the other five students in the room. Not a single one of them had their mouths half-open, as I did.

One of the sure signs that somebody is completely lost in a situation is if somebody has his or her mouth half-open. When a dog doesn't understand something, such as what in the hell you are talking about when you say, "Here, poochie, poochie, poochie" (Since the dog's name is "Jerome"), the dog will cock his head to one side and look at you like you're nuts.

But when people find themselves in that situation, they half-open their mouths. I sat there in Dr. What's-his-name's Honors Psych 101 class for fifty minutes and never took a single note. That's because I had no idea what to write down in my notebook.

A few minutes before class ended, Dr. Strangespeak asked the class, "Are there any questions?"

I wanted to say, "Yeah, I've got one. What in the name of God have you been talking about for the last forty-five minutes?"

One hand did go up from one of my fellow

students, a fat girl. I didn't even understand her question, much less the instructor's answer. A boy with terminal acne then raised his hand and asked the instructor a question in something that sounded like Chinese. The instructor answered in Portuguese.

Finally, I raised my hand, and asked, "Did Sigmund Freud have a dog?"

I dropped out of Honors Psych 101 the very next day and signed up for a course called Earth Science Survey. We talked about what causes lightning and thunder. I could deal with that.

Lightning is caused when cold air bumps into hot air and the clouds catch on fire. Thunder is caused by God beating His drum. I would make an "A" in Earth Science Survey. The instructor had a sense of humor.

Honors Math 105 turned out to be the same mismatch for me Honors Psych had been. The real problem may have been that the instructor was a male. I had taken all my algebra from the sex symbol of my high school faculty, the lovely Miss Fleming, she of the tight sweaters and skirts.

Somehow, a man in a pair of baggy pants didn't stir my interest in, or recollections of, algebra. I dropped Honors Math after the first day of class and enrolled in Introduction to Goat Roping over at the Ag school. To this day, I still think I could rope a goat much easier than I could solve some mathematical problem, such as "If Darryl leaves Chicago headed for Des Moines, a distance of 330 miles, driving at 55 miles an hour and he gets 22 miles to the gallon in his Corvair and gasoline costs (this is 1964), 37 cents a gallon, what is Ralph Nader's shoe size?"

Introduction to Journalism, on the other hand, turned out to be a wonderful change.

It was taught by Dean John E. Drewery, the distinguished and learned dean of the Henry W. Grady School of Journalism. Dean Drewery was an elderly man who wore three-piece suits and peered down over his glasses. He was John Houseman with a classic, to-the-manor-born southern accent.

The Grady School had, in effect, risen to national prominence under his guidance. The Grady School, then and now, hands out the prestigious Peabody Awards each year, broadcast journalism's Pulitzer prizes.

Dean Drewery, it was widely rumored, had the credentials to have risen to the presidency of the university, but an indiscretion that received a great deal of publicity had kept him in his deandom.

There are many versions to the story, which every student in the School of Journalism knew by the second day of enrollment. My favorite went like this:

Dean Drewery was having an affair with his secretary in the early sixties. He was married at the time. One afternoon, between classes, the dean and his secretary gave in to passion's urging and decided to have at it right there on top of the dean's desk.

At some point during their lovemaking, the door to the dean's office opened suddenly, and there stood Mrs. Dean Drewery with a pistol.

Before the dean, who was on top with his pants down, could say, "This isn't what it seems to be," his wife opened fire. She aimed at her husband's bare hindparts and put three bullets into her target.

The dean's secretary, despite the fact she was shielded by the now-bleeding dean, was also hit.

When the ambulance arrived, Dean Drewery is said to have commented to the attendants, in his best stentorian southern, "Do hurry. We've been shot."

Dean Drewery recovered from his wounds and obtained a divorce from his wife, who left Athens and was never charged in the shooting.

The trial would have been terribly messy. After his divorce, the dean married his secretary, who was much younger than he was.

By the time I was in school, the dean no longer drove. Each afternoon, he would stand in front of the Commerce-Journalism Building, and his wife would drive up to take him home, and off they would putter in what I think now was a large black Buick, an automobile befitting a man of Dean Drewery's style and position.

I don't recall very much of what I learned in Introduction to Journalism class my first quarter in school. I know I learned the name of the first sportswriter in Journalism History class. (You'd think I would have remembered that name for the rest of my life. Unfortunately, I soon forgot it, along with a lot of information about Ben Franklin and the Penny Press.)

But factual information wasn't what good Dean Drewery was all about in the first place. He was an entertainer. Never a day passed in one of his classes that he didn't send his audience into great convulsions of laughter.

Dean Drewery calling the roll was even memorable. All his classes—he also taught courses in journalism ethics, magazines, and advertising—were held in the spacious Commerce Journalism Building auditorium, which seated three hundred students. He addressed us from behind a podium on a raised platform. Classes were fifty minutes long. Because his voice was cane syrup, dripping slowly, the dean normally took twenty minutes to call out the names of his three hundred students.

It went something like:

"Miss Ad-eee-son."

"Here."

"Mr. Awwwwl-brite."

"Here."

The dean also was one of the few people who pronounced my name the way I pronounce it, the first time he stumbled upon it.

It's been tough having a name like Grizzard. My family always has pronounced it with the emphasis on the second syllable, as in "Griz-*Zard.*" Unfortunately, about 8 million people have pronounced it as *"Griz*-zard," (rhyming with *"Liz*-ard") when first confronted by my last name.

Not Dean Drewery. He said my last name in the manner I am certain God intended.

"Mr. Griiii-ZAAAAAARD," the dean would call forth.

One morning I answered, "I'm right here, Dean."

He replied, "Mr. Griiii-*Zaaaaaard,* a simple

'here' will suffice," and went directly to, "Miss Ham-illl-tun."

"Wuhhhhhds [words]," the dean would say. "You must learn the value of 'wuhhhhds.' Without them, you are lost. Wuhhhds are the tools of your trade. You must love wuhhhds, cherish wu-uhhds, and use them with a mind toward economy with the gallant purpose of meaningful communication.

"The use of some wuuhhds often confuses me. I heard our bright students use a wuuhd describing a very warm environment. I hear them say, 'It's hot as ———." Certainly, that is a suitable metaphor. But then, I also hear them say, 'It's cold as h———.' It cannot be both. Let us choose wuuhhds with great care, so as not to confuse the listener or the reader. 'It's cold as a polar bear's posterior.' Isn't that much better? Wuuhhds."

As much as the dean may have preached the economy of wuuhhds, he didn't always follow his own mandate. He was the master of using fifty words when one or two would suffice. But that somehow had a marvelous appeal to me.

On the first day of the Introduction to Journalism class, someone asked the dean, "Is it okay if we smoke in your class?" "Yes" or "no" would have been the very essence of the gallant purpose of communication. But Dean Drewery took another route:

"Fire," he began. "A wonderful wuuhhd, 'fire.' The mere sound of it conjures so many images. A roaring fire. Ah, yes. Quiet evenings with a good book in a chair near the roaring fire.

"Fire and Brimstone. One can almost feel the heat and smell the sulfurous, acrid smoke. Go to church Sunday, class. One can't be too careful in regards to the hereafter.

"The wind-swept fire. With fire in his eyes. Ready, aim . . . *fire!*

"Mahvelous word, fire. There will be no fire in my class."

He was once lecturing on press coverage of the Kennedy assassination. He began by saying, "A young man went to Dallas. . . ." Then, lowering his voice and peering over his glasses at us, he added the ominous, ". . . But he nevah returned."

You never knew in which direction Dean Drewery might go. One day, during his lecture, he would walk to his right and turn and peer out one of the two doors of the auditorium. He would return to the podium, and a few moments later walk to his left and peer out of the other door. At midsentence, twenty minutes into his lecture, he interrupted himself and said, "I am sure there are those of you who are wondering about my interest in the two doors today. I feel I owe an explanation.

"I have been reading a great deal in the periodicals recently concerning the possibility of visitors from the outer reaches of space.

"Last evening, as I pondered this possibility further, it occurred to me that if visitors were to land in this area, they obviously would come here to the University of Georgia, the center for learning in our great state.

"And upon landing on campus, what would be their first stop? Why here, of course, to the Henry Grady School of Journalism, where our business is communication.

"What I have been doing is occasionally looking out each door to see if any such visitors have descended upon us. I feel it would be my duty, as dean of the school, to be the first to greet them."

The only time I actually saw Dean Drewery explain his thoughts without starting in France and ending up in Outer Mongolia, was on one of the School of Journalism's most festive days—Henry Grady's birthday.

Henry Grady was editor of the *Atlanta Constitution* during the turbulent post–Civil War days. He was a visionary who saw the possibility of a

New South emerging from the ashes of the old one.

There would be cake and punch in the School of Journalism library on Henry Grady's birthday. Balloons would grace the halls of the school, and the dean often would read something from Grady to his class.

During my sophomore year, the dean came into class on Grady Day and began to call the role.

He was somewhere near "Miss Tal-eee-fah-row," when two radio-TV majors seated in the back of the class turned on a tape-recorded message. It began, "This is the ghost of Henry Grady. . . ." and went on to offer his appreciation for the observance of his birthday and a few other messages from journalism's Valhalla.

Dean Drewery never looked up from his roll. The laughter from the class died quickly when the recorded interruption ended. Was the dean offended? Was this day so hallowed humor had no place in it? As the dean continued to stare at his roll, offering no comment whatsoever, there was much throat-clearing and seat-squirming. Finally, the dean broke through the silence by simply continuing to call the roll.

"Mr. Tahhh-lee-vor . . ."

When he finished, he looked up and said, "Class . . ." Then, ever so subtly, he lifted his eyes skyward and said, ". . . And honored guest . . ." and went directly into his lecture. It was his only mention of the prank. I thought it perfect.

In such a few words, he had acknowledged the cleverness of the effort and had given his approval of it. If I learned nothing else from Dean Drewery, I learned an appreciation for both overstated bombast, as well as the effectiveness of subtlety.

I'm not certain if Dean Drewery did it for all his graduates, but he obviously kept an eye on my career. Each step I took in it was accompanied by a note of congratulations from Dean Drewery. Each was poignantly short-winded.

One said, "You make me proud." Another, "Well done." And yet another, "Bravo."

In 1987, long after the dean's death, I received the John E. Drewery Award from the Grady School. The plaque said, FOR DISTINGUISHED ACHIEVEMENT IN JOURNALISM.

It's on the wall of my office. Even as I type these words, I can look up and see it. It hangs over an autographed photo of Bear Bryant. When I am low, I often go to my wall for an ego lift. I won the Drewery Award, and Bear Bryant recognized my existence with a personalized autograph on his photo.

What treasures.

6

The student newspaper at the University of Georgia was *The Red and Black*. The Journalism School looked over its shoulder, and journalism students put it out twice a week.

There were two problems I saw in working for *The Red and Black*. One was, it paid even worse than real newspapers. I needed money.

I wanted to get my mother off the financial hook. The more money I made, the less I would have to depend on my mother to pay my college expenses. I wanted to relieve her obsession with having the money to pay for my education. Also, the phrase "I worked my way through college" was something I could use, perhaps, when I had children of my own.

"Daddy," one of my children might say, "All the other guys at the fraternity house are driving Mercedes convertibles, may I have one?"

Of course, I would eventually buy my son such

a car because I would want him to have a better life than I did, but first, in order to inflict guilt upon him, every parent's right, I could say, "Young man, I had to work my way through college."

Somehow, I also thought working for a real newspaper, not one produced by journalism students, would be more beneficial to me in my quest for practical experience. Journalism, I reasoned, was not something you could learn entirely from a book, or a newspaper with training wheels. What good would it do me to know about Johannes Gutenberg if I didn't know any sportswriting clichés? A sportswriter with no clichés would be like a Junior Leaguer with no station wagon.

I suppose before going any further with this, I probably should offer some examples of sportswriting clichés, which, I am sad to say, are no longer operable on today's sports pages. That's because the sportswriters of today all have college educations; don't get drunk, then try to write; actually have read something besides *Sports Illustrated* and the Larry Bird autobiography; had rather write about the plantation mentality of big-time college athletic programs than Georgia versus Auburn; are married to women with double last names; drive BMWs;

wear shirts that don't have frayed collars; write on a computer rather than a manual typewriter; have no idea who Smokey Burgess was, eat salads for lunch; don't smoke; have never seen *The Babe Ruth Story,* starring William Bendix, and have no idea who William Bendix was.

Clichés. First there were the terms you could use when describing participants in various sports. You didn't always say, "The Georgia football team," for instance. Also available was the Georgia "gridders," the Georgia "11," and, if the team was having a great year, the Georgia "juggernaught" or the Georgia "dreadnaughts."

Basketball Players: The home five, the basketeers, the roundballers, or the hoopsters
Trackpersons: Thinclads. Cross-country runners could also be described as "harriers," but I don't know why.
Baseball Players: The home nine, the visiting nine, and, in a real pinch, the diamondeers
Bowlers: Kegglers
Fishermen: Anglers
Golfers: Linksters
Tennis Players: Netters
Race-Car Drivers: Leadfoots
Boxers: Pugilists
Wrestlers: Grapplers
Swimmers: Poolmen

Growing up in the South, I never had occasion to learn clichés for hockey players. If I had to invent some, I'd probably go to "icemen," "pucksters," or "stickmen."

I hadn't heard much about soccer at that time, either. Soccer would come to the United States and make an absolute nuisance of itself a few years after I was out of college.

There was an Atlanta team in the North American Soccer League when I worked for the *Journal.* I think our soccer writer described them as "booters" once, but I'm not really sure, and the North American Soccer League went out of business anyway.

If there was, or is now, a cliché to take the place of "gymnasts," I don't know it, and the same goes for rowing, kayaking, skiing (both snow and water), marble shooting, chess, bicycling ("peddlers"? "wheelers"? "Spandexers"?), ice skaters who don't carry hockey sticks, polo (water and horse), volleyball, Ping-Pong, archery, clay-pigeon shooting ("pigeoneers"?), synchronized swimming ("dingbats"? "treaders"?), canoeing, bobsledding, ("crazy fools"?) fast-walking ("prissers"?) curling, dog-sled racing, rodeo (including bronc-busting, bull riding, and calf and goat roping), and truck-pulling which, thank God, introduced itself long after I had been out of the sports business.

Sportswriting clichés certainly don't end with "hoopsters" and "gridders." There are about a zillion clichés that can be used in place of the word "beat." Let's say I'm covering the Georgia-Florida football game and Georgia beats Florida, as it often does.

In place of "beat," I can use:

Georgia upset Florida.
Georgia pummeled Florida.
Georgia crucified Florida.
Georgia nipped Florida.
Georgia smashed Florida.
Georgia embarrassed Florida.
Georgia stormed past Florida.
Georgia slipped past Florida.
Georgia swept past Florida.
Georgia nailed Florida.
Georgia annihilated Florida.
Georgia made mincemeat of Florida.
Georgia downed Florida.
Georgia killed Florida.
Georgia stuffed Florida.
Georgia toppled Florida.

These are pretty typical. If you really want to get exotic about it, you could write:

Georgia picked up Florida and shook it like
a dog playing with a dead squirrel.
Georgia tiptoed past Florida like a thief in the
night.
Georgia sent the Florida faithful home shak-
ing their heads.
Georgia made believers of Florida.
Georgia dashed Florida's bowl hopes.
Georgia put a big bite on Florida's hopes for
a Southeastern Conference title.
Georgia swarmed over Florida like white on
rice.

There are also clichés to use instead of the
simple "game."

A close game can be a "cliffhanger," a "nail-
biter," a "heartstopper," a "barnburner," or a
"thriller." One night I was listening to Skip Caray
do a telecast of a tight professional basketball
game, and he said, "This game could make coffee nervous."

A one-sided game can be described as a
"laugher," a "rout," a "massacre," a "run-
away," a "walk in the park," a "mismatch."

The term "game" itself can be replaced by
"tilt," "battle," "annual meeting," "get together," "shoot-out," "tussle," "fracas," or
"backyard brawl," as in "Neighbors Auburn and

Alabama battle today in their annual backyard brawl."

A football may be called "the pigskin," "the slippery oval," or "the mail," as in "Nobody ever carried the mail any better than Red Grange."

A baseball can be the "apple," the "pill," "horsehide," or the "aspirin tablet" as in "All Nolan Ryan served up to the Expos Friday night was a steady diet of aspirin tablets."

Basketballs are "roundballs." Golf balls are often "pellets," boxing gloves are "mitts," and I saw this written once: "McEnroe sent the yellow fuzzy-wuzzy sphere past Borg with a vicious topspin backhand."

Baseball probably has the most colorful clichés, however.

What do the following mean?

1. Can of corn
2. Frozen rope
3. Circuit clout
4. Hot corner
5. Keystone
6. Hit for the circuit
7. Tools of ignorance
8. Just a long strike
9. Circus catch
10. Texas Leaguer

11. Port-sider
12. Chin music
13. Sunday hop
14. Grizzled veteran
15. Rabbit ears
16. Fireman
17. Skipper-pilot
18. Clubhouse lawyer
19. Tribe
20. Solons
21. Chisox
22. Bosox
23. Dem Bums
24. Ruthian clout
25. Timber
26. Sidewinder
27. Submariner
28. Senior circuit
29. Junior circuit
30. Grabbed the gonfalon

The answers:

1. Easily caught fly ball to the outfield.
2. Ball hit hard on a line.
3. Home run.
4. Third base.
5. Second base.

6. Hit a single, double, triple, and home run in one game.
7. Catcher's equipment.
8. Long foul ball.
9. What Willie Mays used to make all the time in center field.
10. Short fly ball that falls in for a hit.
11. Left-handed pitcher.
12. Pitch thrown near the batter's head.
13. Ground ball that takes a big hop and is easy for an infielder to handle.
14. An old guy who hasn't retired yet.
15. A player who listens to the opposing dugout screaming obscenities at him and questions his manhood and gets upset about it.
16. Relief pitcher.
17. Manager.
18. Troublemaker.
19. The Cleveland Indians.
20. The old Washington Senators.
21. The Chicago White Sox.
22. The Boston Red Sox.
23. The old Brooklyn Dodgers.
24. A home run reminiscent of the ones Babe Ruth used to hit.
25. A bat.
26. Pitcher who throws sidearm rather than over the top.

27. Pitcher who lets it go around his knees.
28. National League.
29. American League.
30. Won the pennant.

Television sportscasters, and their accompanying analysis, have introduced a number of new clichés to sports, and let's not get into the use of the word "great," because we'll be here all day.

But here are some relatively modern television sports clichés and what they mean:

1. *Hang-time:* How long it would have taken Alabama fans to hang football coach Bill Curry if he hadn't split to Kentucky.
2. *Role-player:* A guy who has something on the general manager because he still gets to pinch-run on occasion and he can still pick up his fat paycheck when he should be in Double-A.
3. *Aircraft carriers:* What basketball analyst Al McGuire, who used to coach, calls large basketball players who could dunk their Porsches.
4. *Possession time:* How long Olphonsio McGree, the brilliant linebacker of the Rams, will be in jail for getting caught with cocaine while going 175 miles an hour down a suburban street in his Porsche.

5. *My good friend and colleague:* What the announcer calls the ex-jock who keeps interrupting him with a bunch of non-sense during the game.
6. *Game of the Decade:* There are about thirty of them each year.
7. *Quality starts:* A pitcher lasting five in-nings without getting shell shock before being relieved by some guy who throws split-finger fastballs for $176 million a year.
8. *Lance Ten Brook:* Some golfer you never heard of who is leading the San Antonio / Bisquick / Federal   Express / Wild Russian Vayna/Oreo/Republican Party/Tidy-Bowl/Salvation Army/Perry Como / Cher / Hard Rock Cafe / Fuji / Alaskan Board of Tourism / Häagen Dazs/Open when Saturday's broadcast of the third round begins.
9. *Rising star in women's golf or tennis:* Any player with large breasts, thin legs, and a pretty face who hasn't had a les-bian affair yet.
10. *Graduation rate:* What a losing college coach can point to when he's just had an awful season and the alumni want his house back. He'll still lose his job, but

liberal editorial writers can point out he is the sort of individual college sports need more of.

11. *Car salesman:* The coach's next job.
12. *Exploitation of black athletes:* "A Jaguar? Clemson offered me a Rolls-Royce."
13. *Burner:* Member of the University of Miami football team with an arson charge pending.
14. *Speed merchant:* Sells drugs to fellow players.
15. *Paternity suit:* What Steve Garvey will wear at his trial.
16. *Graphic:* What television announcers call the things that come on your television screen showing Nebraska lineman LaMont (Big Hawg) Jackson is 6–11, weighs 350 pounds, leads the team in tackles and dormitory sexual assaults, and is majoring in asphalt paving.
17. *Top of the show:* Televisionese for "When we came on the air," as in "At the top of the show, I thought Howard was too drunk to get through this thing."
18. *Time-out:* "Get some black coffee in Howard."

19. *Nonqualifiers:* "I know the sumbitch can't read, but he'll knock your jock off."

20. *Jesus Christ:* Fixes games, as in, "If it hadn't been for my Lord and Savior, Jesus Christ, I'd never have made that three-pointer at the buzzer."

These were much simpler times in 1964, of course. One never read of agents, arbitration, training-camp lockouts, drug abuse, or Brent Musburger. Sportswriters were doing columns on the infield fly rule (Just as I was about to catch the ball, a fly got in my eye!), and sportscasters were still saying things like, "He won't hang up his spikes until they tear the uniform off his back," which translates as, "This time next year, he'll be pumping gas."

* * *

Before I move on here, I need to stop and give a little credit to a couple of other people who helped me with my Start—not as much as Ed Thelinius did, but they certainly contributed.

Charlie Harris was the head football coach at Newnan High. Charlie had played end at Georgia and was known as the Gliding Ghost of Goodwater. Goodwater being Goodwater, Alabama, Charlie's hometown. After college, he'd played service football and got a job in the pros when the American Football League was formed. I'm not clear as to exactly how he wound up at Newnan High School, but it was a break for me.

I didn't play football in high school. I was afraid to. But I did take Charlie Harris's informative health class my senior year.

I don't know what they teach in health classes today, although I did write a column once about parents in Bowdon, Georgia, losing it when they found out a local nurse had demonstrated to a class the proper way to use a condom by putting it on a banana. It could have been worse. She could have used a cucumber.

This was before such things as rampant teenage pregnancy, AIDS, and rock music with filthy lyrics that cause our children to go into immediate heat upon hearing them.

In Charlie Harris's health class, we learned the proper way to brush our teeth, the names of the various food groups, what causes dandruff, never to mash a pimple, and that alcohol is a depressant while coffee is a stimulant. Or was it the other way around?

It doesn't matter. Coach Harris recognized early the fact I was a bright and promising young man, a fact that went over a lot of other people's heads.

I knew of his background at Georgia, and he

knew of my future goals. Nice guy that he was, he wrote a letter to Dan Magill, sports information director at Georgia, introducing me as a bright and promising young man who never mashed a pimple.

Magill, meanwhile, turned the letter over to his crack assistant, Loran Smith, who wrote me late in my senior year at Newnan and said, "Dear Louis [I later forgave him for this oversight], Coach Charlie Harris tells me you are a bright and promising young man who wants a career as a sportswriter. Come to see me when you arrive at Georgia and if there is anyway I can help you, I certainly will."

It took me about eight seconds to locate Loran Smith when I arrived on campus. Incredibly, Loran Smith did a Thelinius on me. Yet another miracle.

But first, some background:

Everybody in the state of Georgia knew the phrase "them lyin' Atlanta newspapers." It was first introduced by Georgia governor Eugene Talmadge in the thirties. Whenever the papers would criticize him, he would go to South Georgia somewhere and talk about "them lyin' Atlanta newspapers."

In fact, Talmadge would put a plant in his audience to bring up the subject.

"They say I stole! Well, I did! But who did I steal for! I stole for you, the poor people of Georgia, that's who!"

At which point, Talmadge's plant would scream out, "Tell 'em 'bout them lyin' Atlanta newspapers, Governor," and Talmadge would reply, "I'm a-comin' to that."

(Incidental to that is the fact that in the movie *Blaze,* the story of Louisiana governor Earl Long and his romance with stripper Blaze Starr, Paul Newman, who portrayed Long, says to his constituents: "The poor people of Louisiana have only three friends: Jesus Christ, Sears and Roebuck, and Earl Long." I grew up hearing this quote attributed to Gene Talmadge, and I'm sticking with him.)

In the 1950s, the afternoon *Atlanta Journal,* owned by the Ohio Cox family, acquired the morning *Atlanta Constitution,* giving the family what every newspaper owner longs for, a monopoly.

What further stirred the white masses of Georgia was the fact Ralph McGill, publisher of the *Constitution,* was given a front-page column, and he used it to assail segregation. McGill later won a Pulitzer Prize and achieved international acclaim as a man of courage, kindness, understanding, and vision. But that's not what they thought in most of Georgia's 159 counties. Ralph McGill became "Rastus" McGill, and that often was lengthened to "that nigger-lovin' Rastus McGill."

The Atlanta papers took a liberal editorial stance on most all subjects. They endorsed John Kennedy for president in 1960, further rankling many of their readers who saw Kennedy as a threat to the continuance of segregation, and a president who would get his orders direct from the Vatican. (There weren't many Catholics in rural Georgia. In Moreland, there was only one Catholic family, and a lot of people were afraid of them because of the rumor that Catholics went around kidnapping babies.)

As the civil-rights movement began to move in earnest and the Civil Rights Bill was being introduced, a score of wealthy white conservatives started a third newspaper in Atlanta, the *Atlanta Times.* It had been publishing for less than a year in the fall of 1964.

But here's what else:

The *Atlanta Times* also had a sports section, and Loran Smith said to me at our first meeting, "I think I can help you. Al Thomy's the assistant sports editor at the *Times,* and he's looking for an Athens correspondent."

I didn't ask what the job paid, what I would be

asked to do, or if I would have to vote for Barry Goldwater. It didn't matter.

The next day, Al Thomy came to Athens to do a Georgia football story, and we met. He explained that I would cover Georgia football practice whenever a regular *Times* staff member was not available to do so.

I would file feature stories, the head coach's comments, updates on injuries, and any other pearls of information I came across. For this I was going to be paid ninety dollars a month. I nearly wet my pants in the excitement of the moment.

It didn't stop there. The local paper was the afternoon *Athens Banner-Herald.* It might not have been the worst daily in the country, but it had to get dishonorable mention. Local readers referred to it as the *Athens Boner Herald,* or the *Athens Banana Herald.* (Making up funny names for newspapers is sort of a universal exercise, I would learn. The *Atlanta Constitution* often was the *Atlanta Constipation,* and the *Atlanta Journal* was, what else, the *Atlanta Urinal.*)

The *Banner-Herald* had been in operation for several thousand years (I think Johannes Gutenberg served his internship there). It was owned by an old Athens family that really didn't give a damn. If it had, it would have been terribly embarrassed.

The *Banner-Herald* was dull, full of errors, and didn't pay its employees squat. When I was offered a job there, I accepted it in a heartbeat, however. It was still better pay than the *Red and Black*, and it didn't have training wheels.

Wade Saye, a journalism graduate in his middle twenties, was sports editor of the *Banner-Herald.* He was an Athens native and didn't want to leave, which was the only conceivable reason he continued to work at the paper, receive lousy pay, and not be able to rent a motel room when he covered the Masters golf tournament in Augusta, which was eighty miles away. He drove over to each round in the morning, returned to Athens to write his story, and I'm not even certain he was reimbursed for his mileage, which was nothing compared to when Dan Magill, introduced earlier as sports-information director at Georgia, was the fourteen-year-old sports editor of the *Banner-Herald.* He was paid in free movie passes.

Wade had begged and pleaded with the paper to allow him to have an assistant. He was routinely doing eighteen-hour days, getting paid minimum wage for only eight hours of work. Overtime was not an operable term at the *Banner-Herald.*

Finally, after Wade became quite pale and began to lose weight, I suppose the paper wondered where it would find somebody else to take Wade's place when he died from exhaustion, so they gave in on the assistant thing. Wade could hire somebody to work for a dollar an hour, twenty hours a week.

I had just walked out of the broadcast booth at halftime of the Georgia-Clemson game to get a free piece of fried chicken and a Coke when Wade Saye walked up to me, explained the details of the job, and asked if I were interested. I mentioned earlier how long it took me to accept.

Four mornings a week, I reported to the *Banner-Herald* at six-thirty in the morning and worked until eleven-thirty. Wade taught me how to write headlines, how to call the Georgia sports information office to find out how the wrestling team did on the road and write a four-paragraph story on it, and what glue pots were for.

Before newspapers discovered high tech, the glue pot was an essential tool. You wrote a three-page story, and before you sent it to the Linotype operator to cast your words in lead, you pasted the three pages together. And if you took three stories off the wire and put them together to make one, you pasted those pages together.

Some bad things could happen if you didn't know anything about glue pots. First, there was a brush that went through the lid to the glue pot. You unscrewed the lid, pulled out the brush, and applied the glue to the pages.

The key was to make certain the brush got back into the glue pot. A brush not returned to the glue pot would become dry and rigid. *Very* dry and rigid. Leave the brush out of the glue pot and when you tried to paste pages together, it was like trying to paint with a yard rake.

Another bad thing that could happen is if you forgot to put the lid and the brush back into the glue pot, there was the chance you could knock the glue pot over and get glue all over everything.

This happened to me. I was editing a wire story about the World Series, and I knocked over the topless glue pot. Glue got all over the story, my desk, my clothes, Wade's shoes, and the floor. It took an hour to clean up the mess, and Wade had to cut himself out of his shoes before he could go to bed.

I also think glue pots had a lot to do with sportswriters often exhibiting odd behavior. You pass that glue pot around, you obviously are going to inhale some of the fumes from the glue. I think a lot of sportswriters used to get high on glue fumes, then do things like actually pick up a bar tab, wear paisley ties with striped shirts (with frayed collars), and ask for the bowling beat.

I swear I was told about a bowling writer up North somewhere whose name was John "Skid" Rowe. His bowling column was entitled "In the Gutter, with Skid Rowe." There's an overturned glue pot in that story somewhere.

And as long as I brought up the immortal Skid Rowe, I might as well expand on other names that further indicate inhaling gluepot fumes may be at the bottom of a great deal of questionable creativity.

I knew a guy in South Georgia who wrote a column called "Disa and Data."

I also would like to say I once saw a hockey column called "Up Your Ice," but I never did. I also never saw a column about prostitute bridge players called "Trumps 'n' Tramps," a wrestling column entitled "Inside the Tights," a baseball column dealing with overweight, spoiled bums making $3 million a year who hit .228, "Brats 'N' Balls," a mixed-doubles tennis column named "Jocks and Jills," an auto-racing column called "In the Pits," a horse-racing column known as "Out Behind the Barn" or "Manure Matters," a dog column called "Licks 'N' Ticks," or a golf column entitled "Never Up, Never In," which also would make a good name for a column offering sexual advice.

However, I *didn't* make this one up: The sports editor of the Gainesville (Georgia) newspaper wrote a column he named "Who Cares?"

There was a man who obviously knew his readership. A lot of columns, both sports and otherwise, could have been entitled "Who Cares?" Unfortunately, nobody would have noticed the name.

* * *

I took on too much my freshman year at Georgia: three jobs (radio spotter, Times correspondent, and Wade Saye's assistant), a full academic load, and, worse, no car. Freshmen were forbidden to have cars, the thinking being that if they had them, they would be even more dangerous than they already were.

This theory didn't come to me until I was an upperclassman, but the reason freshmen are so dangerous is most of them are away from the parental nest for the first time in their lives. That first surge of freedom can make a person do some odd things, such as eating library books, pouring lighter fluid under the door of another dorm room and lighting it, taking the sand out of a hall ashtray and making a tee out of the sand and hitting golf balls down the hall at three in the morning, going to the movie with three bottles of fifty-nine-cent Red Hurricane wine and throwing up in the box of popcorn that belongs to the person sitting next to you, and stealing pigs from the School of Agriculture and letting them loose in the sorority house where the girls tended to be fat and have mustaches.

Giving freshmen cars would have been akin to giving terrorists their own airline. With mobility, college freshmen could have done such things as leaving the dorm at midnight to drive to Wyoming, just for the hell of it, or running over science majors, who dressed funny, weren't in fraternities, and *still* had a face full of zits.

Again, forgive me for leaving the subject at hand for a brief move elsewhere, but I can't allow the subjects of zits to go by without further discussion.

Like all teenagers, I had zits. I often wore enough Clearasil to clog Hoover Dam. However, by the time I reached college, most of my zits had disappeared.

Then something awful happened. A friend of mine fixed me up with a girl from Macon, who didn't have any zits but did have large things that rhymed with them.

A day or so before my date, I awakened with a zit on the end of my nose. It got bigger by the hour. In Geography 104 class, my first of the day, it was the size of the taillight on a 1954 De Soto. By Georgia History, it was blocking my view of the blackboard. By Introduction to Journalism, my classmates were hooting at me and calling me "Rudolph." By the time I got back to the dorm and hid under the covers to hide it, my zit was no longer a zit. It was a bulbous growth the size of the tomato that could win "Best of Show" at the annual country fair and agriculture exposition in Gooberville, Arkansas.

How could this be happening to me? I'd gone all through high school having to deal with zits, but I thought they were behind me forever now that I was in college.

There were a couple of things I considered: One, I would stay in bed and under the covers as long as I had my zit, I didn't care if it took three weeks.

But there was the matter of class and work, and I did so much want to keep my date with the buxom lass from Bibb County. So I decided on surgery. Charlie Harris had taught me not to try the mash technique. I found a safety pin and sterilized the sharp part with a match. (I earned a first-aid merit badge in the Boy Scouts.) Then

I went to my mirror and made several painful incisions into my zit in order to drain it. I will spare you any details of what resulted from my incisions.

When the draining was over, I washed off my nose. I still had my zit, but at least it was flat now and didn't protrude six inches ahead of me. Then I applied a coat of rubbing alcohol. I bit down on the hot-water handle of the sink until the pain subsided.

After that, I applied a coating of Clearasil I had purchased from the drugstore. After that, I applied a large Band-Aid. I realize a person with a Band-Aid on his nose looks silly and will be asked a thousand times, "What happened to your nose?" but it was better than walking around with a zit the size of Jefferson City, Missouri, while people laughed, pointed fingers, and made references to unicorns. At least, I thought so at the time. But the first thing my date said to me was, "What happened to your nose?"

"I ran into a door," I said.

"You sure it's not a zit?" she asked.

"Positive."

Zit denials are hard to pull off. Later in life, one of my wives, in her thirties, got a zit. She denied it, of course. It was a zit and she knew it and I knew she knew it. But still she insisted it wasn't.

Me, too. I spent my entire date with Miss Chest O'Plenty (there was a stripper named that once) denying I had a zit, but what finally did me in was running into a friend who asked, "How's your zit?"

I was dead.

"Okay," I said to my date, "it *is* a zit, but it's the first one I've had since my junior year in high school."

"Why did you lie to me?"

"I was afraid if you found out, you wouldn't like me," I answered.

"Just because you happen to have a zit on the end of your nose doesn't mean you're a bad person or I wouldn't like you," she said, quite sincerely.

"Does that mean I can still fondle your breasts?" I asked.

Her fist caught me squarely on the my nose zit. When it stopped hurting and I could open my eyes again, my date had returned to her dorm. Unfortunately, she had taken her breasts with her.

* * *

The fact I couldn't have a car gave me serious problems. I had to walk everywhere I went, and I had to go to a lot of places.

Here was my schedule:

5:00 A.M.: The alarm goes off. My Reed Hall roommate screams at me from the top bunk, "Why don't you switch to animal husbandry? The chickens aren't even up at this hour!"

5:15 A.M.: My roommate threatens to kill me. I have hit the snooze button, and the alarm is back on.

5:30 A.M.: Shower. (Do you know how eerie it is to be in a giant shower stall big enough for a hundred guys to use when all of those guys are asleep? At least there's nobody's hair on the soap yet.)

5:45 A.M.: Dress. "Cut off that light," says my roommate, who is thinking of transferring to the University of Arizona.

6:00 A.M.: Walk a mile to the *Banner-Herald*.

10:30 A.M.: Walk back another mile to the campus.

11:00–3 P.M.: Walk all over the damn campus, which has large hills, to classes.

3:00–3:45 P.M.: Walk to the opposite end of the campus from the *Banner-Herald* office to cover Georgia football practice.

5:30 to 5:35 P.M.: Interview head football-coach Vince Dooley, who doesn't like being asked stupid questions such as, "Well, Coach, who looked good in practice today?" by some seventeen-year-old.

5:35–6:00 P.M.: Type my story on Georgia football practice for the *Atlanta Times:* "Georgia Head Coach Vince Dooley said today that nobody looked good in practice and he was sick and tired of my stupid questions."

7:10–8:00 P.M.: Hoof it another mile back to town to file my story to the *Times* at Western Union.

8–8:30 P.M.: Stop by the Varsity resturant on the way back to the dorm and eat all the grease $1.50 will buy.

8:30–9:15 P.M.: Walk back to the dorm.

9:15–9:20 P.M.: Study, then fall asleep.

5:00 A.M.: The alarm goes off again.

My roommate made plans to purchase a firearm, and I gradually began to hate this schedule. There was one instance where I thought about giving up journalism, becoming an archeology major, and calling my mother to ask for money for a shovel.

It was raining when I stepped out of Reed Hall at dawn, on my way to the *Banner-Herald.* I was sleepy. I was wet. I thought, Why am I torturing myself like this?

I stopped. I looked back at the dorm. Turn back, or go ahead? The rain had soaked me down to my underdrawers. Nothing like wet underdrawers to sap one's ambition.

But I went ahead. Underdrawers dry out, and

I was convinced all this would pay off later. When I arrived at the *Banner-Herald,* I took a good stiff sniff of glue and told myself I had made the right decision.

It got easier. I went to see the assistant dean of men and told him my schedule and begged him to waive the no-car-for-freshman rule in my case, because if he didn't, I'd be in a wheelchair by quarter's end, having walked myself into paralysis.

He was a kind man. He said I could have a car if I didn't lend it to any other freshman, if I never allowed any other freshman in it, and if I promised not to set foot in Wyoming until I was at least thirty-five.

I agreed to all this, and my stepfather, who was selling cars at the time, let me have the 1958 blue-and-white Pontiac he had bought from the dealership where he worked.

I suddenly became the most popular person in the entire freshman class at the University of Georgia. Complete strangers came from two dorms away to ask to borrow my car, and you can, in fact, get fifteen college freshmen in a 1958 Pontiac. I proved it on many occasions.

Luckily, I never got caught bending any of the dean of men's rules. Since I have always enjoyed an occasional walk on the wild side, I even went to Wyoming for the first time when I was thirty.

The car made it easier. I vowed to avoid walking as much as possible for the rest of my life, which is one thing that hurt me in the three marriages I would have. Wives have this thing about walking, as in, "Honey, why don't we take a walk?" Whenever one of my wives would say that to me, I would run and get under the bed in the fetal position.

When countless marriage counselors asked me, "Lewis, why won't you take a walk with [either No. 1, No. 2, or No. 3]?" I would reply, "Have you ever covered a college football practice?"

When they would reply, "No," I would say, "I rest my case," and No. 1 or No. 2 or No. 3 would start crying. That's one of the reasons I could never stay married.

And speaking of life with disruptions. The *Atlanta Times* went out of business during winter quarter of my freshman year. They still owe me ninety dollars for the Georgia basketball games I covered. The *Atlanta Times* never had a chance against the *Journal and Constitution.*

It had never occurred to me before that newspapers could go broke and close down. I thought they were eternal, like savings-and-loans.

I took the closing of the *Times* hard. It wasn't simply the matter of the ninety dollars. I was making a couple hundred a month by then with my new business, Lewis's Friendly Freshman Rent-a-Car Service. But I had seen my own by-line in that newspaper, a big-town daily. (I was using "Lewis Grizzard, Jr.," at this point, Lewis Grizzard, Sr., owed a lot of people a lot of money.) I was never even inside the *Times*'s newsroom, but I knew it must have been a fine place, a noisy and busy place where the tele-type machines raced, phones rang, and glue pots got turned over.

I had never thought of newspapers in a busi-ness sense. It never occurred to me they had to make money to survive. It had never occurred to me one paper could snuff the life out of another.

The primary function of a newspaper was to print the news and raise hell, I thought. But I learned the truth. The primary purpose of a newspaper was to make money and stay in busi-ness. How many daily newspapers were there in New York twenty-five years ago? Seven, eight, nine? Now, there are only four and one of them, the *Daily News,* is fighting for its life.

Chicago is down to two newspapers. The *Her-ald Examiner* folded in Los Angeles. Competing newspaper towns continue to dwindle in num-ber.

I suppose if I owned a newspaper and had to concern myself with the business end of the business, I might feel differently. But all I have ever done is *work* for a newspaper, and when I happened to be in an area where there was competition, it made it better.

Twenty-five years later, I still insist the most fun I ever had working came as a result of some crazy people who had the idea to start a competing morning newspaper in Athens, Georgia, of all things and of all places.

I've said it a thousand times in my life: "If I could go back, I'd go back to Athens and do it all over again."

"The People Paper." It had one helluva run, and thank God and Gutenberg, I was a part of it.

But more about that in a little while.

7

I've never been very good with machinery. And machinery, in my mind, at least, is just about anything you can't eat, wear, or read. I am the man, I think, who inspired Brother Dave Gardner, the late Deep South comedian and philosopher, to quote a mother speaking to her son and saying, "James Lewis, get away from that wheelbarrow! You know you don't know nuthin' about machinery!"

Wheelbarrows confuse me, too. Do you pull or push the thing? And shovels and rakes and hoes and post-hole diggers and sling blades. Forget it. In fact, one of the primary reasons I've never committed any crime to speak of is I am actually afraid of sling blades, which is what prisoners use to cut back the grass on state and county roads.

A sling blade is this thing with a wooden handle and a sharp, rectangular blade on the end of it. The idea is to sling the blade down onto the grass. If you are still confused, recall that in the marvelous movie *Cool-Hand Luke* (Paul Newman, George Kennedy, and Strother Martin as the warden), the prisoners often were taken out on state and county roads to cut the grass with sling blades.

What always frightened me about sling blades was the idea I might sling the blade down at the grass and hit my leg, ankle, or foot instead, thus causing myself great pain. It could happen. I'm so bad with machinery I can't tell you how many times I have nearly cut my throat while shaving with one of those disposable razors.

All a disposable razor is, is a sling blade for whiskers. Once I was late for a party I was giving downstairs in my house, and in my rush to finish shaving I cut a place just above my Adam's apple. The blood ran down my neck and onto my chest. I tried everything to make it stop bleeding. I applied direct pressure to the wound, something I learned about in the Boy Scouts. That didn't help. I tried washing the wound with cold water, something I didn't learn about in the Boy Scouts, but it seemed to be a good idea at the time. That didn't help.

So I tried an ancient form of trying to make shaving wounds quit bleeding. I tore off a small piece of toilet paper and stuck it on the place on my Adam's apple. Gross. The little piece of toilet paper instantly became saturated with blood, and when I removed it from the wound, the blood gushed faster than it had been gushing before. That's when the doorbell started to ring, indicating my guests had begun arriving.

Then, I thought, Band-Aid! I found a box of Band-Aids in a drawer beneath my sink, where I also keep other items to be used in emergencies, such as condoms and peanuts. (You never know when you will be practicing safe sex and an elephant will walk into the room. What you do is give the elephant some peanuts to keep him busy until you're through.)

The problem, however, was I couldn't get the top off the Band-Aid case, and now blood was running down my chest into my abdominal area.

The instructions on the Band-Aid case said that in order to get the lid off I had to press down on the edges with my thumbs. But that didn't work, so I went to the drawer where I keep my burglary tools, found a crowbar, and beat the case open.

Another problem with Band-Aids is that damn little string. You're supposed to pull that little red string and the outer cover of the Band-Aid will come off, but that never works for me. Either I pull the string the wrong way, or it detaches from the Band-Aid altogether and I have to remove the outer covering by hand and the part of the Band-Aid with the sticky stuff on the bottom gets folded and then it won't stick on wherever it is you're trying to apply the Band-Aid to.

I went through three or four Band-Aids before I was able to remove the outer covering successfully. My next problem was this: The basic flaw in Band-Aids is they don't stick well to a place that isn't flat.

Try to get a Band-Aid to stick on a knuckle, for instance. The knuckles are raised above the skin, and if you try to put a Band-Aid there, it will stick at first, but as soon as you move the hand where the injured knuckle is, the Band-Aid will come loose.

Same with the Adam's apple. I put the Band-Aid on my Adam's apple, but as soon as I said, "That ought to do it" and my Adam's apple moved, the Band-Aid came loose.

What I did next was curse the Band-Aid. All those who are machinery-impaired like myself know that when all else fails, curse at whatever it is that is giving you a problem. (Paul Newman again. In the movie *Blaze,* he couldn't get his lawnmower to crank, so he cursed it. Then he went one step further. He went and got his shotgun and shot the lawnmower.)

I also knew a guy who got fed up with a car that would take thirty minutes to crank every time he tried to crank it. He got tired of all that and began cursing his car. Thirty minutes later, when the car finally cranked, he drove it to the nearest railroad crossing, shut off the engine, got out of the car and left it on the tracks so a train would hit it.

When he heard a train coming, he said to his car, "Good-bye, you suhbitch."

The engineer of the train, however, saw the car on the tracks soon enough, and was able to stop the train before any collision could take place. The engineer got out of the train and asked the man, "Is that your car?"

The man said yes.

"Well, get the damn thing off the tracks," said the engineer.

The man, realizing he might be guilty of some sort of Interstate Commerce Commission violation, got back into his car and attempted to crank it.

It wouldn't crank, of course.

The engineer, becoming ever more impatient, finally said, "Push that damn thing off the tracks. I've got a schedule to keep."

So the man put his car in "drive," got behind it, and pushed it off the tracks. Unfortunately, the road went downhill on the other side of the tracks, and the car began to roll, picking up speed. The man chased his car and attempted to get inside and put on the brakes, but it was too late. His car rolled into a Dunkin' Donuts place, knocking out the window front and coming to rest in the glazed and powdered section of the doughnut rack behind the counter.

The man wound up having to pay two thousand dollars in damages, not to mention paying for a tow truck to come pull his car out of the doughnuts. It wouldn't crank, naturally, when he tried to back it out of the Dunkin' Donuts.

What the man did to his car next was set it afire in his backyard. Noxious fumes covered the entire neighborhood, and somebody called the fire department, who came and put out the fire. The man was charged with burning without a permit, and now he had this half-burned piece of machinery in his backyard.

What he finally did was call the towing company again, and they charged him seventy-four dollars to tow the car over to a junk dealer who said he'd give the man ten dollars for the car.

"I'll take it," said the man.

"This is the last time you'll embarrass me," the man said to his car.

He called a taxi to take him home. On the way, the taxi got hit from behind and the man suffered whiplash. He sued the driver of the other car, but when he told Judge Wapner his side of the story, Judge Wapner said, "I had a car like that once, too. What I did was roll it off a pier, which is what you should have done. I rule in favor of the defendant."

And I'm still bleeding. All my guests had arrived by now, and were complaining about the meatballs. "Damn things are probably made of soybeans," I heard one of my guests say.

How I eventually got my Adam's apple to stop bleeding is I prayed. I once saw faith healer Ernest Ainsley pray and a little girl that had one leg that was shorter than the other, suddenly had legs of the same length, and she jumped up and did the Jerk, right on the stage.

I said, "God, if you will make my Adam's apple stop bleeding, I'll never try to save a few bucks by serving meatballs made out of soybeans to my guests again."

The bleeding stopped. A miracle. My guests at least liked the bean dip I had sitting next to the bowl of Fritos.

So how did an individual who has also had trouble with which of the knobs is for cold and which is for hot on unfamiliar sinks, hasn't mastered a Mr. Coffee machine or a plastic ice tray that doesn't have a handle, wind up driving a forklift in the summer of 1965?

It was Ronnie Jenkins's fault. When spring

quarter ended at Georgia, I no longer had a job with the *Banner-Herald.* Wade didn't need me because school was out and all that was left to cover in Athens was boys' baseball, an occasional swim meet, and the Saturday night auto races at Athens Speedway. The *Atlanta Times* had gone out of business, and football season didn't start for three more months.

I decided to go back home for the summer. Ronnie had quit his job at the bank in Atlanta by then, and had also moved back home. He got a job in the accounting department at a Newnan plant that made plastic tabletops. Ronnie said, "I can get you a summer job at the plastic plant."

I had some experience in accounting myself, thanks to my career in the loan-payment department the summer before. And the company put out a newsletter. Perhaps I could edit and write that? Or how about public relations?

Ronnie, who got to wear a tie to work and sit in an air-conditioned office, got me a job driving a forklift for minimum wage, $1.25 an hour.

The first forklift I ever saw, I was driving. A forklift is this vehicle that has two forks in front of it. There's a handle near where the driver sits that makes the forks go up and down.

The idea is that things that needed to be lifted,

moved to another place and then lowered onto that place sat on wooden platforms called "skids." Each skid had two openings. You drove up to the skid, lowered the forks into the openings, then raised the skid and whatever was resting on them.

I likely was one of the few employees out in the plant with a high school education. I am certain I was the only one with any college experience.

In fact, I was so much smarter than everybody else, they finally had to paint a little sign next to my lowering and lifting lever so I wouldn't forget which way to push it for up and down.

"For a college boy," my supervisor, Lonnie (Goat) Smith, a twenty-year veteran of the plant with terrible B.O., said to me one day, "you sure are a dumb suhbitch."

"I'm a journalism major," I said to Lonnie (Goat) Smith. "I have seen my byline in a metropolitan newspaper. The fact that newspaper no longer exists is irrelevant here. What is not irrelevant is I should be over there in an air-conditioned office wearing a tie like Ronnie Jenkins, but instead, I'm sitting out here on this machine and it's hot, I am perspiring profusely, and the gas fumes are making me sick to my stomach, but at least they smell better than you do.

"Now, the only reason I am here in the first place was I needed a summer job and they are onto my clever ruse of last summer at the bank in Atlanta. So I will drive this snorting tool until September, when I will return to the University of Georgia and continue my meteoric rise as a sportswriter. Now, why don't you leave me alone and go have your armpits steam cleaned?"

Actually, I didn't say any of that to Goat, because if I had, two, and possibly three, things could have happened.

One, Goat wouldn't have understood a word I was saying. Two, he might have understood I was being a smart-ass, and there's nothing a supervisor of forklifts dislikes any more than a smart-ass college boy, and he would have hurt me. Three, I also could have got fired, which wouldn't have been that bad a circumstance had I been Dan Quayle, who's about my age, at the time.

If I had been Dan Quayle, I could have called Dad and he could have called the plant and had Goat Smith cleaning toilets and me switched over to planning and development where I could have spent the summer going around saying things like "What this company needs is a good slow-pitch softball team."

Unfortunately, I was Lewis Grizzard and didn't know Dan Quayle's father, so I simply agreed with Goat that for a college boy I was a stupid suhbitch and continued to punch in at seven each morning for my eight-hour shift.

I never did come to master my forklift. I had the arrows to show me which way to push the lever, but I was still able to inflict much damage. I never hurt a person, but I did manage to destroy a fair amount of property. There was the day the shipment of resin arrived.

"Go back to the loading dock and unload the resin shipment out of the truck," Goat instructed me.

The resin came in many paper bags that sat on skids in the back of a truck. I didn't have any problem with the unloading part. I lifted each skid of resin, backed my forklift out of the truck, and deposited the shipment nearly inside the plant.

"Who's goin' to sign for 'is?" the truck driver said to me as I was backing the last skid out of his truck.

"You would want to see Mr. Smith about that?" I asked.

"Well," said the driver, "tell him to git his ass out here, I ain't got all day."

I found Goat.

"The truck driver said for you to git your ass out there and sign for the resin, he ain't got all day."

I might not have been able to drive a forklift with great skill, but I was developing a good ear for quotes, and my communication skills were improving even outside the classroom.

I drove back out to the loading dock to see if Goat and the truck driver were going to have any words, forged by the truck driver's impatience and the fact he had referred to Goat's ass.

"What you in such a got-damn hurry about?" Goat asked the truck driver, who wasn't as big as Goat and certainly didn't smell as bad, but who did have a tattoo with the words "Born to raise hell" on his left forearm.

"Got-damn," said the truck driver, wrinkling his nose, "when's the last time you took a bath?"

"You sayin' I stink?" Goat responded.

"Either that, or you got a dead dog in your pocket," shot back the truck driver.

"I ain't above whippin' yo' ass right here," said Goat.

"Hell," said the truck driver. "Your smell already 'bout knocked me down."

With that, Goat took a swing at the truck

driver, who dodged the blow and countered with a right to Goat's belly. Goat doubled up, and fought for his breath.

When he was able to speak again, he said to the truck driver, "Where do I sign?"

I started laughing. I couldn't help it. I just sat there on my forklift and howled, and after Goat had signed for the resin shipment and the truck driver had departed, Goat said to me, "There's nothing I hate more'n a smart-ass college boy."

At this point, I realized that I didn't have a single tattoo on my person and could not handle Goat with the same ease as the truck driver, so when he added, "Git an empty skid and take it over to the paper press," I stopped laughing and drove to where I happened to see an empty skid.

As soon as Goat was out of range, however, I started laughing again, and failed to notice there was a large nail sticking out of one side of the empty skid. Goat had often warned me, "Make sure you check over the skid and see there ain't no nails stickin' out."

I had never paid attention to much else Goat had told me, so why was I going to make a lasting mental note about this bit of instruction?

I lifted the skid and started driving over to the paper press. I drove past the bags of resin I had unloaded out of the truck. I drove too close to the bags of resin I had unloaded out of the truck. The nail sticking out of the skid ripped open about eighteen bags of resin before I realized what was occurring. Resin was pouring out the bags and getting all over the floor. Goat saw what had happened, rushed over, and said, "Son, you ain't study'n to be no doctor, are you?"

I assured him I wasn't.

"Good," he answered.

Later I thought, That was pretty funny what Goat said about me studying to be a doctor. His implication was that if I was dangerous driving a lift fork, what would I be with a scalpel in my hand?

Another time, I was carrying a skid of finished tops over to shipping and hadn't pushed the forks far enough into the openings to the skid. As a result, the plastic tops fell, and many were scratched and rendered unshippable.

Goat asked, upon surveying the results of my improper forklifting, "What are you study'n over at that college?"

"Journalism," I said with some degree of pride. "I'm going into the newspaper business."

"Well, I hope you can walk while you're deliver'n, 'cause you couldn't drive a boot up a mule's ass with directions written on the heel."

To be quite honest, I began to both admire, and feel sorry for, Goat as the summer wore on. He was actually fairly patient with me, and I am certain now, in retrospect, he must have felt there was at least some hope for my becoming a good forklift driver. He kept saying to me, "As soon as you catch on to this, I'm goin' to teach you how to flush the commode in the men's toilet."

The *Newnan Times-Herald* was the local weekly. It was always winning prizes. The *Newnan Times-Herald* was doing amazing things with color and printing twenty years before other newspapers, even the big ones, figured out a brighter package would help sell a product more.

The paper was, and still is, owned by the Thomasson family. Editorially, it was like most small-town weeklies. There was, as I discussed earlier, the news of the various communities and county, and there was news of who died and who was born and who got married and what local son had just completed his basic training and who spoke to the weekly Rotary meeting.

The paper took on a major project in the spring of 1965, the centennial year of Coweta County. The paper decided to print a special edition, covering the history of the county.

The family hired a woman with impressive

credentials to write and edit the special edition. She was a flop, however, and it was the middle of July and the edition was due in a few more months. I was over at the plastic plant on my forklift.

I was never quite certain how Mr. Thomasson, the editor and publisher of the newspaper, got the idea to hire me to work on the special. I seriously doubt he went back through the files and found my work covering my little baseball league. But I came home from work one afternoon, and my mother said Mr. Thomasson from the paper had called me and wanted me to call him back.

I did. Here was the deal:

The fancy woman was gone, he was in a bind, and would I come help work on the centennial edition for the rest of the summer?

What, and leave my forklift?

I said, "When do you want me to start?"

He said, "Tomorrow."

I reported to the plastic plant at seven the next morning, told Goat I was going to go to work at the newspaper, and he said, "Hell, you wasn't cut out for this kind of work no way anyway," but he said it with a smile and even parted with a "Good luck."

I wore my regular clothes into the plant that

morning. I certainly would report to the *Times-Herald* in a jacket and tie, but I didn't want to show up that way at the plant and give off some message that said, "You poor suckers are stuck here, but I'm moving on to bigger and better things." I'd decided I didn't really want to be a smart-ass college boy after all.

What I did for the *Times-Herald* was write histories of the local communities. One of these communities was once known as "Wahoo Creek."

I wrote, "Nobody remembers exactly how the village came to be called Wahoo Creek, but perhaps, when the first settlers arrived and saw the beauty of the sparkling creek that ran there, one was so overcome with joy, he jumped and said, 'Wahoo,' and that's how, etc. etc."

Okay, okay, I know—but I was eighteen at the time, for goodness' sake.

I did the history of Arnco-Sargent, Sharpsburg, Grantville, Welcome All, and my hometown, Moreland, which used to be called Puckett Station before a guy named Moreland moved into town and promised the residents he would bring in a Popeye's fried-chicken franchise and get the Jefferson Salt Company to paint everybody's barn red if they would change the name from Puckett Station to Moreland.

Well, they did, but there's still not a Popeye's fried-chicken franchise in Moreland, and there turned out to be a hitch in the barn-painting thing, too. The Jefferson Salt Company said it would paint everybody's barn red, but that it would also paint JEFFERSON ISLAND SALT on the top of the barns for advertising.

Most people in Moreland who had barns didn't want JEFFERSON ISLAND SALT painted on the top of their barns. Most of them already had SEE ROCK CITY, anyway.

The townspeople finally ran Mr. Moreland out of town. Some of them wanted to change the name back to Puckett Station, but they had already put up the new name of the town at the Atlanta and West Point Railroad Station, so, according to one elderly lady I interviewed, "They decided it was too late to screw with it."

In my history of Moreland, I also wrote a lot of stuff about cows and chickens and mules and picking cotton.

That's because horses, cows, mules, chickens and cotton picking were big deals in Moreland before the boll weevil came and ate all the cotton, mules gave way to tractors, horses got too expensive to keep a lot of them around, and most people quit raising cattle and went to work in either the Moreland Hosiery Mill or Cole Shop

in Newnan, or they opened a beer joint, which
is what Steve Smith eventually did in Moreland,
which is also where I drank my first beer, but I
didn't mention that in my history.

At the end of spring quarter at Georgia, Wade
had assured me I would have my job waiting
back at the *Banner-Herald* in the fall. With the
ten dollars a week I'd get from spotting for
Georgia football broadcasts and the money I
had saved over the summer, I figured to get by.

A couple of weeks before I was to return to
Athens, I got another message from my mother.
"A man called you from Athens and wants you
to call him back."

It was Wade. I called him back in Athens at
the number he had left. Only the operator didn't
answer, *"Athens Banner-Herald."* She answered, *"Athens Daily News."*

The Athens Daily what?

Wade filled me in briefly. He said some men
from Columbus had got together with some men
in Athens and started a shopper, basically a
newspaper with nothing but ads.

They had then decided to change the shopper into a six-times-a-week-daily and call it the
Athens Daily News. He had been trying to find
me all summer to come back to Athens and go
to work for him.

"I'm the sports editor," he said.

"You left the *Banner-Herald?*" I asked him.

"Wouldn't you?"

Wade knew I had gone back to Moreland, but what he didn't know was my mother had remarried and our phone number was under the name H. B. Atkinson, my stepfather. He finally called the university, tracked me down, and now wanted to know if I could come to work as soon as possible.

"I'm swamped," he said. "Georgia has started football practice, and I need you to cover Athens High."

I finished the last history for the *Times-Herald,* told everybody how much I had enjoyed it, and drove back to Athens. It was the beginning of the best newspaper experience of my career. Nothing that came later matched it.

A Columbus man who owned some radio stations joined with a couple of Columbus newspapermen and an outdoor advertiser in Athens and conspired to start the new morning paper in direct competition with the afternoon joke, the *Banner-Herald.* Athens was ripe. The university and the town were growing.

There was also an untouched opportunity in the surrounding northeast Georgia area, largely ignored by the *Banner-Herald* and dabbled with only ever so slightly by the *Anderson* (South

Carolina) *Independent,* just across the state line.

The *Banner-Herald* had been asleep for fifty years. The *Daily News* came with thunder and smoke.

Claude Williams, the Athens outdoor advertising man, was the publisher. Glenn Vaughn, who was a part of the Pulitzer Prize the *Columbus Enquirer* won for its coverage of the Phenix City, Alabama, story, was the editor.

Phenix City, Alabama, just across the Chattahoochee River from Columbus, was full of rigged gambling houses, prostitutes, and seedy bars that attracted soldiers from nearby Fort Benning in the early 50's. The corrupt local city government ignored citizens' cries for reforms. Finally, a state investigation closed down the Phenix City joints with the help of troops from Benning, and years of murder, thievery, extortion, and various other wide-open illegal practices came to an end. The *Enquirer* had crusaded for the reforms that finally came.

Wade Saye had sports. Larry Young, former police reporter for the *Augusta Chronicle* was city editor. Gerald Rutberg, who was to have interned at the Columbus paper that summer under Glenn Vaughan had, instead, followed him to Athens.

Gerald had just graduated from Auburn University, where he had been editor of the school newspaper. Glenn made him society editor. Glenn's wife, Nancy, did whatever it was that needed doing.

And that was the editorial staff that put out the first issue of the *Daily News* on June 17, 1965. The thing was charmed from the beginning.

Larry Young was in his late forties. He was straight out of the mold. He was a tall man with a deep, thick South Carolina accent and he smoked one cigarette after the other. He would hold the telephone between his shoulder and his cheek and interview a police chief while beating out the quotes on the old manual at his desk. He could do that with a cigarette in his mouth, and the longer he talked and typed and the longer the cigarette remained in his mouth, the more his face would go into contortions from the smoke of the cigarette billowing toward his eyes and nose.

It was only when the smoke teared his eyes to the point he could no longer see that he would take one of his hands off the typewriter in front of him, pull the cigarette out of his mouth, take a deep breath, and dump the ashes onto the floor. Then the cigarette would go back into his mouth, and I can hear him now, "Chief, if anything breaks on this, how 'bout calling me first?"

Larry even dressed the part of the veteran small-town reporter. His clothes never seemed to match, and he apparently had only one pair of shoes, beige Hush Puppies. But his appearance didn't matter to him, and, obviously, money wasn't very high on his list, either, since small-town reporters might expect to make $120, tops.

He was divorced. He had a history of problems with the booze. If his marriage had worked and he'd never looked for an answer in the bottom of a glass, he wouldn't have fit the mold.

Glenn Vaughn had rescued Larry. The drinking cost him his Augusta job, but Glenn had hired him anyway. When he was sober, he could get the news. Glenn simply hoped the sober days outnumbered the other ones.

Larry Young had no college degree in journalism, or in anything else. (Today, with no college degree, you might land a job in the mail room.) Larry simply could do what all good reporters can. He could make people tell him things and then convince them not to tell anybody else. Cops, politicians, members of the city council, bartenders, night clerks, the president of the university—Larry Young could talk all of them out of whatever story he was seeking. Remember Abe Lincoln's line about Grant? "Find out what kind of whisky he drinks and give it to my other generals." Glenn Vaughan might have said the same about Larry Young.

Shortly before the first edition of the *Daily News,* Georgia's senior senator, Richard Russell, died. Richard Russell had been a power in the Senate for years. They used to say, "If Richard Russell hadn't been from the South, he would have been president."

Russell's home was Winder, Georgia, twenty miles west of Athens. His funeral and his burial would be there. Larry Young got on the phone. He asked a Russell aide what Washington names would likely fly down for the Russell funeral. The aide told him, "We expect the president."

Larry, a few hours from deadline, phoned the White House, and it was confirmed Lyndon Johnson would be flying to Winder for Russell's funeral.

The *Banner-Herald* had missed the story in its afternoon edition. The President was coming, and Larry Young had the story. *Scoop.* It was a delicious newspaper term that has given way now to "exclusive," and mostly it is used by television news. So few towns still have competing newspapers anymore, there's nobody to scoop. The best a reporter can hope for is some prize for an in-depth series on the troubles in Lower Slamdunkovia.

But this thing in Athens would become as competitive as any other newspaper battle to the death. On a much smaller scale, yes, but a fight is a fight, regardless of the stature of the combatants.

Glenn Vaughn, the editor, was the perfect editor for this perfect newspaperman's dream. He was a graduate of the university. He had worked in Atlanta and on the *Columbus Enquirer.* I've never known a man who loved newspapering as much as Glenn Vaughn. Newspapers consumed him. He rarely talked of anything else. The *Daily News* was his and was whatever he wanted it to be. I don't know when he slept or ate.

And how much he looked his part, too. He wore suspenders long before stockbrokers and lawyers all started wearing suspenders. He wore thick glasses, and his hair usually was down over his forehead. He dressed better than Larry Young, which basically meant his taste in shoes was better and he had more than one suit.

He edited in green ink. He had been known as "Foggy" to his Georgia classmates in the early fifties. Glenn often seemed to be in the Newsroom Out Yonder. He was absentminded, messy, and given to forgetting what the conversation was about. He also came at you from places no one else ever did, ever could, or ever will.

After I'd been at the paper a year or so, I walked by his office one day, and Glenn said, "Lewis, you got a minute?" his standard way of saying, "Come into my office."

I sat down at the chair in front of his desk. Whenever Glenn had a new idea and was enthusiastic about it, he would beat a fist into the palm of his other hand, which is what he began to do soon after I sat down.

"What," he began, "would be the biggest local story we could ever have at the *Daily News?*"

I thought for a minute. "The university burning down."

"Bigger than that."

"Georgia winning the national football championship."

"Even bigger than that."

"Twenty-five sorority girls indicted in a sex-ring operation."

"That's big," said Glenn, "but not as big as what I have in mind."

"I give up," I said.

"What if," he followed, pounding his fist into his palm even harder now, "the Second Coming took place in Athens?"

I didn't have time to answer the question.

"It's got to happen somewhere, doesn't it?" he went on. "A lot of people might think it would happen in New York or some other large city, but why not a small town?"

I didn't have any argument with that. Nothing I had learned in the Methodist Church had indicated where Jesus might actually touch down on that Great Gettin'-Up Morning. If I had been asked to guess, though, I really wouldn't have selected Athens. New York, sure. Start with the big sinners and then work on down.

I knew Glenn had a reason to be asking me all this. He did.

"In case the Second Coming did happen in Athens," he continued, "we've got to be ready for it."

Right. We certainly would want to beat the *Banner-Herald.* Lyndon Johnson coming to town was big, but this, this would dwarf even that.

Glenn said, "I've already drawn up the front page."

He showed me the layout sheet. Across the top of the page was an eight-column, one-line 124-point headline. The higher the point size, the larger the headline. *The New York Times,* even today, rarely goes over, say, a 48-point headline, even when a president dies.

Underneath the headline, Glenn had drawn the newspaper's masthead. To take a headline or a story "above the mast" was to put the story in the category of stupendous, colossal, and far-reaching in its effects.

Down the left-hand side of the front paper was our usual "Georgia Datelines" feature. It was a two-column compendium of Georgia news, taken off the United Press International wire. Even if the Second Coming was the main story, Glenn had reasoned, we couldn't take "Georgia Datelines" off the front. There might be a big fire in Atlanta or a killing in Americus.

The other six columns of the front page were taken up by a large photograph that went nearly to the bottom of the page. Glenn explained:

"As you know, we get our UPI Wirephotos from the mail. So, if one of our own photographers didn't get a photograph of the actual ascension, we'd have to wait a day for UPI's. So I went over to the library and took out a book on religious art, and found what I thought was the best and clearest portrait of Christ.

"I brought it back and had a Velox [a picture of the picture] made. It's just a head shot, but we can paste it right on the front page in a matter of seconds. I've also already written the headlines and had them made up. We can paste them down right away too and be on the streets with a special edition before the *Banner-Herald* knows what hit them."

I knew he would show me the headlines. He did.

The eight-column over-the-mast, 124-point head said:

"HE'S BACK!"

Underneath the Velox of Christ, there was a small headline that said,

"DETAILS, PAGE 2."

"I want you to write me a cut-on line [caption] for the head shot of Jesus," Glenn said.

I wrote, "Christian Savior Jesus Christ Returned to Earth Today."

"Needs more pizzazz," Glenn insisted.

I wrote, "Biblical Prediction Comes True: Son of God Returns."

"Still not right," said Glenn. "It needs a local angle."

So I wrote, "Athens Set to Give Hero's Welcome to Returning Son of God, Jesus Christ (pictured above)."

Finally, Glenn rewrote the cutline himself. His

said, "Athenians say 'Glad to Have You Back' After Surprise Drop-In by Jesus. Larry Young's exclusive interview inside."

"Do you think Larry could get to him first?" I asked Glenn.

"No question," he said. "I've already told him to make sure he has at least a half of tank of gas in his car at all times, just in case."

What Glenn Vaughn thought a community newspaper should do is cover the community first. He figured you could wrap up most of the national and international news in a brief summary inside the paper. It was rare a nonlocal story ever made front page of the *Daily News,* and if it did, it had to be the sort of story no other newspapers could carry out front.

"I remember the old wire editor in Columbus," he told me once.

"He'd go through the wire and find some incredible story, pass it around, and say, 'Here, read this.' It would be a helluva story. But as soon as everybody had read it, it would go back to the wire editor, and he would throw it in the trash."

"Why was that?" I asked him.

"Because the story wasn't on the wire budget," he explained.

Each day, the wire opens with its summary of

what editors considered to be the top stories of the day. This was the budget. Not to carry a story that was on the wire budget was considered a manifestation of poor news judgment.

"You know how the wire budget probably gets made up?" Glenn asked me. "Somebody in New York says to a copy boy, 'Go around and see what everybody's got today and make me up a budget.' There's some nineteen-year-old kid who's determining what wire stories are on the front page of newspapers all over the country."

I first walked into the *Athens Daily News* building in the morning of August 22, 1965. I was nineteen. The *Daily News* building had once been an automobile agency. The showroom, with huge glass windows looking out onto the street and directly at the Open House Restaurant (open twenty-four hours a day, all the grease you could eat and breathe), had been turned into a newsroom.

There were six desks. On each desk sat a manual typewriter. Facing the window, Gerald Rutberg had the far desk on the right. Larry Young's desk was the closest. Nobody was in the far desk on the left. Wade Saye had the near desk on the left.

There was another desk to the left of Wade.

Next to that desk was the UPI teletype. That's where Jim Sheppard, the managing editor, worked. He stripped the wire, edited copy, handled assignments, and laid out what pages Glenn hadn't already taken his green pen to.

I went to Wade's desk first. He said, "You need to go in and meet Glenn Vaughn, the editor."

Glenn's office was to the right as you stepped up from the newsroom. It probably was the office of the sales manager when the place was still an automobile dealership. You know the sales manager. He's the one the salesman talks about when he's trying to sell you a '64 Plymouth and he says, "My sales manager is going to kill me for this, but I'll let you have it for nine-hundred-fifty dollars."

I knocked on the door.

"Wade said you did a good job for him at the *Banner-Herald*," he said to me.

"Well, sir," I said, "I worked as hard as I could. I feel practical experience is very important when one is seeking a career in journalism."

I was proud of myself for saying that. I sounded like a young man who knew what responsibility was all about and who could be trusted not to sniff a glue pot intentionally.

"I can give you twenty hours of work a week," Glenn said. "At a dollar twenty-five per hour."

I went back to see Wade. He said, "Athens High is practicing at one. Cover it."

So I found some brown typing paper—we weren't provided notebooks at the *Daily News*—folded it, and put it in my back pocket. Then I found a red copy pencil, put it behind my ear, and got into the car I'd bought over the summer in Newnan, a red-and-white 1954 Chevrolet. The salesman had said, "My sales manager is going to kill me for this, but I'll let it go for four-hundred-fifty dollars."

I drove over to Athens High and watched practice. When it was over, I walked up to Weyman Sellers, the head coach and a former Georgia star, and introduced myself. Weyman Sellers was a large man.

"I'm Lewis Grizzard of the *Daily News*," I said.

"Grizzard?" he asked back. "What kind of name is that? What are you, a Japanese exchange student?"

I would have a lot of trouble attempting to interview coaches during my sportswriting career. I might as well have started here.

I asked Weyman Sellers, "Coach, what kind of team are you expecting this year?"

He looked at me as if I were crazy.

"You sure you aren't from Japan?" he asked.

I assured him that I wasn't. "Grizzard" is a

French name. My mother's ancestors were Scottish and Irish.

"How do I know what kind of team we're going to have?" he went on. "Right now, we've got so many people hurt, we can't even scrimmage."

Ah, so, my angle. I asked him to name the key players hurt, and I wrote down the players' names on my brown copy paper with my red editing pencil, said it was nice to meet him and that I would be covering the team the entire season.

"You believe that, Frank?" he said to his assistant, Frank Malinowski, who'd also played at Georgia. "We're going to have a Jap with us all year."

Frank just laughed.

I drove back to the *Daily News.* Wade told me to sit at the empty desk across from Rutberg.

I wrote:

By LEWIS GRIZZARD JR.
Daily News Sports Writer

"Oooh! Ouch! Oh!"—familiar interjections at the Athens High Trojan football practice yesterday.

I learned the word "interjection" in English class my senior year in high school and never had had an opportunity to use it. I had filed it away, however, awaiting just the right moment. This was clearly it.

Wade ran the story without comment.

I would work for the *Daily News* for a thousand days. Each of those days were precious. Like nothing before, like nothing since. I have cried in reminiscence more times than I remember. If only it, like so many things, could have lasted.

There was the story about Dr. Aderhold's wife's chicken. Dr. O.C. Aderhold, was president of the University of Georgia, and he lived in a stately mansion on Prince Avenue.

Mrs. Aderhold had a pet chicken. I seem to remember the chicken's name was Hilda, but it could have been Rhonda. No, Rhonda was the waitress at the Open House who didn't have any teeth and used to sit at the counter during her breaks gumming pickles out of the counter pickle jar, which was something to see and something the *Daily News* should have done a story about. Hilda was a girl who worked back in the mail room, I think. It was twenty-five years ago. Who cares what the chicken's name was?

Anyway, one day, Mrs. Aderhold's pet chicken (maybe it was Veronica) climbed up in a tree in Mrs. Aderhold's yard and wouldn't come down. Mrs. Aderhold tried to get her chicken down out of the tree for hours, but the chicken wouldn't budge. Mrs. Aderhold was afraid the chicken would catch cold at that altitude, or would be carried off to the Casbah by a lecherous chicken hawk. You know how they are.

When she panicked, she did what any wife of the president of a large southern institution would do when she couldn't get her pet chicken (Florence?) to come down out of a tree.

She called the fire department.

Larry Young covered the story. We had photographs. Glenn Vaughn made it the lead story in the *Daily News* the next morning. Who remembers what the *Banner-Herald* led with?

"THE RESCUE OF MRS. ADERHOLD'S CHICKEN"

screamed the 72-point, eight column headline.
    And then:

By LARRY YOUNG
Daily News City Editor

A pet chicken owned by Mrs. O.C. Aderhold, wife of University president Dr. O.C. Aderhold, wouldn't come down from a tree in front of her stately Prince Avenue home yesterday, so the Athens Fire Department came to the rescue.

Answering a call from Mrs. Aderhold at 2:17 P.M., Athens fireman arrived on the scene at exactly 2:20 and had the chicken safely out of the tree in a matter of moments.

"I just love that chicken," Mrs. Aderhold said. "I don't know what I would have done had it been carried off by a chicken hawk. You know how they are."

The chicken was rescued when hook and ladder engine No. 8 was driven under the tree and fireman Arnold Spintz was hoisted to the limb where the chicken was perched. With great care not to injure or alarm the chicken, he brought it down and placed it into the waiting arms of Mrs. Aderhold.

As for President Aderhold, he had no other comment except to say he appreciated what the fire department had done and was going to sleep.

The story had Athens talking for weeks. Some reacted, of course, by whispering, "How could the wife of the president of the university become so attached to a chicken?" Others simply thought it was pretty funny, while others called in with their own chicken-in-a-tree story.

A man from nearby Comer, Georgia, called to say, "Any fool knows a chicken will come down out of a tree soon as it gets hungry enough."

A Watkinsville woman commented, "Mrs. Aderhold ought to go ahead and eat that chicken before she becomes even more attached to it.

"I had a pet chicken once, but the preacher came to eat one Sunday, and Daddy went out an' wrung its neck and Mama fried it and served it to the preacher. I wouldn't eat none of it myself, on account of I was so attached to it, and I was hungry all Sunday afternoon until Mama opened a can of Spam for dinner."

A journalism professor of mine said it was embarrassing to see a daily newspaper carry a story about a chicken rescue as the banner, but that he'd had a pet chicken once and his dog killed it trying to have sex with it.

How stories get on the front page of most morning newspapers goes like this:

There's a late-afternoon news meeting of the

editors. The managing editor usually conducts the meeting, and he asks each of his or her various underlings what stories they are preparing for the first edition. Once all this information is in, there's a roundtable discussion to decide which stories are important enough go to on the front page.

As I mentioned earlier, there is the wire budget to consider.

The managing editor will ask the wire editor, "What's on the budget?"

The wire editor will respond, "Congress has voted to give statehood to American Samoa, the Supreme Court (which the budget always refers to as SCOTUS—you figure it out) has ruled it's unconstitutional to turn right on red, the Russians have invaded Argentina, there's a piece on tangerines causing cancer, and Willie Nelson has decided to shave off his beard."

Then the city editor will come forward with the local stories of the day:

"City Council is studying a proposal to sell the entire town and all its citizens to the Japanese; something ate an entire garbage truck. Lon Dinkle's pit bull "Skippy" is the prime suspect; the mayor has admitted he is a homosexual and will seek reelection as a Whig; a sinkhole swallowed the bowling alley and the entire Pin-Busters team; and a drive-by mooning incident has been reported by the weekly meeting of the United Daughters of the Boxer Rebellion."

The managing editor will decide all these stories are much too interesting to go on the front page ("This ain't no tabloid," he will say), and the editors will be told to go back and find a lot of stuff about South Yemen and rezoning hearings.

That's not the way we did it at the *Athens Daily News.* Glenn, ever the journalistic pioneer, insisted every story on the front page was worth reading, shocking other journalism instructors, who said, "If the *Daily News* keeps this up, it won't last six more weeks."

But we never let up. For instance:

* In neighboring Jackson County, the local solicitor had decided to crack down on an infamous car-theft operation. One morning, he went outside and cranked his car and his car blew up with him in it. We covered it like the Second Coming.

  Three men were arrested in the incident, but a fourth was still at large. Fearing for his life because of the outrage the bombing brought, the suspect finally called Larry Young and said he would turn himself in to the newspaper if we could guarantee his safety.

The headline went something like:

"BOMBING SUSPECT GIVES UP TO DAILY NEWS"

Scoop.

* Georgia was to play at Clemson the following Saturday. On Sunday morning, I happened to catch *The Frank Howard Show.* Frank Howard was head coach at Clemson and talked as if he had a mouth full of mud, which was really tobacco.

I wrote a Tuesday column, lampooning the show and quoting Coach Howard saying such words as "Heah" (here), "co-atch" (coach), "big-un" (large person), as in "Jawja's gone brang in some big-uns ovah heah Satdy and Co-atch Dooley always has his boys ready to play."

Wednesday morning, I was having lunch at my apartment. The phone rang. I answered it. A gravel mixer on the other end asked, "Yo' name Grizzud?"

"That's close," I said.

"This is Co-atch Frank Howard at Clemsun, and I done read what you had to say 'bout me, and I'm gon' sue you butt."

Having not yet taken Journalism Law and knowing very little about libel laws, I panicked and drove quickly to the office to tell Glenn about the phone call from Co-atch Howard. I assumed he would go into a rage and say, "This could cost us millions." Instead, he started hitting his fist into his palm and said, "This is great!"

He interviewed me, wrote a story, and the next day we lead with, "Clemson's Howard Threatens Suit Against *Daily News.*"

Of course, there never was a suit, but it beat the *Banner-Herald*'s lead on rioting in South Yemen.

One evening, there was nobody but me to go to a neighboring community and investigate what various callers had told us was the local police chief running a speed-trap operation.

It was my first nonsports assignment for the paper. I had no idea what to do, since there's no press box to sit in when you investigate a police chief operating a speed-trap operation.

What I did was drive to the little community, walk into the one-room police station, and ask the man I saw sitting there, "Are you the police chief?"

He said that he was, and I said, "Glad to meet you. I'm Lewis Grizzard of the *Athens Daily News,* and I wonder if you would comment on the fact we've had several calls about you running a speed-trap operation."

The chief responded with something that went like this: "Get your ass out of my office, and if I catch you back in my town again . . ."

I didn't hear the rest of the quote because I was halfway back to Athens by this time.

"What did you get?" Glenn asked me when I got back to the office.

"Nothing," I said. "The chief told me to get my ass out of his office, and that if he ever caught me back in his town again . . ."

Glenn didn't need the rest of the quote. By this time he was writing a story that appeared on the front page the next morning under the headline

"POLICE CHIEF THREATENS
DAILY NEWS REPORTER"

Charges eventually were brought against the chief, incidentally, and he was run out of town. Journalism at work.

Glenn would take risks.

Dr. Aderhold had retired as president of the university, and the Board of Regents had launched a search for his replacement.

The Sunday *Atlanta Journal-Constitution* had run a story naming eight finalists for the job. The new president was to be introduced at an Atlanta news conference Wednesday morning.

Tuesday afternoon, Glenn said, "We've got to find out who it is. I want the new president's name on the front page in the morning."

Glenn got on the phone. Larry Young got on the phone. They called one of the candidates at his home in Missouri. The man was there, so he was ruled out. The new president would be in Atlanta, waiting to be introduced at the press conference the next morning.

For one reason or the other, six of the candidates were eliminated. That left two, a guy from Ohio or someplace and Dr. Fred Davison, vice-chancellor for the University system of Georgia.

Glenn and Larry couldn't find either one of them by phone. It was nearing deadline.

"It's got to be Davison," Glenn said.

"But what if it's not?" Larry asked him.

"Sometimes," Glenn said, "you've got to roll the dice."

The headline was above the mast the next morning. It read:

"DAVISON TO BE NAMED UNIVERSITY PRESIDENT TODAY"

The Atlanta news conference was scheduled at eleven. Glenn and Larry, armed with copies of the paper, drove to Atlanta to be at the conference.

I had a nine o'clock journalism class that morning. One of my professors said, "If you're not right, your paper is going to look pretty stupid."

The *Banner-Herald* had only speculated the day before. Neither the *Journal* nor the *Constitution* had gone out on a limb, either.

There was an Associated Press teletype in the journalism building. At eleven, I walked over to it and waited for the Georgia split (national and international news would be interrupted for state news).

My loyalty to Glenn and the paper had grown to living-and-dying proportions by this time. What if we were wrong? Would we go out of business? Would Glenn be fired? Would my future be clouded because of my association with a newspaper that might be deemed irresponsible if we had guessed and missed?

The AP machine typed the dateline, "AT-LANTA . . ."

This was it. The first letter was a *D*. The second was an *r*. A period followed.

ATLANTA—Dr. Fred Davison, vice chancellor for the University system of Georgia, was named president of the University of Georgia. . . .

I skipped my next class and went directly to the paper. When Glenn came back, he was ecstatic:

"You should have seen it!" he laughed, beating his fist into his palm. "We were standing there with all those Atlanta reporters, and as soon as Dr. Davison was announced, I started handing out copies of the paper.

"They couldn't believe it. They couldn't believe a little paper in Athens had scooped the world."

Glenn also had sent a reporter to the Davisons' home. She came back with an exclusive interview with Mrs. Davison for the following day's paper.

The beer was cold that night. We stopped celebrating when the sun came up and Glenn had a great idea (most ideas that were crazy, and worked, were Glenn's) about a catfish with false teeth.

Yeah, a catfish with false teeth.

If you can make the lead story in a daily newspaper a report on a chicken that wouldn't come down from a tree, certainly you could run a story about a catfish with false teeth.

In late March, Glenn said to Larry, Wade, and me over a grease burger at the Open House, "We need to do something for April Fool's."

Other newspaper editors sit around and ponder series on China, suburban sewerage problems, the environment, large cracks in the earth, needed changes in the tax codes, and the coming crisis someplace in Chad, which you thought was a folk singer not a place.

Not Glenn Vaughn. Every day's newspaper presented him with the opportunity for an adventure. If there were more newspaper editors like Glenn, there actually would be a lot of interesting things to read in the paper, like somebody broke into Lurleen Furgesson's house down the street last night and stole her La-Z-Boy recliner and skinned her cat. Who cares about Chad when there is great stuff like that?

So Glenn had this idea. He dispatched Larry Young and a photographer out to Pete Dickens Lake, west of Athens. Pete Dickens had one of those lakes where you could pay a dollar or so and catch all the catfish you could haul out of the lake.

Catfish make tasty eating, unless you've seen one up close. Up close, they look like skinned, slimy cats. It's also unappetizing to see somebody clean a catfish. What you do—and I'm not making any of this up—is you find a tree and nail the catfish's head to it.

Then you take a tool like a pair of pliers and you pull the catfish's skin off the catfish. Then, of course, you have to cut the catfish open and remove everything you wouldn't want to eat, such as the catfish's gallbladder.

I've seen catfish up close and I have seen catfish being cleaned, but I have a strong stomach and I still have been able to eat catfish through the years, which also has something to do with newspapers other than the obvious tie-in that newspapers make great wrapping for fish.

Most newspapers have started to pay decent wages, but in 1965 a person could starve on a newspaper salary. That's where all-u-can-eat catfish places come in. All over the South there were those kinds of places with names like "Catfish King" and "Catfish Corner," that advertised "All the Fried Catfish U-Can-Eat, $2.95."

That usually included all the French fries and

coleslaw you could eat, not to mention all the rolls, butter, and iced tea you could consume.

I would expect that I ate catfish around thirty times a year during my early career as a newspaper man. I also used to hide some of the rolls in my pocket and walk out with them. I tried getting out with a couple of extra catfish one night, but the waitress noticed a dorsal fin sticking out of my back pocket and summoned the manager. He made me put it back on my table, but at least some of the tartar sauce was left to give the roll a little flavor.

So Glenn's idea was for Larry to catch a catfish out of Pete Dickens Lake, put on it a pair of false teeth—procured from I know not where—then have a picture taken of it.

I'm not certain how much the catfish Larry caught weighed, but it was a fairly good-sized catfish, certainly too large to fit inside anybody's back pocket.

Somebody, I'm not clear who, hit the catfish on the head with a hammer, rendering it unconscious, which is a good idea when you're trying to put a pair of false teeth into a catfish's mouth. Otherwise, the catfish will be jumping all around with all that slime, which makes them hard to hold on to. Plus, catfish will fin the dickens out of you, unless they are dead or knocked out.

Larry put the false teeth in the comatose catfish's mouth (Good name for a catfish restaurant, huh? The Comatose Catfish), and the photographer took a picture of it.

We ran the picture of the fish on the front page of the paper the next morning, accompanied by a story written by Wade Saye that began:

Anglers from all over the Southeast were astounded to learn that a catfish caught out of Pete Dickens Lake, west of Athens, was wearing a pair of false teeth.

The story went on about a fictitious fisherman who caught the fish.

"Dangest thing I ever saw," the fisherman was quoted as saying.

Fictitious game and fish wardens were also quoted, and the story came off as completely straight.

We got a call from Australia. A local minister phoned and said it was a sign the world was going to end soon.

I answered one call. The man said, "Y'all made that up about the fish, didn't you?"

I said, "Absolutely not."

And he said, "Come on. You can tell me the truth. Y'all just made it up, didn't you?"

Again, I assured the man the story was for real.

The man said, "Hold on a minute." Then he turned away from the phone and said, "Earl, come over here. This man at the paper said they just didn't make that up about that fish."

Then he talked to me again, and said, "I told Earl y'all didn't make that up about that fish, but he won't believe me."

Earl came on the line.

"Y'all didn't just make that up about that fish?" he asked.

"It's all true," I said.

"Caught on a red wiggler or a Loosiana pink?" the man asked.

"Wiggler," I answered.

"Blue cat?"

"Channel."

"You ain't shittin' me?"

"I'm not."

"Well, 'bye."

"Good-bye," I said.

The fish captured Athens's imagination. It was the main topic at Rotary. Bubber, down at Bubber's Bait and Beer Store, said, "I caught a fish one time in Florida, and when I cut him open, there was a man's watch inside. I wonder if the paper wants to do a story on me?"

A week after the April 1 catfish story ran, Glenn put the photograph back on page one with a headline that said, "APRIL FOOL, ATHENS!"

Nobody got mad.

Somebody did phone in to say he had spotted a large black bear on the outskirts of Athens. Page one. For several days.

"BEAR STALKS ATHENS"

We never knew if there was a bear or not, but people talked about it for days, and Glenn milked the story for all it was worth.

There was a legendary whorehouse in Athens, known to generations of University of Georgia students as Effie's. When Effie died, Glenn put her obit on page one, under a headline that said, "PROMINENT BUSINESS WOMAN DIES." Later, when they tore down Effie's old place, somebody went by and loaded a trunk with bricks from the house and passed them out with a plaque that read, "A LITTLE PIECE OF EFFIE'S."

* * *

Newspapers really should print more rumors. There's nothing like a good rumor to attract readership.

Sportswriters are best when it comes to planting a rumor. On a slow news day, you simply call the manager of, say, the Atlanta Braves, and ask him, "Is there any truth in the rumors that say you're going to trade Dale Murphy to the Mets?"

The manager says, "Are you crazy?"

And then you write a story with a headline that says, "BRAVES PILOT DENIES MURPHY TRADE RUMORS."

I don't think Glenn made up the alleged Jeane Dixon rumor in Athens, but he did have a good time with it.

The rumor was simple: Clairvoyant Dixon was supposed to have predicted the University of Georgia coliseum would fall in during upcoming graduation ceremonies. Most newspapers would have ignored such a rumor. Not us. We reported the rumor, then investigated and ultimately told our readers Jean Dixon had forecast no such thing. A good story, a public service, and, twenty-five years later, the coliseum is still standing.

The *Banner-Herald,* under its old ownership, was an easy prey for Glenn Vaughn's aggressiveness and understanding of what a small-town daily should be, above all a mirror of the community.

But the *Banner-Herald* was sold in 1965 to the Morris newspaper chain, out of Augusta and Savannah. Naturally, the *Daily News* reported a story that people from Augusta and Savannah were buying the *Banner-Herald,* and what does that say to you? It says, "We're Athens. We're your local paper."

The new owners of the *Banner-Herald* put a new staff in place, moved the offices to a modern building, and changed over to offset printing, from the old hot-type method. The *Daily News* had been offset from the beginning, which, for one thing, enabled it to reproduce much clearer photography than our competitor.

The Morrises even attempted to buy the *Daily News* after they had acquired the *Banner-Herald.* When the owners wouldn't sell, the *Banner-Herald,* with much greater resources than the *Daily News,* simply vowed to run us out of business.

It wouldn't happen. By this time, the *Daily News* had become the legal organ of the county, and its ad lineage was way ahead of its competition.

And, as I mentioned earlier, we were charmed. The Newspaper God saw our need and filled it. He sent us Brown Cline Stephens.

9

The Athens Daily News lasted for thirty months as an independent newspaper. The charmed life it led during that period had to have had its origin in a cosmic force that brought to it an assortment of people who, even it they had been fictional, would have challenged the imagination.

Glenn Vaughn had to have come down from the sky. Larry Young fell out of a tree and into the newsroom. My uncle doesn't come home from the hosiery mill with a newspaper every day, and who knows if I would ever have made it there? Wade Saye should have left town years before, the way he was treated at the *Banner-Herald.* Why he stayed long enough for the *Daily News* to rescue him must be written in the stars somewhere, too.

Gerald Rutberg wanted to be a veterinarian as a kid. Then he goes to Auburn, becomes

interested in the school newspaper, expects to
intern for Glenn in Columbus, and all of a sudden, he's in Athens, available for any duty from
writing wedding announcements to covering
local news and sports with an energy and creativity that would mark the rest of his life as well.

And they kept coming, from backgrounds as
diverse as their abilities and personalities. Some
would even change my life.

I'll start with Browny:

There are as many photograph clichés in
newspapers as there are examples of worn and
tattered writing.

First, there's the Firing Squad shot. That's
where the Ladies' Garden Club is giving out its
annual awards.

The publicity chairman calls the newspaper
and says, "We're giving away our annual
awards. Would you please send a photographer
to take a picture?"

So the photo editor, or whoever, awakens a
photographer and dispatches him.

It angers the photographer that he's not off
covering a war or a moon shot somewhere, so
when he gets to the Garden Club luncheon, he's
as irritable as can be and wants to get out of
there as soon as possible and have a drink. (In
fact, just about everybody drank when I was

actively involved in the business, and that's one of the reasons why: It made the long hours and low pay easier to bear.) So the photographer puts all the ladies who won awards side by side, like the Germans used to do when they were going to shoot prisoners, and takes their picture.

If you've seen one photograph of the Ladies' Garden Club Awards winners, you've seen them all, and that goes for the new slate of chamber of commerce officers, a group of new Eagle Scouts, a winning bowling team, and the twenty-eight members of the Get Down Baptist Church choir that is off to sing at the Democratic Convention just before Jesse Jackson makes a three-hour speech.

I'm not certain how long there has been such a thing as the newspaper photographer, but I do know the Firing Squad photos have probably appeared in more newspapers over the years than photos of Earl Scheib trying to sell you a paint job for your car.

A variation of the Firing Squad shot is the Shake-Hands-and-Look-Like-You're-Talking-to-One-Another setup.

This is often used when there is a photograph to be taken of the outgoing Rotary Club president shaking hands with the incoming Rotary Club president.

Even the laziest photographer will tell the two individuals, "Okay, shake hands and look like you're talking to one another."

That's hard to do. It's hard for one person to look another person in the face for a photograph and pretend to be talking. It's a little uncomfortable and embarrassing. And look like your talking? How can you talk normally when you know somebody is taking your picture?

One other thing, however: It is easy to figure out which one is the outgoing president of the Rotary Club and which is the incoming in the paper the next day, even without the caption. The outgoing president will have a sense of relief all over his face. The incoming president will look constipated.

Another newspaper cliché photograph is the Now-Just-Point-to-the-Sign shot. This is where the city has decided to put up a billboard near the city limits sign that says, "HARD BOTTOM, ALABAMA, HOME OF JAKE (NUB) DINKENS."

Jake (Nub) Dinkens will be the local state senator who introduced a bill in Montgomery when the state legislature was in session to outlaw anything that was fun, being the strict fundamentalist that he is.

He will have been a guest on *CBS This Morning* and whoever the hostess is (I won't name names since, like everyone else who was ever hostess, she'll probably be fired before you read this) would have made him look like a complete idiot, but he wouldn't know that, and neither would anybody else in town who agreed with him.

So they will think Nub, whose bill didn't pass ("But at least he tried, and that's what's important to the Good Lord"), is the best thing to hit Alabama since cable television let you get faith healer Ernest "Isn't-Jeezus-wondahful" Ainsley every Sunday morning.

So there will be an announcement at the church to collect money to immortalize Nub with a billboard. Mayor Filroy Gimple will be standing by the sign, and the photographer of the local paper, *The Hard Bottom Blabber,* will say, "Okay, Filroy, point at the sign and smile," which he will do, and the picture will appear on the front page of the next edition of the paper with an accompanying article that notes, "Unfortunately, Sen. Dinkens could not be present at the dedication of his billboard because of pressing business in Atlantic City doing His work."

Sports photos can also be worn and tiresome. Ever really look at a newspaper photograph of a bunch of guys playing football?

It usually looks more like a big pile of laundry

than anything else. You can't see anybody's face. You don't know if the action came on a pass play or a running play or on a fumble or when the referee was calling a penalty for one team having too many guys with weird names like Olphonzio and Hugehamism and Euphrates on the field at one time.

Basketball photographs mostly show a lot of hairy armpits. Baseball photographs are mostly one guy sliding into a base. I got a shot one night of a local high school game where the player tagging the guy sliding had applied the tag square on the slider's privates.

I wanted to run the photo with the following caption:

Stinky Marshall of Monroe Area applies Tag to Madison County's Farley Denton, former bass in the Boys' Glee Club.

You had to be very careful with photographs of trackmen, especially high hurdlers. What could happen there was that a high hurdler could be caught by the camera just as he stretched over the hurdle—and you *know* how they wear those very thin shorts (recall "thinclads" from a previous chapter).

Well, if the camera angle was just right, it could capture whatever might be dangling under the hurdlers' shorts. Sometimes those guys forget to put on their jock straps.

That happened to a friend of mine who was putting together the sports pages of a newspaper that should not be named here. He said when he first looked at the photograph, he didn't notice what the camera had captured.

"So I ran the damn thing in the first edition," he told me. "The managing editor came out and went crazy. We replated (took the picture out) immediately, but it still made it into a lot of papers. We got about five hundred calls the next day, and at least that many letters with the photo and the object that shouldn't have been in it circled.

"The managing editor made me write back to everybody who wrote in and personally apologize. I didn't, though. I wrote everybody back and said it wasn't what they thought it was, it just was just an ill-placed shadow. A guy wrote me back and said, 'I've got a shadow just like that, but it still doesn't have any business being shown in the paper.' "

If I had ever had my own newspaper, I would have hired some great photographers and filled my newspaper with their work. A still picture often can tell more than one that moves. A still picture can capture a moment because there is time to study each detail, to pick up every nuance of an event.

Show me Henry Aaron's eyes following the

ball when he hit home run number 715 and
broke Babe Ruth's record. Let me study the
face of a suspected VC man as he is being shot
point-blank in the head in Vietnam. Give me a
still so I have a long enough time to dwell with
the portion of the Zapruder tape that shows the
moment Lee Harvey Oswald's bullet shattered
John Kennedy's skull.

And give me some life in a still photo. *The
New York Times* and *The Washington Post* run
too many photographs of guys in suits making
speeches or of one guy in a suit welcoming another guy wearing a suit as he gets off an airplane.

I also hate grieving-widow shots. All grieving-
widow shots look the same. I was on a plane
from Atlanta to Melbourne, Florida, four hours
after the *Challenger* explosion. The plane was
full of reporters and photographers from all over
the country.

I never found out what paper this particular
reporter and this particular photographer were
from, but as we walked out of the plane, the
photographer asked the reporter, "Anything
special I need to shoot?"

"Just find the nearest grieving window," said
the reporter.

The New York *Daily News* has always been

"New York's Picture Newspaper." The little *Athens Daily News* played the same role in Athens.

The new offset printing method made reproduction of photographs much better than the old method, so Glenn Vaughn decided his newspaper would say it with photos.

In that first edition, when the *Daily News* got the Lyndon Johnson scoop, not only did Larry Young write the story, but Glenn used ten of his photographs to accompany it. Still, it would be a while before Glenn decided that the paper needed and could afford a full-time photographer.

The *Daily News* used some weird free-lance photographers in the early days. One was a funeral director. Another was an absentminded old guy who actually would shoot an assignment, and do everything perfectly, except for one very important item—loading film in his camera.

He was shooting an Athens High baseball game one night that I was covering. He brought along a lawn chair and sat down in it next to a light pole along the left-field line, where he promptly went to sleep, with his head resting on the pole. Several innings later, somebody hit a line-drive foul ball toward left. It struck the light pole inches above the sleeping photographer's head. He never budged.

After the game, I went down and awakened him. He said, "I've got some great action."

What he had was one out-of-focus shot of a girl buying a Coke at the concession stand. I had to blow up a head shot of the guy who hit the home run that won the game.

But then came Browny. Brown Cline Stephens. He came from outer space, too.

Browny was a native of Chattanooga. He enrolled at Georgia, in journalism school, in the early fifties. He got by working in an Athens bakery. After he paid for his food and his schooling, there wasn't enough money left for even a dorm room, so Browny slept in the bakery on an army cot.

After he graduated, he began an odyssey that would take him to more towns and more newspapers and more jobs than even he could remember.

I doubt there are many people left in the newspaper business today like Browny Stephens. There once were a lot of them, people who bounced from one paper to the next, always seeking another ten bucks a week here, a publisher who wasn't as tight there. Browny worked the small-town circuit. I doubt he ever in

his life made over $250 a week as a newspaper-
man, and I doubt he ever worked any place the
publisher wasn't tight, and I doubt he ever
worked any place where it didn't require sixteen-
hour days, seven days a week.

He told me once he went to work for a man
in Ohio who had planned to start a weekly newspaper. Browny was his staff. He worked for a
month getting ready for the first edition. The
man said he would begin paying Browny his
check when the first edition came out.

Browny wrote scores of feature stories, took
a like number of photos. But when the month
was over, the man said he still wasn't ready to
start up the paper.

So Browny kept working. Another week, another, and then another went by. Still no date for
the first edition. Browny finally headed for another stop.

"About a month later," he said, "somebody
sent me a copy of the first edition of that paper.
Whoever put it out used everything I'd done for
six weeks—for free—in that first edition."

Browny was slaving away for pauper's wages
in a forgotten place called Haleyville, Alabama,
in the late fifties. There had been an earlier marriage that had lasted only a couple of weeks—
Browny's first wife had decided there was

maybe a better future with the likes of a sawmill worker or a used-car salesman. That's what small newspapers did for a lot of marriages, I suppose.

There was a small restaurant in town where Browny ate dinner every night, and there was a waitress there. Nancy was her name. She would flip quarters with customers in order to play the jukebox.

If she lost, she put her quarter down the slot in those five-plays-for-a-quarter days. If the customer lost, he paid for the jukebox with his quarter, but Nancy got to choose the songs. You did what you could for kicks in a small northwest Alabama town in the late fifties.

But the waitress never flipped Browny, even though he was there every night for his supper. The cook had asked Nancy, "Why do you never flip that guy?"

She said, "He looks too much like a stick-in-the-mud." *"Stick-in-the-mud"* was late fifties Alabama for nerd, I suppose.

But one night, she figured what the hell. (No, the late fifties in Alabama. *Heck.*)

"Wanna flip for the jukebox?" Nancy asked Browny.

He would recall later, he nearly fell out of his chair trying to get a quarter—"one of my last"— out of his pocket.

After that, he and Nancy would talk when he came in for dinner. One night, he was paying his bill at the cash register and noticed a photograph of a little girl on the counter.

"That's Kathy," Nancy said to Browny. "She's mine."

Cleverly, Browny asked, "Does she look like her Daddy?"

"She ain't got no Daddy," Nancy answered. Daddy had split.

"I'd like to come see her sometime," Browny said. "I've never seen a prettier little girl."

Nancy would say later, after she and Browny married, "I've always told people Browny fell in love with Kathy and then married me."

From Haleyville, Nancy and Browny and little blond Kathy made more stops than the Greyhound between Little Rock and Dallas.

Browny saw an ad in the newspaper industry's *Editor and Publisher* for a sports editor's job in Butte, Montana. Browny was out to see the world, and Nancy hadn't seen much more than Haleyville, so to Butte they went. Later, Browny left Butte for a job in Billings.

"We loved Montana," Nancy would say. "But I knew we couldn't last there. Browny was a sucker for a sad story, which is one reason why we moved around so much. Anybody who called him and said, 'I really need you,' he would be

there. We left Montana to go back to Fort
Payne, Alabama, which is one of the last places
I wanted to go.

"I remember when we pulled out of our driveway and headed back, I started to cry. I was
holding Kathy in my lap. She said, 'Mama, don't
cry. We'll move again. We always do.' "

So there was, in no particular order, Fort
Payne and then Pasadena, Texas, and San-
dusky, Ohio, and Cedartown, Georgia, and
someplace in Michigan, and then back to Alabama, and then back to Texas or Mississippi or
Louisiana.

By then, Nancy and Browny had two more
children to go with Kathy. Daughter Miranda
(Browny had named her after a camera) came
first. Then a son, Clark.

The camera thing is important here. Browny
had to do it all on the small papers where he
worked. He wrote, he edited, he laid out the
pages, and he took all the photographs. It was
photography he enjoyed the most.

By 1966, he had become sort of legend on the
back-roads newspaper circuit, and what they
were saying is, if you wanted a guy who would
work cheap and churn out great photography,
he was your man.

Glenn found him in Kingsport, Tennessee, in
1966, and said, "I need you."

Browny and Nancy packed themselves, their belongings, and their three children, and moved to Athens. Glenn gave him a raise—albeit small—built him a tiny darkroom and told Browny what he'd been wanting to hear for years:

"You take pictures. That's all you're responsible for."

Browny and his photography would cut a swath through Athens and the Georgia newspaper community. He could make the Ladies' Garden Club Carnival Awards thing look like the raising of the flag on Iwo Jima. No Firing Squad shots. Browny would focus the ladies behind a flower. He would mount a chair and shoot down on them while they looked up. He would have had them form a human pyramid with awards in hand, if they had been able to do such a thing.

The Oconee River flooded in Athens. The *Daily News* ran two open pages of nothing but Browny Stephens photographs. The one I will always remember is the rooster perched on a fence. Flapping its wings in defiance of the rising water.

There was something at the University of Georgia known as Sigma Chi Derby. The fraternity sponsored a tricycle race for coeds. Browny got a shot of the winner, head forward like a thoroughbred stretching for the wire, that we ran six columns on the front page. It remains one of the best action photographs I've ever seen.

Browny didn't take photos of laundry piles at Georgia football games. He got the strained looks on coaches' faces. He got a running back turning a flip in the air after being tackled.

He got fans with silly hats, players on the sidelines, their helmets off, looking up and cursing the sun when a defeat became apparent.

Browny's old open-air Jeep had given way to a VW Beetle by then. But he was in such demand, was sent on so many assignments, even a VW Beetle became cumbersome. He had to find a place to park it, had to get out with all those cameras around his neck, had to get back in and hustle to his next stop and find a place to park again. So Browny got himself a motor scooter. It was blue. I can still see him riding off to Prince Avenue or to the campus, or to somebody's farm in Watkinsville to get a picture of an eleven-pound squash, Browny with his crash helmet on, his cameras around his neck, pencils and notepads bulging out of his pocket, a man on a mission.

Browny and I became friends. Maybe our relationship was more journeyman-takes-apprentice-under-his-wing than simply friends.

Whatever, I loved his stories about where

he'd been and what he had done. When the paper was closed around midnight, I would usually wind up at Browny's little rented house east of Athens. If you got off work at five, you wouldn't rush home and go to bed. Same if you got off at midnight.

I had discovered beer, and there was always plenty of it in Browny's refrigerator. Sometimes we would talk until dawn. Other times we would play pre-dawn Ping-Pong on Browny's table. I never beat him. His forehand smash always was more than I could handle. How I managed to stay in school—or even stay awake for classes—after eight hours at the *Daily News* and then those mornings I greeted at Browny's house remains a mystery. I suppose I got by tap dancing and using mirrors.

After Browny came Frank Frosch. Frank Frosch wasn't a real person, either. He was created by some screenwriter, and he came to the *Daily News* by some unexplained magic I've long ago forgotten about trying to trace.

Frank Frosch was from Speedway, Indiana. He had graduated from Virginia Military Institute, but he had a year off before he had to take his commission into the army. He decided to use the year, 1966—67, teaching English and working on a Master's degree at Georgia.

Frank Frosch played something like twenty-five musical instruments. He spoke four or five foreign languages. One was Russian. I used to say, "Frank, let me hear some Russian." If he didn't know it, he could have fooled me.

Frank had two basset hounds. He lived in another neighboring county, Oglethorpe, to the east of Athens.

Frank discovered there wasn't a band at tiny Oglethorpe County High. So he said he would organize one for free. That was Frank Frosch—leader of the band.

And Frank was a writer. He already had published one book, a novel, and he wanted to write more. So, one day he called Glenn, introduced himself over the phone, told Glenn of his background and his desire to find a place for his writing. Glenn, ever with the instincts, was intrigued.

What came from all that was something called "Dateline: Lexington." Lexington was the small county seat of Oglethorpe; Frank was our-man-in-Lexington. Frank may or may not have been paid for anything he did, but what he wrote captivated our readership.

Frank could do a gentle piece on a dying farmer. He could dig up a hundred-year-old hanging of a black and rile the living relatives of those long dead who were responsible for the incident.

Frank was visiting his own relatives during Indy 500 week in Speedway. He sent back a story on a camper city outside the speedway, and one of my journalism professors called it "the best piece of sportswriting I've ever seen."

But after a year at Georgia and the *Daily News,* Frank had to take his army commission. Vietnam was starting to boil over.

Frank had those two dogs, those two basset hounds. The female was Patsy. The male was Plato. I loved those two drooling, howling dogs, and Frank knew that. His mother-in-law had promised Frank she would keep the dogs back in Speedway when he entered the service. Then, as he packed to leave Lexington, his mother-in-law called to say she had thought the dog thing over a time or two and had decided she would take only Patsy. Plato was much the rowdier of the two.

Frank called me.

"Want to keep Plato while I'm gone?" he asked.

I should have consulted my bride, but I was afraid Frank might change his mind, so I agreed, with much pleasure.

Before it was over, Plato won Paula over, too,

despite the drooling and the howling and the wandering and the eating of panty hose and the sleeping on the bed.

After Frank left, Chuck Perry came. Claude Gibson Perry. He was seventeen when I first met him, only two years younger than I was. He had been born and raised in Athens. His father delivered candy. His mother stayed home and raised the five kids. Chuck was the eldest. He was born with the same affliction I was—the tendency to take on more than one person could possibly handle and remain fairly sane. Please note I said *fairly.*

When the *Daily News* began publication, Chuck was a rising senior at Athens High. He was hired to work part time in the mail room, stuffing sections of the paper together and running the address machine that sent the paper out to the subscribers.

But Chuck was also the Athens High place-kicker. In August, football practice began. Two-a-days. No matter. Chuck would still report to the mail room at ten in the evening and work until the wee hours.

Chuck was on the team I covered for Wade Saye my first years at the *Daily News.* I'd run into him in the mail room a few times. We had become friends, too, and it got me a few meals at his Mama's table. The woman could cook.

Chuck turned out to be more than just the Athens High placekicker. He was one of the top high school placekickers in the country and set a national record for points scored by a kicker in 1965.

Weyman Sellers, the Athens coach who had mistaken me for a Japanese exchange student, had a power in 1965. Athens won a game 86–0, and they went all the way to the state finals. They were to play Valdosta on the Athens High field on a freezing Friday night. Valdosta was then, and remains, a high school football factory. When somebody started giving out such a thing, Valdosta even won a national high school championship.

The state championship game led the *Daily News* on Friday morning. Glenn went to his typewriter and came up with the banner heading that read, "OKAY, VALDOSTA: YOU'RE NEXT!"

But Valdosta didn't go quietly. As a matter of fact, with five seconds to go in the game, Valdosta led 14–7. But Athens scored from the one with no time left on the clock. That made the score 14–13. Chuck Perry came on the field in front of twelve thousand people to kick the extra point to tie the game and make Athens and Valdosta co-state champs.

Chuck had kicked something like fifty straight

extra points. The college scouts were drooling. The ball went sideways. Athens lost.

When people hear Chuck's story, they always ask him, "What on earth did you do after the game?" And he always tells them, "Went to work in the mail room at the *Daily News.*"

Chuck never got his football scholarship, either. After missing on the big kick, he went on the unwanted list. He would wind up in the newspaper business, instead of in pro football.

There were constant staff changes going on at the paper. People came. They left. They came back. Larry Young started hitting the bottle again. Glenn then moved Wade to managing editor and made me a nineteen-year-old sports editor of a daily newspaper. He even allowed me part-time assistants and gave me a nickel-a-week raise. The *Daily News* budget held together only because so many of us would have worked there for nothing, I suppose.

I hired Johnny Futch, another journalism student. And I hired Chuck in 1966. He had enrolled at journalism school after graduating from Athens High. I covered Georgia. Futch handled layout, editing, and enjoyed writing about track, which I didn't. I gave Athens High and golf to Chuck. He wrote the celebrated "Around the Green" column. He also reminded me of myself. When did he sleep?

There are so many names.

Jones Drewery. Glenn hired him as a reporter. He was a classical pianist who had suffered some mental distress as a result of service in World War II. Jones chain-smoked. When he finished his cigarettes, he would toss the butt, still afire, in a trash can that sat next to his desk. The trash can usually was filled with discarded copy paper. It was never a matter of "whether" Jones was going to set his trash can on fire, it was "when."

Colleen Kelly: Another journalism student Glenn found. She was gorgeous. I tried to date her, but I didn't get very far. I later married and brought Paula to Athens, and Glenn hired her as our receptionist. Somebody told my wife how charmed I had been with the lovely Colleen, and there were many fits of jealous rage. Ah, the start of a pattern in my life.

And Sharon Bailey. She had moved to Athens so her husband could do graduate work. In order to make it possible for him to concentrate on his studies, Sharon came on as a reporter. She was indefatigable, a quiet, frail woman who could bleed the news out of a city-council turnip and he would never know what hit him.

And Fran Smith. Another student. Another reporter. I never got to know her very well, nobody did. She always seemed troubled, somehow.

But she could get a story. And that's what counted.

Thirty months of energy, aggression, colossal scoops, insane antics. Thirty months of camaraderie, competitiveness, and there was even some love then. It was grand.

Then Christmas Eve, 1967, it all came to an end.

10

After the Morrises bought the *Banner-Herald* and began upscaling it, ad salesman for the paper began telling clients the *Banner-Herald* would soon be able to run color photographs and color ads and that the *Daily News* would never be able to compete with that.

The *Banner-Herald,* which did have a superior production plant to ours, announced it would change over from hot type to offset and be able to produce four-color photographs. Newspaper color photography at that time was in its infancy.

Even weather maps were black-and-white, as hard as it may be to believe today.

Glenn got anxious. It was his move. He had to counter.

He called in Cecil Dill, his head pressman, and asked if he could figure out a way on our small press to run processed color. I still am not certain how all that works, but it had to do with turning pages around here and back through here and there wasn't all the technology we have today, and Cecil was this quiet little guy who always had dirty hands from fooling around with our press.

But Cecil was also some kind of genius pressman. In the press room at the helm of his machine, Cecil could make the thing talk.

Cecil said he would give color a shot, and what Glenn needed now was a proper color photograph. Of course, he had his sources and the word came down that the *Banner-Herald*'s next Sunday edition would feature a color photo of the old Civil War cannon in front of the courthouse.

" 'Still' color photography," Glenn mused, the fist-in-the-palm routine going again.

"What about 'action' color?" he asked Browny. It was nearing our Saturday deadline, and Glenn wanted color in the *Daily News* before it appeared in the Sunday *Banner-Herald.*

He dispatched Browny on his motor scooter. "Just go out there and find something," Glenn told him.

There was very little sunlight left. Browny had to hurry. He came upon a Little League baseball game. You know the scene. Parents in the stands.

As I said, we were charmed.

What Browny got was a masterpiece. The biggest kid on the team had just slugged a grand-slam homer to win the game. As the big kid stepped on the plate, his teammates swarmed him. He dwarfed them.

The photograph showed several of the kids' feet off the ground as they jumped to congratulate their slugger. In the background, parents were standing and applauding. Norman Rockwell.

The incredibly clear color photograph came out on the front page of the *Daily News* the next day. This was a quarter of a century ago. It would be *years* before *USA Today* would even occur to somebody. Cecil had pulled off a miracle.

The photo reproduced so well, I can still remember that one of the parents standing and applauding in the background was wearing a blue shirt with an emblem over one of his pockets. This was *in the background* of the photo. You could actually make out what the distant emblem said. It said, "Gulf." The guy worked at a service station.

"Action Color," Glenn called it in the paper that day.

The *Banner-Herald* came out late the next day. There were all sorts of production problems. If you looked hard and long enough, you could, in fact, make out that the color photo on the front page was some sort of large gun. That was about it.

The *Banner-Herald* began referring to itself as "No. 1", or "the Big One" in promotions. The message was that they had a bigger staff (even an Atlanta bureau that served the *Banner-Herald* and other Morris papers) and a bigger plant. They covered the world, and we, well, did whatever it was we did. But whatever the *Banner-Herald* tried, Glenn was one step ahead of them.

Glenn had another stroke of genius. He cornered an Athens artist named Don Smith, and out of that union of creativity came the concept of "the People Paper."

On one side "the Big One."

On the other "the People Paper."

"We care about what's happening in the world, too," read our promotion ads, "but we also care about what's going on down your street. The *Athens Daily News,* the People Paper."

There were People Paper bumper stickers and People Paper pins, and there was even a radio jingle that went:

> *The People Pay-per*
> *Is the Pay-perr*
> *People pick.*

Kids were singing it all over town.

When the Georgia Press Association annual awards came, the *Daily News,* the first year it entered, swept through it and won more awards than any other paper in the state, including the dailies of the larger cities.

We won best local photography, naturally; and best local sports coverage and best local this and best local that, and we also won the most prestigious award, that for first place in community service, for getting a new state park built near Athens.

To celebrate these awards, Don Smith came up with another promotion. Said the headline:

"EVEN PAPER PEOPLE PICK THE PEO-
PLE PAPER."

For all the things Glenn Vaughn and the *Daily
News* did that were a little crazy, it also had a
profound effect on the city and area it covered.

* A Glenn Vaughn editorial supported a
  mixed-drink and liquor referendum in
  Athens, and voters passed it something
  like seven to one.
* A *Daily News* stance saved Athens's old-
  est residence from being torn down.
* It forced an expansion of the school board.
* It discovered the weakness of the local
  library and led to a huge new one, "certainly more appropriate for the learning
  center of the South."
* It helped get a new, unpopular fire chief
  canned.

The *Daily News* even outsold the *Journal* and
Constitution in Atlanta one day.

In 1966, a black Washington, D.C., educator
named Lemuel Penn was driving through
Athens one evening, headed back to Washington after two weeks of National Guard summer
camp at Fort Benning. Penn had no connection
with the civil-rights movement. According to Bill

Shipp, who wrote a book about the incident called *Murder at the Broad River Bridge,* Penn deliberately steered away from activism.

"He was just a hardworking guy who didn't want to cause anybody any trouble," Shipp told me.

As Penn drove through Athens, three locals with Ku Klux Klan connections noticed a black man driving a car with Washington, D.C., license plates.

Said one of the Klansmen, "There goes one of Lyndon's boys. Let's get him."

They followed Penn into rural Madison County. As he drove across the Broad River Bridge, they pulled along next to him and one of the Klansmen fired a twelve-gauge shotgun blast into the car, killing Penn.

It quickly became a national story. The three men were arrested and brought to trial for murder in Madison County. The trial was a complete joke, according to Shipp. The three men were acquitted. But the *Daily News* stayed with the story and wrote several editorials regarding the fact justice hadn't been done.

One of the Klansmen involved, as a matter of fact, was part owner of the Open House restaurant across the street from the *Daily News.* We could often see him and his various friends drinking coffee through the glass door of the restaurant.

I kept wondering, What if these guys decided to fire in here? My desk was directly next to the huge window overlooking the restaurant.

I could see the headlines: "DAILY NEWS SPORTSWRITER FELLED BY SHOTGUN BLAST." All I was writing at the time was whether or not Georgia could win the Southeastern Conference football championship.

The Klansmen eventually were brought back to trial—in federal court in Athens—and charged with violating Lemuel Penn's civil rights. The trial was covered by every major news outlet in the country. Shortly before one-thirty in the morning, the jury came in with a verdict of guilty. Glenn had held the *Daily News* crucially late to see if we could get a verdict.

GUILTY! said our headline the next morning.

That same day, there had been a wildcat strike of one of the production unions at the Atlanta papers, and there was no competition on the street that morning.

Circulation manager Roy Holliday and reporter Pete Trigg left Athens at five the next morning with a station wagon load of *Daily News* editions. They hawked the papers in front of the *Journal-Constitution* building.

"Little paper comes to the big town!" they said. The Atlanta papers went for a dime each then. Roy and Pete made sure they gave out the message, "And it only costs a nickel!" They sold out of papers.

We started hearing the rumors in the fall of 1967. The *Banner-Herald,* it was obvious by then, was not going to take complete control of the Athens market while the *Daily News* simply fell rotten to the ground. So the word was out— the Morrises were trying to buy the *Daily News.*

A lot of bitter feelings began to boil.

What would happen if we were sold? Would we still have jobs? Why the hell had we been busting our butts for so little pay all this time when they're going to just up and sell us to those bastards up the street? What about our loyalty? What about the blood and guts and the beer we used to drink after work, still talking into the morning about how we could whip the *Banner-Herald?*

I didn't know the details then. I was still a college kid who would have worked at the paper for nothing, simply for the experience, the cama-raderie, the utter thrill of it all.

The *Daily News* had passed the *Banner-Herald* even in ad lineage, and we were in the black. But the thing had been started on a shoestring in the first place, and the reserves were small. There had even been a number of last-second loans to meet Friday payrolls. That's a little scary, even as I consider it now.

The debt service was heavy. And the owners didn't want to incur any more.

After bargaining sessions that went on even into December, the Morris people finally agreed, according to Millard Grimes's *The Last Lino-type,* a book about Georgia newspapers, to pay $443,000 for the *Daily News* and assume its debts. The sale was announced on Christmas Eve, 1967.

"And all we get," said a *Daily News* staffer, "is screwed."

You have to have worked at a newspaper to really understand. A newspaper is a living, breathing thing, and to pick up yours, as it comes off a press when it is still warm, is to hold your newborn. We were all in this together, we thought. We gave our sweat for so little pay, but we did it without complaint. And we hated the *Banner-Herald.* We *hated* it. A thirty-seven-year-old managing editor of the *Banner-Herald* had a heart attack and died during the battle. Somebody said, "You'd have a heart attack, too, if you had to get up every morning and see how you've gotten your ass beat once again."

It hadn't been Ben Hecht and *The Front Page,* but it had been ours and we had relished the fight and gloated unashamedly at what we constituted every victory, no matter how small.

And it was over.

I couldn't go anyplace else. I was still six months from graduation. There were others, like Chuck, in the same position as I was.

As much as we hated to see the struggle end, we certainly were relieved when the Morrises announced the *Daily News* would not be absorbed into the *Banner-Herald.* We would still be published as a morning entity. Except it wasn't going to be "we" anymore.

Glenn would move over as editor. I got the sports editor's job. I could take Chuck along. But Wade split. He couldn't stomach going back to the paper where they had tried to starve him to death. Browny was off to a newspaper somewhere in Louisiana. There were others in production and circulation and accounting and the ad department who weren't offered jobs.

Even Larry Young got to go. He had straightened himself out again, and the new owners knew of his value.

One cold January night, we put out the last *Athens Daily News* in the old building across from the Open House restaurant.

I had covered a Georgia basketball game. I can remember the makeup man finishing the pasteup of my last sports page.

"You want to take one last look before I send it back?" he asked.

I looked at it. There were tears. He picked up the board with my work pasted upon it and walked it out of my sight. There would be a lot of moments of feeling staggering loss in my years to come. But this moment was up there, it was up there.

The sons of bitches made us move our own desks. After we finished the last edition of an independent *Daily News,* we had to pick up our desks and chairs and our typewriters and our files and we had to load them into the newsroom at something they call 1 Press Place. The Big One, my ass.

We finished about four that morning. They paid us off, maybe five of us, with a case of beer. Schlitz.

I skipped my morning class and slept. I reported to my first day at work for the new owners at two that afternoon. We got a paper out the next day. I'm not certain how. It was a fire drill. We didn't know how they did it, and they didn't know how we did it, and the first *Daily News* under new ownership was awful.

Glenn said to me, "It will get better."

For the first time, I didn't believe him.

I managed to stay in touch with Browny. He eventually moved out of Louisiana and went to work in Tennessee, I think, or was it Arkansas?

I missed the *Daily News,* as once it was, and I also missed Browny Stephens on that motor scooter, Browny Stephens coming back from some sports event and putting world-class photography on my desk for the next day's edition.

I missed the nights-that-turned-into mornings at his house, where we'd go after the paper was finished.

It was Browny who bought me my first legal beer, as a matter of fact. October 20, 1967, the day I turned twenty-one. We left the paper for dinner, walked over to a joint, and Browny ordered us a pitcher of cold Ballantine, which is a lot better than Schlitz, at least.

Browny asked, "Does it taste as good legal as it did the other way?"

"No," I said.

As I sit here and think about it, Browny was around for a number of firsts in my life.

He took me to New York City for the first time: Paula and I went to visit him in Vineland, New Jersey, where he had wound up editing a poultry industry magazine. We drove from Atlanta, and it was also the first time I'd ever been in New Jersey. I expected hundreds of square miles of urban expanse and a lot of guys named Raoul with tattoos. Newark is what I was expecting.

But as I drove to Vineland, I passed through miles of rolling hills and farms and I said, "Aha! This is why they called it the Garden State."

One day during our visit, I happened to mention neither my wife nor myself had ever been to New York, and we were already twenty-two. As I mentioned earlier, there were always some suspicions on the part of those who grew up in the hinterlands that there really was no New York City.

We didn't know anybody who had actually been or anybody who knew somebody who had actually been there. What if it were nothing but a clever hoax? What if *The Ed Sullivan Show* came to us from a warehouse on the outskirts of Greenville, South Carolina? Who could be certain?

Browny took me and Paula to New York-by-God-City the very next day. We drove to Staten Island in his VW bus and rode the ferry to Manhattan.

There, we rode a subway. Browny knew I liked trains.

"How did you enjoy your first subway ride?" he asked me.

The suhbitch scared me half to death is how I enjoyed my first subway ride, I told him.

Are the lights *supposed to* go on and off like that? Is it supposed to go so fast and screech like a hyena from hell? And who were those other people on there? Recent escapees from a Turkish prison? There was a man on the subway talking to his hands. That was nothing. There was a woman talking to her shoes.

We went to see Grand Central Station. We caught a bus there. I scheduled my next subway ride at some point in the twenty-first century, at the earliest.

My wife brought a blouse at Saks Fifth Avenue. Browny took her picture handing over several of my twenty-dollar bills to a clerk who looked like a female version of Basil Rathbone.

The first time I ever went to the bathroom in New York City was at Saks Fifth Avenue. Basil told me where it was. I stole a couple of hand towels from the rest room. It was all I could afford.

We saw the Empire State Building and Rockefeller Center, and my wife kept saying to Browny, "Take our picture here."

I, of course, was embarrassed. You start lining up in front of street signs to get your picture taken in New York City, they know right away you parked your turnip truck on Staten Island and took the ferry across and you're some kind of bumpkin or hick or geek or hillbilly, and a taunting crowd will gather and tell you to go back home. I actually posed for only one photograph—one of me looking down a sewer drain to see if there really was an alligator down there.

On the other end of the spectrum, Browny introduced me to camping, and actually made it fun for me for the first time since I was in the Boy Scouts when we would go to Flat Shoals and stay up all night and go hide behind a tree so the scoutmaster couldn't see us smoking.

I gave up camping after the Boy Scouts because I always felt so tired the next day, and my mouth, from all the cigarettes, felt like an Apache war party had bivouacked there overnight.

My idea of camping out after that was being out of Half-and-Half for my coffee in the morning. (Notice how I didn't write that it was "like sleeping in a Howard Johnson motel with no color TV." I've already said how I despise clichés.)

I was married to my second wife, the lovely Kay, and we were living in Atlanta. Browny had fled from New Jersey and was involved with a small newspaper in Chatsworth, Georgia, near the Georgia-Tennessee line. One day, he called and asked me and Kay if we would like to go up to some river in Tennessee and float down it and camp out.

I had planned to rearrange my sock drawer that day, but Kay was all for the idea. We met Browny in Chatsworth, got back into the same VW bus that had taken me and another wife to New York City for the first time, and drove through a lot of woods and eventually came upon Webb's store in Reliance, Tennessee. As a matter of fact, Mr. Webb's store *was* Reliance, Tennessee, filled with old tires as one edifice.

Next to Mr. Webb's store was the Hiwassee River. I liked Mr. Webb. He wore a Texaco outfit and on his Texaco hat, there was a large red star. I was taken back to Ed Thelinius and his "This broadcast is brought to you by Texaco. Trust your car to the man who wears the star."

Mr. Webb, who had to be in his late sixties, looked exactly like Lester Maddox, who was elected governor of Georgia once. I liked Lester. He once said, "What the Georgia penal system needs is a better grade of prisoner."

In fact, Mr. Webb had a photograph of Lester Maddox in his store, and he would stand next to it and take off his Texaco hat. The resemblance was amazing.

Here was the deal:

We left Browny's bus at Webb's store. Then Mr. Webb, ever the entrepreneur, drove us eight miles up the Hiwassee River and let us out for a small fee.

Browny had two craft we would use to travel the eight miles back to Webb's store downriver on the Hiwassee. One was a small inflatable raft that would seat one uncomfortably. He also had a slightly larger inflatable raft that would seat two and do serious damage to your back.

He had an old bicycle pump that he used to inflate them. He got into the one-person one, and Kay and I got into the double. Browny used a double-bladed paddle, like kayakers. He gave Kay and me a regular canoe paddle.

I was thinking, Have I lost my mind?

I walked over to the river and put my hand in the water. Where were the polar bears? Cold? My God, yes.

So, what I was going to do was paddle this thing with my wife and me in it, eight miles down a nearly frozen river—and I had worn a pair of shorts. *Not* a bathing suit, meaning my underwear would get wet. I hated wet underwear.

We took off.

"Paddle left," said Browny.

I put the paddle in the water, and the raft immediately turned over.

It was like falling into the Volga in January.

Browny retrieved our raft while we swam to the shore. We got inside it, again. I asked Browny, "I think I have made a critical error in judgment. Is there any way we can call Lester and get him to drive us back to the bus?"

There wasn't. I realized if I was ever going to return to civilization again, I had to arrive there upon his blow-up love doll we were using as a boat.

I got better at paddling as we went along, except that since I was sitting behind my wife, each time I would move my paddle to the other side of my boat, I'd hit her in the back of the head with it.

We made it down the Hiwassee River. Once I got over my underwear being wet, I actually began to enjoy the trip.

The water was crystal clear, and there were even a few small rapids I negotiated with ease. Well, okay, so I went through a couple of them backward and once I ran atop a rock and was stuck there for fifteen minutes, but who's keeping score?

We took the boats out of the river back at Webb's store. Browny deflated them and packed them in the bus. We stopped in a shady grove not far from Webb's store to camp.

Browny unloaded all the gear and put up my tent, on account of I didn't know how. When I went camping with the Boy Scouts, I would go out into a thicket somewhere and hide so somebody else would put up my tent. As I mentioned earlier, machinery totally baffles me. It had been a nice day. I was tired. Kay was having severe headaches. Browny put a bunch of stuff in a pot and cooked it over an open fire and it was delicious and we sat up late and stared at the fire. Staring into a fire is a pleasant, soothing experience, except that no matter where you put your lawn chair (Browny had brought several along), smoke from the fire eventually will blow into your eyes. It doesn't matter how many times you move to the other side of the fire.

Browny, Kay, and I upgraded as we went along, camping together. From that first trip on the Hiwassee, we started running the Nantahala River in North Carolina, where the water was even colder and there were some rather serious rapids with which to contend.

Browny's little boats eventually had so many rock punctures, we had to upgrade there, too. Browny and I bought two large inflatable kayaks that were much more durable and were a better match for the larger rapids to which we had graduated.

Browny, incidentally, still inflated our boats, deflated them, put them away in the back of his bus, and put up the tents. I set up the lawn chairs and was in charge of icing down the beer.

Browny and I turned over together once, and both of us lost our glasses. Clark, Browny's son, was twelve or thirteen the time he went through the toughest rapid on the Nantahala while standing and straddling a canoe. He made it with no problem. When Clark was a baby, crawling around on the floor in his diapers back in Athens, if you didn't watch him closely, he would pick up your beer and drink it.

Years later, Clark joined the navy and needed a security clearance. He put down my name as a reference. A man from the Defense Department actually came to see me in my office.

"How long have you known Seaman Stephens?" he asked me.

"Practically all his life," I answered.

"And have you ever seen him exhibit any strange behavior?"

"Sure," I said. "When he was still wearing diapers, he would steal your beer, and when he was twelve or thirteen, he went down the toughest rapid on the Nantahala River standing up and straddling a hard-bottom canoe. I think he's natural for the navy."

Clark got his security clearance.

It was the out-of-doors, Browny would tell me later, that led to his divorce from Nancy. She didn't like paddling down ice-cold rivers and sleeping on the ground. Browny loved it.

It was an amicable divorce. Browny and Nancy remained close, even after she remarried.

Browny did so much for me. And I finally did something for him.

I took him west to Idaho and the Middle Fork of the Salmon River, where we rafted down this often-mighty torrent with an outfitter and other adventurers from all over the country.

Browny loved every minute of it. There was big water and wonderful scenery. Longhorn sheep often came down out of the mountains to drink from the Middle Fork as we paddled past them.

There had been a small tribe of Indians known as the Sheepeaters in this area. But the army didn't have anything better to do a few years after the Civil War, so they went into the area and killed all the Sheepeaters. The called it the Sheepeaters' War. I'm not certain what the Sheepeaters called it. The term "useless massacre" does come to mind, however.

Browny and I had never discussed religion.

We'd discussed everything else, but never religion. Well, we had sung a few hymns after more than a few beers, but we'd never really got into heaven or hell or Jesus or Allah or Billy Graham.

But one morning out on the Middle Fork, the sun had turned the water so clear and green it was breathtaking. And there were the mountains around us and an unpolluted blue sky, and the air was cool, just the right degree of cool to make a person feel incredibly alive.

Browny and I were sharing a large rock on the riverbank while the outfitters cooked breakfast.

"I haven't been to church in years," Browny said. "I don't even remember the last time I went to church. But out here, seeing this, says more to me about a loving God than anything I could learn in church. Whatever and whoever God is, He's also an outdoorsman. How could you look around here and think anything else?"

Yeah, I knew Browny Stephens for twenty-five years. We once walked into a beer joint in Tellico Plains, Tennessee. It was morning, and we were looking for eggs and bacon and grits. We had been on instant oatmeal for several days.

It was barely past nine, but there were a number of patrons already sitting at tables with Formica tops, sipping on cans of Pabst Blue Ribbon. Browny asked the woman bartender, who obviously had had teeth at one point in her life, "Anyplace around here to get a good breakfast?"

"What do you want?" she asked.

"Maybe some eggs?"

"Sit down. I'll be back in a minute," she said.

The woman walked out of the beer joint and into a grocery store next door. She came back with a dozen eggs, a loaf of white bread, some bacon, and a couple of potatoes.

She fried us two perfect eggs. The bacon was good and crisp, and the hash-browned potatoes she made were magnificent. When we were back in the VW bus, Browny smiled and said, "We've got to remember this place. And that woman. I do believe she was an angel."

Perhaps at that moment, Browny was as at peace with his world as anybody can ever be. On the road. Up in the mountains. Canoes in the back. No schedule to keep. No exact destination to reach.

As we drove out of Tellico Plains, he reared his head back and began:

"I'm proud to be an Okie from Muskogee. . . ."

What he lacked in talent when he sang, he more than made up for with his enthusiasm. I sang along with him.

A precious memory, but damned how Lucky Stars can get crossed.

A People Paper epilogue:

First, there was Kathy, that little blond girl Browny saw in a photograph at the Haleyville diner for the first time.

She grew into a beautiful woman, married and moved to St. Louis.

Browny and Kathy's husband became the best of friends. Browny was always going to get him out on a camping trip.

Her husband was out of town on business, and Kathy had driven to the grocery store. She had stopped at McDonald's on the way home and picked up a Coke, a cheeseburger, and some French fries.

They found her in the car, parked in the garage. She was dead of carbon-monoxide poisoning. Her death was ruled a suicide. She was only twenty-two.

But there were all sorts of questions. There was no suicide note. She had exhibited no signs of depression to her husband or to friends. And why would somebody who was going to commit suicide first go out and buy a week's groceries for she and her husband? Why would anybody planning suicide stop by a McDonald's thirty minutes beforehand and pick up a Coke and a cheeseburger and fries?

There are still no explanations. Her mother, Nancy, was bitter at the authorities for years for not trying to answer the questions with a more thorough investigation.

And soon after that, Nancy's third husband was diagnosed with cancer. He went fast.

And then Browny.

One night two years ago, I got a call from Nancy.

"There's something wrong with Browny," she said. "He's been having a hard time using his right arm and hand. We're trying to get him to go to a doctor.

The doctor found a large tumor in Browny's neck. But Browny was going to beat it. There was an operation in Chattanooga, and the prognosis at the time was a good one. But a later checkup revealed other tumors. Browny's doctor said they were inoperable. Browny even went to a clinic in Mexico for help. A friend of Nancy's paid his way.

His medical bills were getting out of hand. His insurance coverage was slight. I got a call from a friend of Browny's from the egg business. The poultry industry was holding its annual convention in Atlanta. He wanted to invite Browny's legion of friends to a reception. There would be a cash bar, and Browny would say a few words and then I would do my dog-and-pony act, and we would ask people for donations to help with the medical bills.

Browny had by then been admitted to a hospice in Atlanta for those with incurable diseases and limited funds. All those years and all those places, working long hours for so little pay, and it had come to this.

I went to visit Browny. We talked about the benefit. The plan was, a couple of days later, for an ambulance to pick Browny up and take him to the World Congress Center in Atlanta, where the poultry convention was taking place. He was going to be wheeled into the benefit, and then he said he thought he might be able to sit up and talk for five minutes. His neck was giving him severe pain whenever he tried to move from his bed.

Nancy would be there. So would Clark, grown and out of the navy by now. Miranda, also grown, had married and was expecting a baby. She'd be there, too. As would all of Browny's friends from the poultry industry. My ex-wife, Kay, was even scheduled to come.

"There will be more people in that room who I love, and who love me," Browny said to me on that visit, "than at any other time in my life. I just want to be able to tell them how much I care for them and how much I appreciate them helping me."

The cocktail reception was scheduled at five. At four that afternoon, Browny's nurse went into his room to get him ready for the ambulance ride.

"He said, 'I'm tired,' " his nurse explained. "And then he was gone."

An hour before the reception, and he was gone.

I was called shortly after he died. When I got to the benefit, few knew what had happened. The word spread throughout the room.

The man who had the idea for the benefit spoke first. Then he introduced me. I didn't do a very good job.

Browny was cremated. The family took a while to determine where to place the ashes as a final resting place. Last winter, Nancy and Clark and Miranda decided to spread them over the Tellico River in the Tennessee mountains, not far from where an angel once cooked Browny and me breakfast.

Browny was fifty-nine when he died. We paid off his bills and set up a scholarship fund in his name at the journalism school at Georgia with what we collected that night.

After Browny died, I decided camping is something I never wanted to do again. Who would put up my tent?

As for the other *Daily News* people: Chuck

Perry received a Master's degree in English from the university and became associate editor of the *Daily News* and *Banner-Herald* and later joined me on the *Atlanta Journal* sports staff. He rose to become an assistant managing editor for the Atlanta papers. He is currently editor of Longstreet Press in Atlanta.

In the early seventies, he married a woman who would receive her Ph.D. in French. And she would join the Emory University faculty in Atlanta. One night, she and Chuck had played tennis on the Emory courts. They were in separate cars. Chuck drove through an intersection and looked behind him to see if she made it through the light. What he saw was another car crash into the side of his wife's car. She was dead when he got to her.

Frank Frosch went to Vietnam as an intelligence officer. Later, he left the service and became a free-lance writer. His inside information made his piece for *Playboy* on the Mylai massacre one of the most compelling stories I ever read.

He eventually went to work for United Press International in Atlanta, and, for the record, he allowed my wife and me to keep his dog, Plato. (She got custody of him in a subsequent divorce.)

Frank later was assigned to the UPI bureau in

PnomPenh, Cambodia. One day, his office received a tip of fighting near the area. Frank and a photographer jumped into Frank's car and went to look for the action. They were found several days later. It appeared they had been dragged from their car, made to fall to their knees, and were then shot in the back of the head.

Fran Smith shot herself dead.

Larry Young got married, quit drinking, and retired as a columnist for the *Daily News* under the new management. A few months after his retirement, he died of lung cancer.

Gerald Rutberg is a successful attorney in his hometown of Orlando. I've written often of his ability to get a ticket to just about anything, and his ability to show up in incredible places.

There was the time Rutberg and I went to the Masters golf tournament for Sunday's final round. I had a press ticket. He had no ticket. The Masters ticket is the most difficult ticket in sports to obtain. It may be the most difficult ticket in *anything* to obtain.

"You'll never get in," I said to Rutberg as I left him at the gate, where there stood a cadre of itchy-fingered Pinkerton guards.

"Meet you at number eleven in thirty minutes," he told me.

After an hour, I went down to 11. There stood

Rutberg wearing an *L.A. Times* photographer's badge. "What kept you?" he asked.

Gerald Rutberg, in a ski jacket, made it onto the presidential platform for Jimmy Carter's inaugural service.

"I just kept walking," he explains.

Georgia played Penn State in the 1982 Sugar Bowl for the national championship. I had a two-bedroom suite at the Sonesta Hotel in New Orleans and two extra tickets to the game. I had moved mountains to get them.

Gerald had got me impossible tickets for years. I wanted to repay the favor. I called and invited him and his wife to stay in one of the bedrooms of my suite. I explained I had two tickets for them.

Rutberg and wife arrived in New Orleans. I handed him their tickets.

"These are in the end zone," Gerald said.

"It took an act of God to get them," I replied.

"No problem," he said, reaching into the pocket of his coat. "These six I have here are on the forty."

He wanted me to see something. He pulled a color photograph out of his briefcase. He had managed to slip into the National Collegiate Hall of Fame banquet in New York City the week before. The photograph showed Richard Nixon on the left and Gerald Ford on the right, both in tuxedos. The guy in the middle with his arms around the two former presidents was Rutberg.

A friend of Gerald's in Orlando called me a year later.

"Gerald's sick," he said. "And it looks bad."

Doctors had found a growth in Gerald's hip. The prognosis was a bad one. If the growth could be removed surgically—which was a large "if"—Gerald likely would be left paralyzed from the waist down. And would be left impotent. If it couldn't be removed, Gerald would die. He went to Mayo Clinic in Minnesota. There were weeks upon weeks of tests.

Gerald Rutberg was the first person Glenn Vaughn hired at the *Athens Daily News.* Maybe that is why there was at least one more miracle left.

The growth turned out to be nonmalignant. Gerald walked out of the hospital. He's now the father of a little blond girl named Leah. She looks a lot like another little blond girl I saw a picture of once.

Me: Okay. I've had too many wives and a couple of surgeries because of a lousy aortic valve in my heart. Compared to the others, I got off easy.

Wade Saye currently works for the Knoxville,

Tennessee *Journal*. Claude Williams, the *Daily News*'s publisher, continues as a successful outdoor advertiser in Athens. Jones Drewery is retired, still lives in Athens, and is still smoking.

Colleen Kelly wound up married to our rival sports editor at the *Banner-Herald.* They later divorced, and Colleen became an assistant managing editor with the Atlanta newspapers. She later sued the papers on a sex-discrimination suit, and the papers settled with her out of court.

Mark Smith is publisher of the *Daily News* and the *Banner Herald* in Athens.

My ex-wife, the *Daily News*'s receptionist, remarried, had a couple of kids, and also had a successful career as a model. I saw her at my mother's funeral in 1989. She looked great.

Glenn Vaughn would become an executive with the Knight-Ridder chain in Columbus, Georgia. He is recently retired.

"I've always had fun in this business," he told me earlier this year, "and I'd still like to have some more."

He always told me, after the *Daily News* was sold, "I'd like to do it one more time."

I told him if he tackled anything, be sure to call me first.

11

I know I've already told you the end of the story, but now I'm going back to tell you the middle, back to when we were taken over by the *Banner-Herald.*

They stuck Glenn Vaughn in an out-of-the-way office at the new *Athens Daily News* head-quarters. His duties were little more than to write an occasional editorial. Little did management realize that was dangerous because it gave Glenn time to do what he was best at—thinking.

He had said it before:

"You know what would be fun? To just start going into small towns with bad newspapers, start a new one, like we did in Athens, and give the old paper hell.

"Then, when we got it going good, we could leave one person in charge and go on to the next town. What we could wind up with is a chain of bright new Georgia community newspapers."

I had an idea, too.

"What we could do," I said to Glenn, "is get us a big tent. We go in, set up our tent, and put a news operation under it. It would be inexpensive, and we could get going overnight.

"When we left there, we could go on to the next place and get us another tent."

" 'Tent journalism,' " said Glenn, pounding his fist into his palm. "I like it."

Glenn's first idea out of his new headquarters had to do with a weekly in Toccoa, Georgia, a mountain town sixty miles north of Athens. Glenn's wife, Nancy, was from Ellijay, another mountain community.

Glenn wanted to buy the Toccoa weekly, owned by an aging gentleman who, rumor had it, was anxious to sell.

"We could buy Toccoa," Glenn said, "then start a five-day mountain daily. We could call it the *North Georgia Mountain Bee*."

"The *Bee*?" I asked Glenn.

"There's the *Sacramento Bee*," Glenn said. "I've just always liked the name *Bee* for a newspaper."

Bee isn't that bad a name when you think about it. There's a spelling bee, of course, and a quilting bee. I don't know if there has ever been such a thing as a sex bee, but you sort of get the idea it would be a lot like an orgy, a lot of people real busy doing the same thing.

I always had a few favorite names for newspapers myself. Names like the *Times, Herald, Banner, Sun,* and even the *Daily News* are pretty commonplace.

I like the name *Plain Dealer,* as in Cleveland. That sort of says, "We shoot straight with you."

And there's the *Hollywood Tattler,* which seems to be saying, "We know it all and we're foaming at the mouth to tell."

Sentinel is kind of boring, as are *Post, Journal,* and *Oklahoman.*

Dean Drewery always enjoyed talking about a small Georgia weekly known as the Hahira *Golden Leaf.* Probably the best name there ever was for a newspaper, however, was *Grit,* the national weekly kids used to sell door-to-door to earn a few extra pennies a week.

I'm not sure whatever happened to *Grit,* but the name implies a newspaper that isn't about to give up on any story and will stomp all over you to get the news. Mike Wallace would have made a great editor for *Grit.*

I've often thought, What would I name my own newspaper if I ever wound up with one?

How about the *Rumormonger,* or the *Believe It or Not,* or the *Busybody,* or the *We Ain't Shit-*

tin' You. There are certain animals you could name a paper for. You could have the *Hound,* or the *Hawk,* or the *Weed Snake,* or the *Barracuda.*

Or how about the *Cat*? Cats look as if they know a lot of secrets. If the truth be known, cats probably sneak into their owners' bedrooms a lot to see what's going on, and they listen to telephone conversations and keep notes on who comes and who goes.

Cats are sneaky and spylike, and that's what a good newspaper should be, too.

I suggested to Glenn that an alternative to the *North Georgia Mountain Bee* might be the *North Georgia Mountain Wildcat.*

"Not bad," he said, pounding his fist into his palm.

Glenn wanted me to go with him if he wound up in Toccoa. His idea was that I would be the managing editor. He also wanted to take along Mark Smith, the boy-wonder advertising whiz, who had also come along with us to our new address.

I went so far as to accompany Glenn to Toccoa to meet with the owner of the paper. Our chat with him was simply to get a reading on just how much he wanted to sell. I wouldn't say he seemed desperate, but he was getting on, and

Glenn said, after the meeting, "I wonder if we could get Browny back as photographer?"

My dream of getting to the *Atlanta Journal* sports department hadn't exactly diminished, but I had found a new angle to newspapering that I liked—being a part of what it looked like, what news it carried, what direction it took. I relished another fight. We go into Toccoa, start a five-day mountain daily, and take on the various community weeklies, as well as the other dailies that tried to appeal to mountain folk.

Working under the new *Daily News* management was terribly boring. It suddenly didn't matter that much anymore what news we broke. There was no longer any competition, any camaraderie, any reason to go beyond a call of duty to make a page look as though the news were jumping off it.

Browny was gone. I was back to getting a lot of armpit shots of basketball games. The only real interesting element of working at our new headquarters was there was an abundance of coeds working in the production department, pasting up pages. It was rather a pleasure to walk downstairs to production to oversee the sports-section makeup. Coeds smile and do your bidding energetically. I would learn later just how important that is for the poor devil in charge of getting a page together and to the presses on time.

At the old *Daily News,* every day was an adventure. At the new *Daily News,* I felt sleepy a lot. The only real action came as a result of a terrible error that slipped past me.

Because the *Daily News* had always attempted to appeal to the surrounding counties, as well as to Athens, I had started an annual *Athens Daily News* All-Northeast Georgia basketball team for boys and girls. I asked the area coaches to vote on the team, and they picked an All-Northeast Georgia player of the year for both sexes.

The results of the voting were in for the 1968 teams, and the girls' player of the year was some quirk of nature who was about six-five and weighed 210 and was named Betty Lou Ann Sue, or something like that.

In those days, there were six players on each girls' high school team. It was a half-court game. Three girls were guards. Their job was to defense the three opposing girls, who were forwards. When they got a rebound, they would then take the ball to center court and pass it off to their three forwards. I suppose they didn't figure girls were strong enough to play by boys' rules back then, which was also before married women were named Henry-Dilmont in an effort to retain their maiden name in some form so as to indicate they might be married but they weren't taking any stuff from their husbands.

On her nomination sheet, I recall quite clearly, her coach had written, "What is amazing about Betty Lou Ann Sue is she hit 75 percent of her shots for the entire season."

So I wrote the story about her being named player of the year, and I quoted her coach in the story: "What is amazing about Betty Lou Ann Sue," said Coach Matthew Grubb, "is she hit 75 percent of her shots for the entire season."

It is amazing there aren't more errors in newspapers. If you could see just how many people have a hand in getting one out on a daily basis, you would understand. You get that many people involved, somebody usually is going to blow it along the way.

Ever been reading your newspapers and suddenly the next sentence didn't have anything to do with the subject matter of the former sentence? That happens when type gets mixed up, and it happens a lot. The makeup man isn't paying close attention, and type that was supposed to go under a headline on page 8 winds up mixed in with a story on page 12. I've always worried that if I ever did win the Pulitzer Prize, the article announcing my award would somehow get mixed up with type from other articles.

My worst fears were that I would win on the same day there was a huge fire at a gay bar and some guy had been arrested for indecent exposure at a major-league baseball game.

The story might read: "Columnist Lewis Grizzard today was named, along with two others with a history of arson arrests, as the yet-unidentified man who exposed himself to a group of nuns at Wednesday's Kansas City–Baltimore game.

"Authorities said that Grizzard, whose jilted lover is reported to have been behind the blaze at *The Boy Next Door,* won the second game of the doubleheader 3–2.

"The popular communist will be arraigned Tuesday."

What happened at the *Daily News* was that somehow the gremlins who haunt newspaper production departments removed the *o* from the word "shots," as in "hit 75 percent of her shots," and replaced it with an *i.*

I didn't see it when I checked the page for the last time. The lovely coed making up the page didn't see it.

But there it was the next morning, and it seemed the whole world saw it.

"What is amazing about Betty Lou Ann Sue," said Coach Matthew Grubb, "is she hit 75 percent of her shits."

Coach Grubb called me. "You idiot," is what he said.

Betty Lou Ann Sue's father called to say, "I'm suing."

The managing editor came over to my desk and said, "Grizzard, you dingbat. Do you know how this makes us look?"

And then a guy called and asked me, "What about her other twenty-five percent?"

I considered suicide. Then I was afraid my obituary might read, "*Athens Daily News* sports editor Lewis Grizzard was found dead Thursday night as the Bulldogs came back with the bottom of the eighth to stop Vanderbilt 3–2 on a suicide squeeze play."

* * *

It was May 1968. Springtime in Athens. Dogwoods and azaleas. The coeds sunning in the front yard of the sorority houses. The beer so good and cold at Harry's, and I was only a few hours short of graduation. I was eighteen hours short, as a matter of fact, and my last spring quarter at Georgia I had only one more journalism course to take. It was a three-hour course called Trade Journals. They would teach us how to put together, say, a weekly company newsletter. We met three times a week, and it was pretty dull stuff. I knew that I would never wind up putting out a company newsletter, so I dozed off a lot.

Then, one day, the professor announced that everybody in the class had to make up his or her own trade journal.

I forget the details of what all was involved, but there were a lot of them, and it seemed to me that here was a thing that was going to take a lot of time and effort, and I didn't want to waste either doing it.

When the professor made that assignment, I knew in my heart I'd never turn in my trade journal. I would find a way to get out of it. I would have the professor shot. Or I would beg out of the assignment on account of having to go to my brother's funeral. I didn't have a brother, but if I couldn't think of anything else, I could always try that.

I was the official scorer at Georgia baseball games that spring. My duties also included manning the public-address system to the handful of fans who showed up for Georgia baseball games.

Georgia was playing some touring team from the frozen north in middle May. I was sitting in the press box, trying to figure out how to get out of my trade journal and how to pronounce the name of the visiting team's center fielder.

Southern names are usually pretty simple. Most of us are Scots-Irish, which means we have names like "McDonald," "Pierce," "Gunterson," or, of course, "Smith." (*My* last name is French, however. It means "wild stallion.") But touring college baseball teams from places up North can have a lot of players who descend from towns where people have names that include a lot of *j*'s and *z*'s mixed up together to form names southerners have no idea how to pronounce.

The center fielder's name was spelled something like "Wjozlfmepzjski." I finally came up with, "Now batting for New Jersey A and M, the center fielder Al 'Wahjahjocowski.' " The batter looked up at me in the press box, and I am certain he was wondering, How did this dumb redneck come up with that?

A man walked into the press box and sat down next to me. He wore a pair of sunglasses, and what had once been a fully-grown cigar was sticking about two inches out the right side of his mouth. The man didn't say anything at first. He just sat down next to me and stared out at the field.

Wjozlfmepzjski singled to left. The next batter

was named Papachini. I had no trouble with that. Most Italian names rhyme with a vegetable.

The man sitting next to me spoke. "Are you going to have to go into the army when you graduate?" he asked.

"No," I said. A heart-valve problem had saved me from getting one between the eyes from some guy named Chow Ding Chu in a rice paddy in Vietnam. They threw Wahjahjocoski, or whatever his name was, out at the plate in the top of the ninth, and Georgia beat New Jersey A&M by a run.

"You want to come to work for us?" was the man's next question.

The man in the press box was James G. Minter, Jr., executive sports editor of the *Atlanta Journal*. I'd read his stuff many times. I'd seen him with Furman Bisher on *Football Review*, Bisher's Sunday television show where Atlanta sportswriters analyzed the preceding Saturday's major southern college games.

He didn't introduce himself to me when he sat down next to me in the press box. I suppose he assumed I knew who he was. There had been no preliminary small talk, save the question about the army. Vietnam was raging. They were shipping twenty-one-year-olds off by the droves.

There was an opening on the *Journal* sports

staff. No use wasting time on somebody who might not live six more months.

Just, "You want to come to work for us?"

It was happening again to me. Out of the blue came the Miracle offer. I'm just sitting there, with no prior knowledge of what was about to happen, and here's Jim Minter offering me a job at the *Journal.*

Again, I have no idea of the exact words I chose to answer him with. There had to have been a "Great Gawdamighty yes," in there somewhere, however.

Minter took the cigar out of his mouth and said, "Be at the *Journal* Saturday morning at nine."

"I'll be there," I managed to say.

He put the cigar back in the side of his mouth, got up, and walked out of the door. I went back to the office, got the sports section out, went home, told my wife we were moving to Atlanta, and called Glenn at home and said I needed to talk to him the next day.

I wouldn't be going to Toccoa with him. I had to see the big time. The good fight at the *Daily News* was over and nothing would bring it back. Ever.

My wife said, "We'll have to find an apartment where they'll let us have the dog."

"That shouldn't be a problem," I said.

"How much money do you think you'll make?" she asked.

"I might get as much as a hundred-fifty dollars a week," I said.

"Let's buy a car with air-conditioning," she said.

The little VW Beetle was a little slice of hell during the summer.

"If I can get a hundred-fifty, a week," I told her, "we can buy a new Pontiac."

Four years earlier, as the southern saying goes, I couldn't have afforded syrup if it had fallen to three cents a sop. And here I was thinking about $150 a week and a new Pontiac with air-conditioning.

Bring on the good life.

The old man in Toccoa decided not to sell his paper, Glenn wound up leaving Athens to move back to Columbus, where he quickly became publisher of the jointly owned papers there.

We both eventually got out of the actual business of getting the paper out every day. I turned to column writing, and Glenn took to working on annual budgets. I ran into him at the Atlanta airport one day years later.

"I wonder what would have happened if we had gone to Toccoa?" I asked.

"We'd have had some fun," Glenn said. That old enthusiasm.

And then he was off to Ottawa or some such place to look at a new press. I caught a plane to San Antonio to address the National Association of Truck Stop Owners. I laughed to myself as I recalled Dr. Aderhold's wife's chicken. I still can't think of the chicken's name, though.

Four years almost to the day that I stood alone in the vacant sports department of the *Atlanta Journal* and vowed to return, I walked back in, older, wiser, and hoping to God I'd get an offer for $150 a week.

I walked into a major crisis.

The *Journal,* an afternoon daily, still published a Saturday edition in 1968, and in the midst of getting that out, there was also the matter of the first Sunday edition, which usually hit the streets around four Saturday afternoon.

This first Sunday edition was known as the "bulldog." As soon as the Saturday afternoon edition was finished, a designated "bulldog man" would then go to the composing room and put together the early Sunday sports section. It would contain stories printed overnight on Friday. All the columns that were to run in every edition went in the bulldog. The rest of it usually included wire-feature stories that had come in all week. They would be pulled in later editions to make room for breaking sports stories.

Furman Bisher's Sunday column went into the bulldog, of course. It always ran down the left-hand side of the front sports section.

There were rules about Furman Bisher's column. Serious rules. Written-in-blood rules.

* You didn't jump Furman Bisher's column from the front to an inside page.
* You didn't cut anything out of Furman Bisher's column.
* You didn't edit Furman Bisher's column. Every word was a pearl.

When I walked into the *Journal* sports department at approximately 9:08 that last Saturday in May, there was panic throughout the place.

Bisher's column was missing, he had neglected to leave a carbon, and he was out of town and couldn't be reached.

The composing-room foreman checked with all the Linotype operators, and they all said they hadn't seen Bisher's column. But the bulldog man swore he had sent it down through the pneumatic tubes Friday afternoon.

I walked in, looked around for Jim Minter. His desk was to the left of the slot, across from

Bisher's office. He was on the phone talking to the composing room when I reached him.

He was telling the composing-room foreman what he thought of him, which obviously wasn't very much. He slammed the phone down, looked up and saw me, and said, "Get a chair somewhere. We've got a problem. Bisher's column is missing."

So I grabbed a chair and just sat there and watched the drama that unfolded in front of me.

After he got through with the composing-room foreman, Minter jumped on the bulldog man.

"You should have made sure Bisher gave you a carbon," he said, sternly. Minter's tone frightened me—and I was just sitting there in a chair watching.

He went back to his desk and to his phone. He called the composing-room foreman again and said, "I know damn well Bisher's column was sent down. Now get off your butt and look for it. It's got to be down there somewhere."

There were anxious moments that followed. If Bisher's column couldn't be found, it not only wouldn't appear in the first edition, but might not make the Sunday paper at all. Bisher would go nuts when he found out about it, and when Bisher went nuts, hell had no like fury . . .

I felt as though I were in an airport-control center and a plane was coming in without its landing gear.

The phone buzzed. Somebody picked it up and said to Minter, "It's the composing room for you."

The office fell silent.

"Well, it's about goddamn time," Minter said into the phone.

The composing-room foreman had found Bisher's column. It was someplace it shouldn't have been. Precious lives had been saved.

"I can pay you one hundred sixty dollars a week," Jim Minter said to me after the Bisher crisis was over.

"How much?" I asked him.

"One-sixty," he said.

My God.

"Bill Clark is coming down from the *Constitution* to cover colleges for us. You'll be number two to him."

That was also good news. The one thing I wanted to avoid was being relegated to the high school beat. I'd covered Georgia for two years and had got a taste for large press boxes, charter flights with the team, and big games in front of thousands in such exotic places as Auburn, Alabama; Jacksonville, Florida; and Jackson, Mississippi.

I suppose if Minter had put me on high schools, I still would have taken the job, because it at least would have got me through the front door. But to be number two on colleges! To work with Bill Clark, whom I'd read for years and seen on Bisher's *Football Review,* was an awesome thought. And 160 big ones a week! God didn't make that much money.

Minter would tell me later how he got my name. He was in Athens speaking with Joel Eaves, the Georgia athletic director. He asked Eaves, "Any young sportswriters around who have impressed you?"

Joel Eaves was a tall, silver-haired man with a deep, commanding voice. He ran the Georgia athletic department with an eye on every penny that came in and went out. He had been brought in to straighten out the mess that was the Georgia athletic program in 1963.

Coach Eaves—which is how he was always referred to—had treated me with surprising respect as sports editor of the *Daily News.* I was nineteen. He had to deal with the Atlanta papers and veterans like Bisher and Minter, but he never refused me an interview, and even fed me a few scoops on occasion.

Coach Eaves had even offered me a job earlier in the spring. There was an opening for assistant sports-information director in the athletic department. The assistant SID kept statistics, wrote press releases, went to get things for the SID, and took sportswriters out for drinks and dinner. Coach Eaves offered me seventy-two hundred dollars a year. But it was too late for me. I was a newspaperman. I had sniffed the glue pot, beat more than my share of deadlines, and had seen combat in a newspaper war. I was committed. He told Minter about me.

Minter would tell me later, however, that Georgia's basketball coach, Ken Rosemond, actually had more to do with the fact he sought me out and offered me the opportunity to join the *Journal.*

Rosemond had inherited a terrible basketball tradition at Georgia. Until 1963, Georgia played its home games in a barn called Woodruff Hall. Finally, the state built the school a new coliseum, but it was the same old losses, just surrounded by a little better scenery.

Rosemond had played on Frank McGuire's 1957 national champion North Carolina team that beat Wilt Chamberlain and Kansas in the finals in triple overtime. McGuire, a New Yorker, had organized a tremendous talent pipeline from New York to Chapel Hill. When Rosemond got to Georgia, he figured he would do the same thing.

What he actually did was alienate every high school coach in the state by saying he couldn't win with Georgia kids. So he went to New York and came back with a cast that didn't do very much better than their home-grown predecessors.

For some reason, Rosemond didn't like me very much. He was tough to interview and very defensive. His team was hosting Georgia Tech in Athens one evening. Tech had a strong team. A large crowd, by Georgia basketball measures, was expected. It was Rosemond's avowed intention to do away with Georgia's image as simply a football school.

The afternoon before the game, Rosemond ran into football coach Vince Dooley in an athletic-department hallway. "Are you coming to the game tonight, Coach?" Rosemond asked Dooley, already on his way to legend status.

"I'm not sure," said Dooley, matter-of-factly. "Who are you playing?"

Rosemond turned fourteen shades of red and stalked back into his office.

Minter had also run into Rosemond the afternoon Coach Eaves had given me his recommendation. Minter asked Rosemond the same question: "Any young writer around impress you?"

Rosemond recommended his manager, who also wanted to go into sportswriting. Minter told me later that he asked, "What about this Grizzard kid?"

"He's a troublemaker," said Rosemond.

"That convinced me," said Minter, who strongly believed that if coaches or players of the team you were covering actually liked you, then you weren't doing your job.

Rosemond's manager, incidentally, was named Henry Freeman. He became sports editor of *USA Today,* and his sections have been so packed with information and organized so well, practically every sports section in the country has stolen at least a couple of his ideas.

Just like that, the job was mine. Less than four years after high school, I had, in a manner of speaking, fulfilled my lifetime ambition, to be a member of the *Atlanta Journal* sports staff. Jim Minter just walked into the press box at the Georgia baseball field, asked me two questions, and four days later he made it official and hired me. I would report to work a week from the following Monday.

And I never did do the trade journal. I told my professor about the job in Atlanta, and there was no way I could be moved in a week and complete the assignment. He was nice about it.

He said, "I'll give you an incomplete. Just try to finish it by the end of summer so you can graduate."

Right.

Paula and I drove to Atlanta in the hot VW the following Tuesday and wound up with an apartment in suburban Smyrna. It was okay to have a dog, the resident manager said. I'm still not certain how we wound up in Smyrna, the Jonquil City, since it was a thirty-minute drive downtown to the newspaper. And I used the term "suburban" earlier. Now, since Atlanta is about six hundred times larger than it was in 1968, Smyrna is suburban. When I moved there however, the term "boonies" fit better.

But there was a good barbecue place nearby, as well as several chiropractors' offices, and a religious bookstore. If I ever got hungry for barbecue and suffered whiplash in an accident on the way to the restaurant and became born-again in the middle of all that, I was in a dandy spot to fulfill all my needs.

My last day at the *Daily News* was a Friday of the last week in May 1968. Nobody threw me any kind of a party. As a matter of fact, that last night was supposed to be fairly routine.

I wrote an occasional front-page column called "Lewis Grizzard on Sportz." I thought misspelling "sports" was a cute idea. It wasn't.

I wrote the obligatory farewell column, laid out the Saturday morning sports section with every intention of getting the section in early and getting out of that place for good. I still hadn't forgiven management for making the *Daily News* staff move its own furniture and then rewarding us with a stupid case of beer.

But early that evening there had been an auto accident, and a friend had been killed.

Carl Gilbert was only twenty-two. He had been a star athlete at Athens High and then had played baseball at Georgia. His younger brother, Paul, was the quarterback on the 1965 Athens High team I had covered my first year at the *Daily News.*

I met Carl Gilbert through another friend, Bill Johnson. Bill did Athens High football and basketball play-by-play for the local radio station, WGAU.

I crashed my car after an out-of-town Athens High football game in 1965, and Bill gave me a ride back to Athens. Carl Gilbert kept statistics for Bill Johnson on the broadcasts. I became friends with both of them. In fact, Bill and I became close. He was married and so was I. We were both working our way through Georgia. He wanted to be the next Ed Thelinius. I wanted to be the next Furman Bisher. He had one of those draft-beer containers in the icebox at his apartment. I thoroughly enjoyed draft beer. It was over many gallons of his draft beer that we discussed our dreams.

"We'll make it," he often assured me.

I took to riding with Bill and Carl to all out-of-town Athens High games. Bill got the WGAU station wagon for those trips, and anything beat driving halfway across the state in that damn VW of mine.

Bill graduated in 1966. He was in the air force ROTC program, and his broadcasting career would have to be interrupted by six months of duty in Texas. The day before he left Athens, we sat in his apartment, poured down the beers, and toasted our futures.

It was nice to have a friend who could relate to my dream. Not only had he done the Athens High broadcasts, he'd also signed on the station on weekdays at the crack of dawn.

"You ever get up in the morning and ask yourself, 'Why am I putting myself through this torture?' " I had asked him.

"When I hit the big time," he answered, "I figure it will all have been worth it."

That last day he was in Athens was the last time I saw Bill Johnson alive. We hugged when

I left his apartment. We would stay in touch by mail.

Bill never did mention anything about his illness in his first letters. I found out from his pretty blond wife, Carol, who had stayed behind in Athens. I dropped by to see her one day and found her alone and crying.

"Bill's real sick," she said to me. She was leaving that afternoon for Texas to be with him.

It had something to do with a virus that attacked Bill's heart. They said he lost a lot of weight before he died, and looked awful. His casket wasn't open at his funeral in his little hometown of Summerville, Georgia, in the north Georgia foothills.

"We wanted his friends to remember him as he was before he got sick," Carol had told me.

I was devastated by Bill's death. My last letter from him had come in early December. He wrote that he was improving since Carol had joined him, and that doctors were considering allowing him to go to the Cotton Bowl in Dallas January 1, to see Georgia play SMU.

But a week or so later, he was dead. We had been in this together. Two promising young men who were willing to work our butts off to get to the place we wanted to be.

As I walked out of the *Journal-Constitution*

building the Saturday morning after Jim Minter hired me, I thought long and hard about Bill. Had he lived, where would he have been at that delicious moment in my life?

He had the voice. He knew the games. And his desire and energy were limitless. He would have made what we considered the big time, too. I was convinced of that. But damn the Fates.

And here I sat on my last night in Athens, and Carl Gilbert was dead, too. We'd traveled all over the state together. Bill usually drove. Carl sat in the front passenger seat, and I took the back. Three of us in that car, and now two were dead. You are going to live forever when you're twenty-one. *But now two of us were dead.*

I found a picture of Carl in the Georgia baseball files and ran it next to his obituary, which I wrote. The pretty coed pasted down the last headline on my sports pages.

I walked back upstairs to my desk. I picked up the box I had loaded with various possessions. The newsroom was empty. There was nobody to say good-bye to. I put the box in the front seat next to me in the VW and drove home by way of the old *Daily News* building, which the new management was turning into some sort of storage area. I pulled in front of the building and sat there for maybe fifteen minutes. I looked over at the Open House across the street. The same old faces sat there drinking coffee and listening to a country song by Jack Green that made its way out of the open door onto the street.

I just sat there and stared at the place where I had spent nearly three years involved in what I still believe to be high on the list of noble human endeavors—putting out a good news-paper.

The place had once been so alive. Now, it sat dark and orphaned.

I cranked the VW, put it in reverse, and backed out into the street.

Then the schoolboy journalist drove away.

12

Newspaper hours are strange. If you work for an afternoon newspaper, you report at the very crack of dawn and you get off when everybody else is having lunch. If you work for a morning newspaper, you report in the afternoon and get off when everybody else is asleep. There are some good points to these hours.

Okay, so I can think of only *one:* You never have to sit in traffic.

Monday morning I walked out of my apartment exactly at six. Of course I remember what time it was. One doesn't meet his destiny without recording each detail.

It was June and it was hot and it was my first day as a paid em-by-God-ployee of the *Atlanta Journal* sports department. Almost four years to the day since I had stood alone in that small office, hallowed be its name, and had vowed to return. Well, not only was I back, I was wearing a new sports jacket.

I had decided I needed one. My old jacket, which I bought to go through fraternity rush at Georgia, hardly seemed right for such a historic moment in my life. It was a tweed sort of thing. And the truth was, it didn't really wow them that much when I went through fraternity rush.

I probably visited fifteen houses and only got invited back to two (I still think they probably got me mixed up with another guy). I wasn't the biggest lizard who went through rush at the University of Georgia in 1964, but I did wear funny glasses, and I had a lot of freckles.

I went to Judson Smith's cut-rate, factory-reject warehouse in my hometown of Moreland to buy my new sports jacket to wear my first day at the *Journal.* Judson dressed almost everybody in Moreland, including the town's two preachers and the grammar-school principal. Judson had a motto: "If you want it, we got it. Let's just hope we can find it."

You had to drive down a dirt road to get to Judson's place. People came from as far away as Hogansville, Grantville, and Primrose to shop there because of his bargain prices. Judson would sell you pillows and sheets, bundles of white socks, six pair for a dollar, shoes, sweaters, shirts, slacks, and if you needed a plumbing tool or a mousetrap, he'd probably have that too.

I selected a forty-long gray sports jacket from Mr. Judson's spring collection. The only thing I could find to identify it as a factory reject was what appeared to be a faulty stitching just under the left side pocket. It was barely noticeable. For twenty-eight bucks, it was practically invisible.

I wore a pair of navy-blue slacks with my gray coat. I also wore a white shirt, a red striped tie, and a pair of brown wing-tip shoes I had shined the night before. I had slicked down my hair with Vitalis, dabbed on some English Leather cologne. And I was gorgeous. Okay, I was clean.

It had never occurred to me where I would park. Jim Minter hadn't mentioned anything about an employee parking lot.

I drove downtown and turned up Forsyth Street, where the *Journal-Constitution* was located, next to Atlanta's Union Station, still suffering from the disappearing railroad blues, as Steve Goodman put it in his brilliant "City of New Orleans," which a lot of people recorded, but Willie Nelson did best.

I circled the block a couple of times—I still had twenty minutes before it was time to report—but I didn't see any parking meters or parking lots. What I did see, however, was a great deal of room in the Union Station lot. Run one dilapidated passenger train a day, and there usually will be a lot of room in your parking lot. I didn't see any sort of guard, so I figured what the hell and parked just above the entrance to the station, where I jumped into the exciting field of sales four years earlier.

Just after dawn, I walked past the station. It hadn't opened yet. But even on the outside, it still smelled of urine, and there were newspapers and wine bottles near the entrance. The place looked like an aging contessa who had let herself go and danced in the darkness of her room alone.

Just past the entrance was some sort of little

cubbyhole that looked as if it might have been a place to check baggage back when the contessa was still a fine-looking lady and the trains were spit-polished and were anxious to arrive "on the advertised"—at the precise hour and minute it had promised its passengers.

As I walked past that area, I heard a voice. It startled me. I sort of had the idea I was the only other person up in the world.

The voice said something like, "Hey, buddy." I looked around. I was the only buddy on the premises. I looked inside the dark little hole. I could make out a human figure. It came out and said to me, "I just got off a freight train, and I haven't eaten in two days. Can you help me?"

The man was as filthy and decrepit as the station. His hands shook. His eyes were hollow. He smelled. Urine and body odor were not my idea of a perfect start to the day. The man seemed more pitiable than menacing.

I pulled out my wallet and gave him two dollars. That left me five. The man seemed genuinely appreciative.

"Where did you come in from?" I asked him. Night trains were especially fascinating to me. I'd heard their distant horns so many nights in Moreland. I'd just lie there and wait for the train to get nearer and the horn to get louder, and then would come the clanking and rumbling as the train passed through town, highballing either south to Montgomery or north to Atlanta on the Atlanta and West Point roadway. Then the horn would grow distant again, and silence would be restored. There was always something peaceful and restful about hearing a train at night. I would lie there under my cover, and sleep was easier. One day I knew I would ride a night train out somewhere covering the Atlanta Crackers on the Southern Association circuit, maybe into New Orleans or Mobile or Little Rock. But as I stood there that morning, the Crackers had been gone from Atlanta for years, and what passenger trains were left were ghosts.

The man said he'd hopped a freight in Nashville. He seemed anxious to get on his way, which made sense. After all, he had said he hadn't eaten in two days.

"Do you know," he asked me then, "what time the liquor stores open?" Oh. I walked into the *Journal-Constitution* a much wiser individual, having learned that in desperation, hunger always comes in second to thirst.

As I rode up in the elevator, alone, to the fourth floor, I wondered, Would I ever leave this place again?

Not likely. I was there to practice the art of

sports journalism, to be the best at it I could be.

I walked in. Tom McCollister, the slot man, pointed to a seat around the rim, and said for me to occupy it. He handed me a wire story that needed a headline. I wrote it. I was official. I had gathered with the eagles, like Bisher and Minter.

Bisher, as sports editor, had run the department for years until the creation of an executive-sports-editor position. Bisher had been a tyrant. There was still a large hole in the bulletin board behind the slot. Former slot man Greg Favre, currently executive editor of the *Sacramento Bee,* was said to have gone to Bisher's office once for the morning ritual of being told what was wrong with his first edition. After this particular session, he had stormed out and put his fist through the board.

Nobody ever set foot in Bisher's tiny office without fear. And nobody ever emerged from Bisher's office with a victory. It was often said, "In that office, Bisher is unbeaten, untied, and unscored upon."

Bisher was a North Carolina man, a robust fellow with black curly hair. His family was in the hosiery business. Bisher grew up in Denton, and as he often mentioned in his column, grew up listening to the dulcet tones of Bill Stern and the early sportscasters on an Atwater-Kent radio. We had that much in common. I had grown up listening to the dulcet tones of Harry Caray and Buddy Blattner on KMOX in St. Louis and Waite Hoyt calling the Cincinnati Reds games on WCKY, which also featured *The Wayne Rainey Show,* where they played a lot of gospel music and sold baby chicks "guaranteed live on arrival." My radio came from Sears.

Bisher originally was sports editor of the *Constitution*. Ed Danforth, who was always referred to as "Colonel," retired as sports editor of the *Journal* in the fifties, and Bisher took his place on the afternoon paper.

Bisher's tyrannical nature (he once walked into the office and said to a staff member he particularly disliked, "Watson, I've got a new assignment for you—find another job.") and his frequent absences as he covered everything that moved in sports, finally led management to the decision to allow Bisher to keep his title and continue to write his brilliant column, but to name somebody else executive sports editor to see to the staff and the daily working of the paper.

Jim Minter got that job.

He had been born into the red clay of then-rural Fayette County to the south of Atlanta, a farm boy who learned the work ethic in his father's fields. He graduated from the University of Georgia and went into the service post-Korea. If he had remained in the service, I am convinced we would have won in Vietnam. No man was ever so born-to-lead.

His father's death took Minter out of the army. He had to return to Fayette County—to the land and to his mother. Both needed caring for.

His family affairs in order, he then followed his own notion to get into journalism. Ed Danforth gave him a job on the *Journal* sports staff, and he wound up running the show.

He was tough. And ornery. A hard man to know. But if you fell in battle, he would come back for you. In madness, he would remain calm.

I hate to jump ahead, but the following example of Minter's toughness fits best here. He eventually left *Journal* sports to become managing editor of the *Constitution*. Reg Murphy, at the time, was editorial page editor.

Murphy, a few years later, was kidnapped by some guy with a mental problem. He stuffed Murphy into the trunk of his car, and then called the newspaper and demanded $800,000 in cash for his return.

He wanted somebody from the paper to meet him with the money. He wanted that person to come in an uncovered vehicle, and he demanded that person come alone.

Minter volunteered to take the money to the kidnapper. It was deep into winter. The Federal Reserve bank, located next door to the paper, came up with the $800,000 in cash.

Minter bundled himself up against the cold and drove to meet the kidnapper in an open jeep, not knowing what might eventually happen to Murphy or himself.

As it turned out, Minter was not harmed and the kidnapper, later captured, let Murphy go.

At a press conference later, a TV reporter asked Minter what he felt like, leaving the newspaper with $800,000 of Cox money.

He replied, "I felt like Furman Bisher on my way to spring training."

Minter demanded good writing. He demanded good layout. There was a way he thought the *Journal* staff should write, and there was a way he thought the *Journal* sports section should look, and he would not allow anything that didn't fit the mold.

And Minter was fiercely competitive.

He wanted news. He demanded news. The *Constitution,* despite the fact it was under the same roof and management umbrella as the *Journal,* was Minter's, and thus Bisher's, mortal enemy. Better to have died a small boy than to walk in one morning, pick up the *Constitution,* and find your adversary had broken a story on you.

We covered the Southeastern Conference with bright and shining light. Nothing escaped us. If the papers in Birmingham, where the conference offices were located, broke an SEC story first, Minter would take it as a personal offense.

The *Journal* and *Constitution* were combined on Sundays, but the *Journal* was responsible for producing the paper. During football season, we covered, with writers and photographers, everything in the South that put on a helmet.

Photographers would fly into, say, New Orleans for a Georgia Tech–Tulane game early. They would shoot the first quarter, then jump on a plane and get the photographs back by early evening. The next day, there would appear a small airplane in the corner of the photographs selected, informing the reader this wasn't any nickel-and-dime operation.

Georgia Tech's legendary head coach Bobby Dodd probably knew how to handle sportswriters and sports pages better than anybody else of his day. If a reporter covering Tech couldn't think of an angle, Dodd would give him one. If

Tech was on the road and the photo deadline was tight, Dodd had a unique way of making the photographer's job easier. He would find out what side of the field the *Journal-Constitution*'s photographer was stationed, and run all the plays on Tech's first offensive series toward that side.

The Braves had moved into Atlanta from Milwaukee in 1966. Atlanta was also granted an expansion National Football League franchise the same year, *and* the St. Louis Hawks of the National Basketball Association came to Atlanta in '68. The city even got a franchise in the North American Soccer League. Atlanta was finally a major-league town.

Compared to today, however, we were woefully short on people and space. Today, most big-league sport departments have wide-open pages, a staff that works inside to produce the paper, and then a covey of writers to cover their various beats. Inside people don't write. Outside people don't edit, and appear only occasionally in the office.

At the *Journal* in 1968, you worked both inside *and* outside, and there was no such thing as overtime (Hold that thought. It becomes important later).

Wilt Browning covered the Braves, Hyland

had the Hawks. Darrell Simmons covered the Falcons. Teague Jackson was the golf writer, Bill Robinson had auto racing and outdoors. Bill Clark and I covered the colleges, Bill Whitley had the high schools. Joe Litsch helped him.

Tom McCollister was assistant sports editor. He ran the slot four mornings a week, then worked Saturday nights producing the Sunday morning edition. He had the worst job on the staff. Basically, what he did was get up at four in the morning four days a week and then work from two in the afternoon until the next morning on Saturday, and if there was anything wrong in the sports section, it was his fault. He is still alive, incidentally.

Bisher wrote his column and still raised hell if there was anything he didn't like in the section. He had accepted the fact he no longer oversaw the day-to-day operation, but did not accept the fact he wasn't supposed to make everybody's life miserable when he spotted what he considered an error in spelling, fact, style, layout, or judgment.

Minter battled Bisher's tantrums and did the hiring and firing. He also gave out the assignments, made up the work schedule, signed expense accounts, reworked the design of the first edition if he didn't like it, covered college football Saturdays, and broke news. He was the first to write that Norm Van Brocklin was coming to the Falcons as head coach.

He got that story when the wife of a *Constitution* reporter bragged to Minter's wife, Anne, that her husband had confirmed Van Brocklin was coming to Atlanta, and was going to write the story in the Wednesday morning paper. Minter came out with it Tuesday afternoon.

Minter was not above any sort of treachery that would net him a scoop. When Georgia was trying to hire a new athletic director, he hid in a room next to where university officials were meeting and planned to listen to what was taking place through a heating and air conditioning duct. Unfortunately, he was noticed by a latecomer to the meeting and his cover was blown. He was first with the story later anyway.

Minter had lost some horses in the late sixties. John Logue had covered baseball and college football and was a brilliant writer, a well-read man whose literary allusions on the sports pages were wonderful. But he had decided to leave and join the staff of *Southern Living* in Birmingham. He has since become a highly regarded editor and writer of mystery novels.

Lee Walburn was gone, too. Walburn had also

covered the Crackers. When the Braves moved into town, Bisher called him into his office with instructions on how to cover a major-league spring training camp. Walburn announced his intention to take his young family with him to West Palm, where the Braves trained.

Bisher was incredulous. How could a man do a job on spring training when his wife and children were around? Walburn recalls Bisher saying, "Lee, you've just got to make a choice—it's either your family or baseball."

Luckily for Lee, before he had to give his final answer, the Braves hired him to run their public-relations department. Walburn later opened his own successful public-relations firm, sold out to J. Walter Thompson, and is currently editor of *Atlanta Magazine.* He is still married, as well.

So here we were that June morning of 1968. My history of falling in with an odd crowd was continuing:

—Frank Hyland, the basketball writer, was in his late twenties. He was originally from Minnesota. He smoked nonfiltered Camels. He had a beautiful wife and two beautiful daughters. Frank enjoyed arguing abut any subject, and there were few subjects about which he didn't have a strong opinion.

I think Frank was always happiest when he

was leaning against a bar with a beer in his hand debating who was the better player, Bill Russell or Wilt Chamberlain. Frank and Bill Clark spent hours on the issue. Frank was a Bill Russell man. Clark defended Chamberlain. Once, I got into the argument and mentioned the fact I was a Bob Pettit man. Frank said, "You have the mind of an earthworm."

—Wilt Browning, the baseball writer, looked a lot like a teacher I had in high school. He had false teeth. He logged a million miles or so traveling around the country with the Atlanta Braves. How he kept his sanity, I'm not certain. He was the consummate professional. He could compose a three-page Braves story at a manual typewriter and never make a typing error. He wrote one of the greatest headlines I've ever seen.

At six-thirty on a Monday morning, Wilt was in the office doing his story on the previous Sunday's Braves game, which they had lost, even then a redundancy.

Wilt's angle to the game was that Mike McCormick, who had pitched for the winning San Francisco Giants, might have an outside chance of winning the Cy Young Award as the National League's outstanding pitcher of the year. McCormick, getting up there in baseball years, had told Wilt, however, that he believed he was too old to hold up during the hot months of August and September.

I was in the slot. I couldn't get a headline I really liked. Finally, Wilt, who didn't have to sit at the desk during baseball season since he was working twelve-hour days anyway, sat down at the rim and said, "Let me try."

He came up with, "Not Young, Cy's Mike." Brilliant.

—Bill Robinson, the outdoor editor and auto-racing writer, had nine children. He never came into the office on time. Seven o'clock, no Robinson. But he always had a great excuse.

Once, he rolled a flat tire into the elevator and then into the sports department to show proof of his latest reason for being late. Legend had it he always kept a flat in his trunk for just such an emergency.

The story went that Greg Favre finally had enough of Robinson being late and told him, "Robinson, if you're late one more time, you're fired. I don't care what your excuse is."

The next morning: Seven, no Robinson. Seven-thirty, no Robinson. Finally, he strolled in at eight, wearing a pair of jeans, a pajama top, and a Pure Oil racing cap.

Favre was livid. He called Robinson to the slot.

"You're fired, Robinson," he said, "but just for the record, what's your excuse this time?"

Robinson never hesitated.

"You know I've been married nine years and I've got eight children," he explained. "This morning was the first time in our marriage my wife had a period, and I had to fix breakfast for the kids because she was too sick to get out of bed."

Robinson didn't get fired.

Robinson was a handsome man, then in his late thirties, whose eyes always seemed to be half-closed. He was originally from Alabama, and held unbending allegiance to the university. Robinson lobbied during the autumn to be assigned to Alabama football games. He covered the Crimson Tide in a Sugar Bowl once and was so thrilled at an Alabama upset, he began writing about the "Crimson Cobras" and the "Alabama Red Snappers," and he forgot to include a final score in his game story.

With the exception of Bisher, Robinson was probably the best pure writer on the staff. I still remember one of his leads from a Daytona 500:

"Nose-to-nose, hubcap-to-hubcap, Cale Yarborough and Richard Petty went into the final lap at Daytona International Speedway as the seconds ticked away, like so many staccato drumbeats."

The problem, however, was nobody was ever quite certain if Robinson had actually attended the event he was writing about. There was the time Minter got mad at Robinson for some sort of misdeed and assigned him to cover a high school football play-off game in the north Georgia mountains on a rainy, cold Friday night, a horrid fate for a veteran sportswriter.

I was in the slot the following Saturday morning. Naturally, Robinson was late. When he finally arrived at the office, I said, "How was the game?"

"One of the best I've ever seen," he answered.

I watched him as he sat down at his desk and opened the morning *Constitution.* I had the feeling then that Robinson hadn't been to the game and was going to rewrite the *Constitution* account of the game.

Unfortunately for him, something had happened to the *Constitution*'s coverage, and all it carried about Robinson's game was a one-paragraph story.

I had laid out a page with a sizable hole for Robinson's article. I also needed a score-by-quarters, who made the touchdowns, and final game statistics. The *Constitution* didn't have that, either.

Robinson put paper in typewriter. The words began to flow.

He wrote a remarkable story. There were phrases such as ". . . North Georgia's hills were alive with the sound of sweet touchdown music" and ". . . the swivel-hipped halfback left tacklers grabbing nothing but the sopping-wet night air . . ."

He also typed out a line score and statistics. Later, he admitted to me he had not been to the game and had made up the statistics. We never received a complaint.

But that wasn't always the case. Robinson wrote a twice-a-week outdoor column. One Sunday, he waxed poetic about a fishing trip with an old pal in South Georgia. According to Robinson's column, the big bass were literally jumping into the boat, and Robinson quoted his buddy through the story.

The following week, I picked up the phone and a man asked for Robinson. He wasn't there.

"Well," said the man, "would you just mention to him he was fishing with a ghost. Ol' [whatever Robinson's pal was named] died two months ago."

—Teague Jackson, the golf writer. He was from the Midwest. His father had worked for the *Chicago Tribune.* Teague always referred to it as "the *Trib,*" as in, "That's not the way they do it at the *Trib,*" which became a catchphrase in the department.

"Hey, Frank, rewrite the National League roundup and put the Dodgers in the lead," McCollister would say to Hyland.

"Okay, but that's not the way they do it at the *Trib.*"

He was a large man, also in his late twenties, who seemed to be in a constant state of dishevelment. You could dress him in a Bill Blass tuxedo, and in three minutes his tie would be crooked and his shirt would be out in back.

Atlanta's newspapers had a history of great golf writers. O. B. Keeler had been the Boswell of Bobby Jones. Ed Miles, who retired shortly before I joined the *Journal* staff, had been there for golf's explosion with Arnold Palmer and television.

Teague was familiar with the tradition, and fancied himself as another link in the chain. But his naiveté kept getting in the way.

Jack Nicklaus's father had died. Teague spent the morning trying to get Nicklaus on the phone. Finally, he did.

We were at very close quarters. Everybody could hear the conversation that ensued:

"Jack?" he began. "Teague."

There was a pause, and then:

"Teague Jackson . . ."

Another pause.

"Atlanta . . ."

Pause.

"Journal . . ."

After Nicklaus apparently had nailed down the identity of the party with whom he was speaking, Teague said, "I'd like to offer you my condolences on your father. I know just how you feel."

There was one more pause and then:

"No, he's still alive."

The best thing about being a golf writer is they play a lot of golf tournaments at nice resorts. Teague was on the phone one morning with a PR type with the women's tour that was to stop at a course on Georgia's coast.

We always listened when Teague got on the phone.

"Yes," he was saying, "I think I should come and cover your tournament. Let me ask the boss if I can. I'm sure it will be okay."

Teague put down the phone and walked over to Minter's desk. Minter was busy. You didn't bother Minter when he was busy.

"Jim," he began, "would it be okay if I went to Sea Island next week to cover . . .?"

Minter didn't let him finish. "You can't go," he said.

"But," Teague argued, "I think the *Journal* ought to be represented. . . ."

"You can't go," repeated Minter.

Teague went back to the phone. "I'm sorry," he said, "but the bosses here at the *Journal* seem to think your tournament is not important enough for me to . . ."

As he rambled on, Minter got out of his chair, walked over to Teague's desk, took the phone out of his hand, spoke into it, and said, "Teague can't go."

He hung up the phone. That was that.

Frank didn't like Teague. It all began when he was out of change and asked Teague for a dime so he could get a cup of coffee out of the machine in the hall. Teague gave him the dime, but as soon as Frank came into the office the next morning, Teague said to him, "Frank, do you have the dime I loaned you yesterday?"

"Jesus Christ, Teague," Frank answered, "it was just a dime."

"Well," said Teague, "I need it back."

So Frank reached into his pocket and forked up the dime. Teague reached into his pocket and pulled out one of those little coin purses and put the dime safely back into it.

Frank shook his head in digust.

Then came the Hawk story.

Teague went to Augusta to cover the Masters. A couple of days before the tournament began, there had been a testimonial dinner for Ben Hogan. Teague wrote a story about it. His lead boggled the mind:

By TEAGUE JACKSON
Atlanta Journal Staff Writer

AUGUSTA—Somewhere in a murky, never-never land, a Hawk circles slowly, licking his wounds, pain gnawing at his vitals as he hurts where only a real man can hurt.

They called Ben Hogan the Hawk, see, and he had been in a car wreck, and he was a bit of a recluse, and . . . And nobody on the desk had *any* idea what Teague was trying to say. We didn't run the article.

While we waited for the first edition to arrive back up in the office, Frank took Teague's piece, sat down at his typewriter, and converted Teague's story into a one-act play. He called it *"The Hawk:* An Original Feature Story by Teague Jackson, Adapted for the Stage by Frank Hyland."

I played the Hawk and pretended to circle

slowly in a murky never-never land. Darrell Simmons made noises he thought sounded like something gnawing on a vital, Robinson played the "veteran pro" Teague had quoted in his story. Frank was the narrator.

We put on the play for Minter, who thought it was a riot. Minter was still reeling, as a matter of fact, from a memo Teague had sent to him a few weeks earlier.

Teague had asked for a day off to go to the dentist and then asked for a "sick day," as he put it.

"How in the hell," Minter had asked, "does Teague know two weeks before that he's going to be sick on a certain day?"

—Bill Whitley, the high school writer. We called him "Doctor Whitley" because whenever he called a restaurant to make a reservation, that's the way he referred to himself.

"Yes," he would begin, "I'd like a table for two at nine. Fine. Put it in the name of Whitley, Doctor Whitley."

"You always get better service if they think you are a doctor," the doctor would say. He was short and round and balding and your basic southern gentlemen. When he laughed, he turned red in the face and lighted up a room.

He was a native Atlantan and a graduate of

Georgia. He was remembered on campus for getting into his MG after an afternoon of drinking beer in the legendary Old South tavern downtown and losing control of his car. It finally came to rest, with him in it, in the Athens bus station. It had gone through the doors to the waiting room, as a matter of fact, and when the dust and glass had settled, Doctor Whitley looked up, smiled and said, "One way to Savannah, please."

The doctor was a Civil War expert. He had seen *Gone With the Wind* about four hundred times and could do practically all the dialogue from the movie.

He and his wife, Miss Margaret, of whom he said, "I brought her down from the hills of North Georgia and put silk underdrawers on her," had a daughter. Her name? Miss Scarlett, of course.

—Joe Litsch, who helped Whitley with the high schools. He was feisty, opinioned, and had a biting sense of humor.

He walked into the office one morning and somebody said, "Did you hear Freddie Steinmark died?"

Freddie Steinmark was a Texas football player who was stricken with cancer. Before he died, one of his legs had been amputated.

When Litsch was told of his death, he replied,

"Well, hell, he had one foot in the grave any-way."

—Darrell Simmons, the pro-football writer, looked like a young Burl Ives. He had come to the *Journal* from Jacksonville, Florida. He smoked Lucky Strikes, spoke so softly it was often difficult to hear what he was saying, but he did do one helluva job sounding like vitals being gnawed in his performance of Teague's Ben Hogan article. I can't spell the sound Darrell made, but I was impressed by his creativity.

Darrell had the toughest beat on the staff be-cause he had to deal with Falcons head coach Norman Van Brocklin, who hated sportswriters. Van Brocklin thought all sportswriters were communists, and his phobia was legendary.

When a soccer-style foreign kicker beat the Falcons with a last-second field goal, Darrell asked Van Brocklin what he thought when he saw the kick was good. He answered, "I was thinking they ought to tighten the goddamn im-migration laws in this country."

—Bill Clark. He was a tall, handsome man in his thirties. I forget what brand of cigarettes he smoked. I think perhaps menthol, though. Didn't we all smoke in 1968?

He had all the college contacts. He was smart and slick and sly. And he helped me. The first time I was ever on Bisher's *Football Review* television program, he said to me, "Relax and don't argue with Bisher."

But Bill Clark would turn the place upside down for a time. I mentioned there was no such thing as overtime at the *Journal.* Once a week, you filled out a time sheet. Under each of the five days you worked, you simply wrote an *8,* and the total was always *40.*

Bill decided that was wrong. He began to ask other staff members privately if they thought they were being taken advantage of.

"How many hours did you work last week?" he asked me one day.

"I don't know," I said. "Who's counting?"

"They're cheating us out of money," he said.

Bill Clark figured there was the time he spent in the office, the time he spent driving to various events, the time he spent covering them, the time he spent eating and drinking with various sources, the time he spent on the phone at night tracking down news, and even, I suppose, the time he spent arguing with Frank about Bill Russell and Wilt Chamberlain.

Me, I was just proud to be there.

Clark began to push for overtime pay. He wrote memos. He argued with Minter. He pushed too hard. Minter fired him.

Clark filed suit.

Each member of the staff was called in to testify at the ensuing trial. It was understood that nobody would take Clark's side. Nobody did. We were loyal to the death, not to mention cross-examination.

Clark's attorney got right in my face.

"Did you help cover the Atlanta Golf Classic on June so-and-so?" he asked me.

"I think so."

"What time did you leave home?"

"I don't know. Nine in the morning."

"What time did you leave the golf course?"

"Maybe six."

"What did you do then?"

"Went back to the office and wrote my story."

"What time did you leave there?"

"Maybe nine."

"So you left your home at nine in the morning, and you were on duty until nine that night. That's twelve hours. How many hours did you put down on your time sheet that you worked that day?"

"I don't remember."

"Don't remember, Mr. Grizzard? What do you mean, you don't remember?"

We were nose-to-nose.

I asked the judge, "Is he supposed to be this close to me?"

"Get out of the witness's face," said the judge.

He finally got me to admit I always put down eight hours, no matter how many I worked.

"If I had wanted to punch a time clock," I managed to get in before the attorney could stop me, "I'd have tried to find a job on the assembly line at the Ford plant."

I got to see ball games and golf tournaments for free and got my byline in the *Atlanta Journal* sports section, by God. Wasn't that and $160 big ones a week enough?

They gave Bill Clark some back pay, and he went off to Florida someplace.

I naturally expected to succeed him as the head college-editor guy. But I had made another mistake, which would send my career in a decidedly different direction. It also changed my life drastically.

I had learned all about graphics and layout and how to get a sports section in on time in Athens. Guys who wanted to cover ball games and write about them were easy to find. Not so, fools who would take on the task of putting the sports section together and then head to the composing room to make certain it got in on time and was relatively mistake-free.

McCollister, the assistant sports editor and

slot man, got one day a week off because he worked Saturday night putting out the Sunday edition.

That meant he had to have a replacement that one weekday he had off. Several other members of the staff filled in for him on that day. Minter thought everybody should have at least some idea of how the paper got put together every day.

I had been at the paper about a month when he said to me, "You've had some layout experience, haven't you?"

I was anxious to please him. I said that I had.

A week later, I sat in the slot for the first time. I had copied the *Journal*'s layout style in Athens. I liked pages where photos and type were displayed horizontally, I didn't think type that ran up-and-down, willy-nilly was very attractive.

When the first edition of my first *Journal* section arrived at Minter's desk, he took a long look at it and then said to me, "You know how we want to look."

I beamed.

Soon after Clark left, McCollister took a job as public-relations director for the Hawks. Minter took me across the street to the Eagle Cafe one morning for coffee. I thought he was going to promote me to Clark's job.

He wasn't.

13

I had but one opportunity to fulfill my dream of riding a train as a sportswriter, which is what I had had in mind, growing up in my mother's house, reading about the Crackers in the *Constitution,* plotting my future in journalism.

My first out-of-town assignment at the *Journal* was to cover Rice playing football against Louisiana State in Baton Rouge. You could ride the Southern Crescent from Atlanta to New Orleans. It left at seven each morning and arrived twelve hours later, through such interesting stops as Birmingham, Meridian, and Slidell. However, I was scheduled to be in the office on Friday. The game was Saturday night, so even if the Crescent arrived in New Orleans as advertised—seven in the evening, Central time—I wouldn't be able to drive to Baton Rouge in time for the kickoff.

I flew. I had flown a couple of times before. I

wasn't afraid of flying. It was the crashing and burning that concerned me.

Okay, I'll admit it. I was terrified to fly. I got it from my mother. Before she and my father divorced, we were living in Fort Chaffee, Arkansas, and my mother became critically ill. She was transferred by the army to Walter Reed Hospital in Washington.

She talked about her own terror so many times.

"They had me strapped in a bed," she said. "It was the first time I had ever flown. We landed and took off three times during the trip. I told God if He would get me off that airplane alive, I'd never fly again."

She never did.

But it was more than my fear of flying that caused my disappointment at not being able to take a train on my first out-of-town assignment for the *Journal.* Airplanes and newspapers didn't fit together for me somehow. Jet airplanes were modern. They involved too much technology. They didn't have names like the Southern Crescent or the 20th Century Limited or the Super Chief. They got you where you were going much too quickly. Whatever happened to getting-there-is-half-the-fun?

Newspapers went with trains. No technology

in the newspaper business, if you throw out telephone and teletype machines. We didn't even work with electric typewriters in 1968.

Trains stayed on the ground, as God intended (Remember: "Lo, I will be with you always." He never mentioned "high"). I understood trains. The engine pulled them. But how on earth does a thing as big as a Howard Johnson motel get into the air and manage to stay there?

Trains meant tradition to me. So did newspapers. Airplanes were television. Trains were the morning paper on your doorstep. You could go to the club car and have a beer served by a man on a train. On an airplane, a lady would serve you a beer, but you had to stay in your seat to drink it, and if you weren't through with it fifteen minutes before landing, that same lady would take it away from you. I still don't understand why they make you give up your drink when an airplane starts to land. Are they afraid if the plane crashes, you might spill something on your suit and the airline would be responsible for your cleaning bill?

When the plane is landing, that's when I need a drink the most. Will the tires hold up? Is the runway long enough? Is there a rookie pilot up there who's never done this with 160 people sitting behind him?

My plane to Baton Rouge didn't crash. I was greatly relieved. LSU beat Rice. The LSU cheerleaders rolled out a cage with wheels on it before the game. Inside the cage was a large tiger. LSU's nickname is the "Tigers."

The cheerleaders rattled the tiger's cage, and the tiger growled fiercely—I could hear it up in the press box because there was a microphone in the cage with the tiger.

Each time the tiger would growl, the crowd, thousands in number, would cheer. This on a hot, humid Saturday night near the banks of the Mississippi.

A guy from the Lake Charles paper who was sitting next to me in the press box said the cheerleaders rattled the tiger's cage before every game. I said, "If that tiger ever gets loose, there's going to be some serious payback time."

The plane that brought me back to Atlanta Sunday morning didn't crash, either. I made a deal with God. If He got me back on the ground safely, I never-under-any-circumstances would build a graven image.

And I haven't.

When basketball season started, Minter put me on Oglethorpe University. Oglethorpe is a small school on the north side of Atlanta. Once, it had football. But football got too expensive, so it was dropped. Basketball survived and flourished, however. A crew-cut guy named Garland Pinholster, of all things, coached it into a national small-college power.

Pinholster had left by the time I got to Atlanta, but Oglethorpe still played quality basketball. At the end of the season, they had won a spot in the national small-college tournament in Evansville, Indiana. Minter said, "Go to Evansville."

Evansville. The Southern Railway didn't have anything, but then I called Union Station, which served the Louisville and Nashville Railroad. The tired old dusty Georgian, I found out, stopped in Evansville on its way from Atlanta to St. Louis.

I left the office on my lunch hour and walked down to Union Station. Same old mess. Same old smell.

The guy behind the ticket window looked at me as if I were crazy when I said to him, "Round-trip to Evansville, please."

"Are you sure?" he asked me.

"Sure," I said.

"There's no food on the train, and it's a long ride to Evansville," he went on.

"I'll bring some food with me," I told him.

"There ain't no water, either."

"I can bring some water with me."

The man wouldn't give up. "All the train is," he continued, "is one car on the back of a freight. There won't be anybody riding with you, and it'll be the middle of the night when you get to Evansville. I don't even know if there will be a light on at the station. I wouldn't ride the damn thing."

If *he* wouldn't, I decided *I'd* better not, either. You never know who is going to be around after midnight.

Browny was living in Nashville at the time, and Nashville was on the way to Evansville. I wound up driving to Nashville, and Browny drove us on to Evansville.

Oglethorpe lasted only one round. I don't remember who defeated the Stormy Petrels (some kind of a bird, I think), but I do recall quite vividly that during an earlier game the giant scoreboard that hung from the roof in the arena fell on the playing floor and shattered into 6 zillion pieces.

Browny took some great photos, but he was working for an egg magazine, and if it didn't cluck, the magazine wasn't interested.

Before I ever got a shot at riding a train to an assignment again, Minter took me over to the Eagle Cafe that morning and said I was his new assistant sports editor, his slot man. I would be getting up at four in the morning four days a week, and working from two in the afternoon Saturday until some ungodly time in the early Sunday morning, fighting with the composing room to get my pages in on time and all that.

I wanted to say to Minter, "Thanks a lot, but I think I'd like to succeed Bill Clark."

But I didn't. Because Minter, when he gave me my promotion, had said, "I want you in the office, so don't ask for Bill Clark's job."

* * *

Assistant sports editor. I got a forty-dollar-a-week raise. Two hundred dollars a week! Two hundred big ones. Two hundred beany wienies. I was a wealthy man.

I bought a 1969 brand-new, interior-smells-so-good, GMAC-financed Oldsmobile Cutlass with power windows, hi-fi radio, and air-conditioning. The car was one of the reasons I wound up divorced a year or so later.

I decided the Cutlass was mine. I made Paula drive the old blue VW, the one where the rearview had fallen off, the gas pedal would get stuck, and Plato's shed hair was three inches deep. And there was no air-conditioning.

Years later, after she had married a man who would never even think of not allowing his wife to take the Cutlass, Paula told me, "One of the first times I really realized that our marriage would never last was when you made me take the piece of junk Volkswagen while you drove the new car. I could have gotten *killed* in that thing. You never did get around to having a new rearview mirror installed, and what if the gas pedal had stuck just as I was approaching a busy intersection?

"And by the time I'd get to work, I'd be wringing wet with sweat and have dog hair all over my clothes. You could really be a thoughtless man at times."

She was absolutely correct, of course. And there was a lot else I did and didn't do. I flirted with a redhead at her company Christmas party, for instance. We were at a downtown hotel. Paula became so angry, she ran out of the hotel and headed down the street. Paula, like other women I have known, was a "runner."

Some women stand their ground when they are angry and jealous; they do things like scream at you or throw whatever object is nearby at you. In many ways, such women are preferable to runners. The screaming will eventually subside, and if you can dodge the flying object, you can avoid any personal injury.

But you've got a major problem with a runner.

First, you have to decide whether or not you are going to run after her. You could just let her go, of course. You know that eventually she will come back.

But she's out there running somewhere, and something could happen to her, and you would feel awful about it. She could get attacked or pull a muscle.

Seconds after Paula hit the air and began running down Spring Street, a busy Atlanta thoroughfare, just as midnight approached, I went after her.

She had a bit of a pigeon-toed gait, and I had retained possibly 50 percent of my high school speed, coming down the court on a fast break or rounding first base, trying to stretch a single into a double. I was what they called "sneaky-fast."

But after I caught her, I still had a problem. She wanted to run some more, and struggled to break free of my grasp.

So, there we were, on a busy street in downtown Atlanta at midnight, and I'm wrestling with my wife. A passing cabbie, who doesn't know she's my wife, stops and gets out of his cab, comes over and puts a half-Nelson on me, figuring I am Lewis the Ripper.

I would have told him it was my wife and he

was intruding on what was a simple domestic quarrel, but I was unable to speak because the cabbie, a rather burly individual, has his forearm pressed tightly on my Adam's apple, rendering me speechless.

But Paula would tell him, of course, that it was okay, I was her husband.

"You son of a bitch!" is how she introduced me to the cabbie. "You and that slut were practically screwing out there on the dance floor in front of all the people I have to work with. I have never been so embarrassed in my life!"

That didn't help my position much with the cabbie. I tried to speak, but I couldn't. I fought for air. My eyes seemed quite serious about popping out of my head and falling, rearview mirrorlike, on the sidewalk.

I did manage to get out one small sound. I'll try to spell it. "Gurrrrq," which meant, "For God's sake, tell him!"

Finally, my wife told him.

"He's my husband," she said. "He was practically screwing a redheaded slut on the dance floor at my company Christmas party."

The cabbie released his hold on me.

"You really do that, buddy?" he asked me.

It would be a few moments before my blood had redistributed itself and I could speak. I finally managed, "She's the one who got so close to me. I didn't have anything to do with it."

"You lying . . ." Paula began.

"Listen," the cabbie interrupted, "why don't you both get in the cab and I'll drive you back to the party. You shouldn't be screaming and fighting like this out in public."

We went back to the party. The redhead was gone, but Paula didn't speak to me again.

My undying ambition and my dedication to my new post at the paper also had a lot to do with our eventual divorce. I didn't talk about much else other than newspapers. And then there were my new hours.

I got Mondays off. But then I was up at four A.M. Tuesday through Friday. I was off each afternoon by one, and Frank and Doctor Whitley and I would be in Manuel's Tavern twenty minutes *after* one. Sometimes those afternoons reached into early evening, past dinner, and on towards midnight. Then I would grab a couple of hours' sleep and be off to work again. The only times I ever went home on time was when I was simply too exhausted to stay out late. I would wind up snoring away on the living-room couch at eight o'clock, which wasn't Paula's idea of a great time, either.

I was having a great time. I knew very little

about neon and the call of the wild, but I was learning. Hyland was a great help. He wound up getting a divorce, too.

I dug deep into my job. Getting an afternoon sports section out four mornings a week and then producing a Sunday morning section was the most difficult, most frustrating task I've ever had. Nothing before or afterward compared to it.

The typical weekday:

The alarm goes off at four. My first thought is to open one eye to see if it's still dark. If it is, I'm okay. If it's not, I'm late and I'll have to throw the section together and Minter will redraw it between editions and the composing-room wiseacres will say, "Why didn't you do it right the first time?"

But it's still dark, and I'm in the office at five. First, I go to the composing room where the printers' union has a Coke machine. Cokes are a dime. They come in little six-ounce bottles. They have ice in them. This is what God had in mind when he created, through some Georgia druggist, Coca-Cola.

I get a jolt from the Coke. I light a Marlboro. I strip the sports wire.

The Associated Press sports wire has been running all night. It has typed out fourteen hundred miles of paper. I have to look at all of it.

I have to determine what needs to go into the sports section and what the readers won't miss. What I would do is take all the paper off the teletype and put it on the floor on the other side of the horseshoe desk, the rim.

I would then put a large wastebasket next to my seat in the middle of the horseshoe. I would then utilize a tool known as the "tear rule." A tear rule is sort of like a lead ruler with one sharp end. You use a tear rule for a lot of things. One use is when you draw the lines of a layout page that shows the printer exactly where each story and photograph goes.

Tom McCollister hit Teague Jackson on his knuckles with his tear rule once. Teague, who was from Chicago, wanted to call the Cubs "Cubbies" in a headline, and McCollister said that sounded silly.

"But that's how they do it at the *Trib,*" said Teague, and McCollister hit him on his knuckles. As far as I know, "Cubbies" still has never appeared on an *Atlanta Journal* sports page.

What else you can do with a tear rule—produced in the composing room—is to tear things. I had to separate each story on the wire. I would hold the tear rule between stories with one hand and rip away. What wasn't going into the paper I'd toss in the wastebasket next to me. What would go I would fold neatly to my left. I would edit each story, mostly for length, and then assign it a headline and pass it to somebody on the rim when the rest of the staff rolled in, in various stages of disarray, an hour or so later.

It would take at least a half hour to strip that wire and pull off the baseball standings, the box scores, the National League roundup, the American League roundup, and so on, depending upon the season.

Then there was the Western Union telex machine. The beat men, working out of Dodger Stadium, or Madison Square Garden, or Lambeau Field in Green Bay, would file their stories back to the office overnight via Western Union telex.

I had to strip that machine, too, and that wasn't so much of a problem, but Western Union sent everything back in capital letters. I suppose that made it easier on the teletype operators. It certainly made it easier on the writers.

If you do a lot of typing, you know how much trouble it is to have to hit that shift key to capitalize. Writers simply did everything in lowercase, which got them out of the press box earlier enough to hit the bars when there might still be some local talent around.

But the poor slot man. Those sons-of-bitches were out there in San Francisco, New York, or

L.A., and here I was at six o'clock in the morning, going through all their stories and underscoring each letter I wanted the Linotype operator to capitalize. God, I hated doing that. It didn't seem fair.

After that, I laid out the section. Here's how that works: The advertising department produces a dummy layout sheet that shows the size of each ad and where it appears on the page. It was my job, basically, to fill in what space was left in the sports section after the ads went in. There was never enough room for what I wanted to do. I'm not certain what the ad-space-to-news ratio was in those days, but it often seemed like 100 to 1.

Even the front page of sports had ads in those days. It was the Wednesday front I hated the most. Every Wednesday, there was a huge, four-column by eleven inches Jack Daniel's ad that took up about a quarter of my front space. You've seen those Jack Daniel's ads. They usually include a photograph of two old geezers sitting on a front porch in Lynchburg, Tennessee, playing checkers. The truth be told, they probably had been in a batch of the stuff over at the distillery and couldn't even hold on to a checker, much less move it into a strategic position.

That ad was so big and that photograph was

so dominant, nothing else I put on the page would catch the reader's eye first.

I had to run Bisher's column all the way down the left side of the page, and what space I've got left goes to the Braves, Al Geigberger shooting a 59, and Richard Petty being on the pole for the Firecracker 400 in Daytona.

I would select the best and most newsworthy photographs I had room for each day, give each story a designated length so as to fit in the space I had allotted for it, and then I would put all my materials in a basket on the side of the rim and scream, ''Copy!''

That was a signal for the lowest of all lows, the boys on the bottom rung, the newspaper version of banking's accounting clerks, the legendary ''copy boys,'' to come fetch what was in the basket and get it to the composing room as fast as possible.

Copy boys usually had a lot of zits, couldn't find a job doing anything else, didn't mind being screamed at or told of their basic worthlessness, and could live on beans and bread, since that's all they could afford on what newspapers paid them.

Copy boys usually were at least a little insane. We had one copy boy at the *Journal,* Ernest, who refused to allow anybody else to push the button for his floor when he got on an elevator.

Ernest would get into the elevator and it would be crowded and somebody near the buttons would ask him, "What floor?" intending to do him a favor by pushing his desired button since it would be basically impossible for Ernest to get through the wad of human flesh between him and the little panel with the buttons.

It didn't matter. Ernest would say, "I'll push my own button, thank you," and then proceed to stomp on numerous toes on his way to push his own button.

Horganmeyer was another copy boy. He was the dumbest human I ever met. He had been at work for about three days, and had dutifully picked up my materials to be sent to the composing room. But the composing room called me and said, "We don't have anything from you."

I screamed, "Copy!" and Horganmeyer showed up. I seem to recall he was drooling.

At any rate, I said to him, "Horganmeyer, you idiot, the composing room says they haven't gotten anything from me. What have you done with all the copy?"

Horganmeyer said, "There ain't no tubes." Materials were sent to the composing room in glass tubes that were sucked down a pipe, or some such magic.

"Well, Horganmeyer," I said, "call the composing room and tell them to send you some tubes back up."

What Horganmeyer should have done was pick up the hot line to the composing room and say, "Send up some more tubes." What he did was go over to the pipe, open it, and scream down inside it, "Send more tubes!"

I had many delicious fantasies about killing Horganmeyer. In my fantasies, I stuffed him inside a tube, and he died.

There was something else that was necessary to the composing room. They were called "shorts." A "short" is a one-paragraph item, a two-paragraph item, even a three-paragraph item with small headlines.

There was a system whereby you could count the number of lines in a piece of copy and determine what length it would make when in type. It wasn't a perfect system, however. Sometimes you would assign a story an eighteen-inch hole. It would turn up sixteen inches long. That's where the shorts came in. You plugged up empty holes with shorts.

Because of an odd configuration of the ad layout one morning, I wound up with a tiny piece of white space, capable of holding a 14-point headline and maybe five lines of type. I was already two minutes past deadline.

"What do you want to put here?" asked the printer working on the page.

"Find a short," I said.

"Which one?"

"Any of 'em. Just plug the damn hole."

He grabbed a short. It was three lines too long to fit in the space. Printers were not known for taking a situation in hand and dealing with it themselves.

"It's three lines too long," said the printer. "What do you want me to do now?"

"Find a period and cut it there," I said.

Type was set in lead. Printers all carried a little tool they used to snip off type.

The first edition of the paper came up. The little short on the front page read, "Cincinnati utility infielder Marvin Snobbs was optioned Tuesday afternoon to the Red Triple AAA affiliate in Louisville, but he never got there."

The first period the printer had come to was after the word "there," and, as I told him to do, that's where he snipped the type.

The rest of the story had explained infielder Snobbs got halfway to Louisville in his car, decided he'd had enough of baseball and wasn't

going down to Triple A, and called the Reds
front office to say he was retiring. But the readers didn't get to read that. We were flooded with
calls the next day.

"What happened to Marvin Snobbs?" they
wanted to know.

Nobody had ever heard of Marvin Snobbs
until they read that story, but I must admit there
was a suggestion of sinister plots and kidnap-
pings in the tantalizing little short that had ended
so abruptly.

One of the best illustrations of deadline frustration was the story about a poor slotman in
Louisville who was trying to get the copy for the
first afternoon edition down to the composing
room on time.

The sports department was partitioned off
from the rest of the newsroom by a rail.

It's late, the composing room foreman has
called seventeen times, and finally, with forty-
five seconds to go before his copy deadline, the
slot man grabs the last batch and decides to run
it down to the composing room himself.

As he is about to step out of the sports department, the foreman appears and says, "You'll
never make it. There's only ten seconds to go!"

The beleaguered slotman suddenly stopped
and threw all the copy—wire stories, headlines,

and photos—over the rail, scattering it across the newsroom floor.

"What in hell are you doing?" asked the foreman.

"I'm throwing the copy out of bounds," said the slot man, "to stop the clock."

The composing room at *The Atlanta Journal-Constitution* was a war zone. There were the long lines of Linotype machines where the operators set each letter of each story by hand. Headlines were cast in another corner. Each page sat on a movable table, so that it could be hustled way toward the presses when it was locked. There was much noise. Machines made some of it. Editors screaming at printers and printers screaming at editors and composing-room foremen screaming at everybody made the rest of it.

The noise and the deadline pressure in the composing room could kill a man. Joel Huff was a soft-spoken, kind man who was an assistant managing editor and supervised the makeup of newsside pages.

I was always amazed how calm he seemed to stay in the composing room. I threw at least one screaming fit daily.

But maybe Joel should have screamed a time or two. He had a heart attack one day and died right there in the composing room, just after he got the first edition in on time.

One hour later, the next edition carried his obituary on page 2. You bust your tail all those years getting the paper in on time. You die in battle and all they give you is a lousy obit on page 2.

The second edition, incidentally, got in on time, too. Joel would have been proud. The rest of us realized that no matter how much our lives might mean to our friends and families, the paper would get the next edition out, with or without us.

The printers, the men who actually picked up the type and put it where it belonged on each page, were members of the typographical union. They moved up only on the basis of seniority. They got paid the same amount of money regardless of how hard they worked or how cooperative they were.

Some of the printers would bust their tails and be pleasant about it, anyway. Others, however, wouldn't.

They didn't give a damn if the paper got in on time or not. But they held your testicles in their hands. Don't get the paper in on time and it costs the company money; the publisher calls the general manager and he calls the managing editor and the managing editor calls you and says, "Why the hell didn't it get in on time?"

All I could say was, "R. D. Cocklesmith made up my pages this morning, and he doesn't give a damn whether the paper gets in on time or not."

Didn't matter—it was still your fault. And there was nothing you could do if R. D. Cocklesmith went into the dreaded four corners on you. The rule was simple: You ain't a member of the union, you don't touch the type. You don't lay one millimeter of skin on one letter. You don't touch the type with something that is affixed to your hand, like a pencil. You don't put your pencil down on the National League roundup and say to R. D. Cocklesmith, "Put that on this page."

There was another rule. If somebody outside the union touched the type, the printer had the right to pick up the tray that held it and dump it on the floor. That was called "pieing the type."

"R.D., listen to me. I just sort of slipped. I didn't mean to touch your type, I swear. R.D., there's only four minutes to go before deadline. Please don't pie that type, R.D. In the name of God, R.D., don't dump that type. . . ."

All over the floor. You would either have to put something in the National League hole like about fourteen shorts that were not related whatsoever, or have the type on the floor reset and risk being late and getting yelled at while R. D. Cocklesmith went to the break room and ate his goddamn lunch.

The one thing I could do to help insure getting my section in on time was give away free tickets to the foremen and printers.

Of course, it was bribery. In desperation, one grabs for any straw available.

The sports department had free tickets out the nose. The Braves gave us dozens, as did the other pro teams in town, and a phone call would produce Georgia Tech and Georgia football tickets as well.

It wasn't like we were on the take. We took the tickets, but we didn't go out of our way to do the teams or schools any favors, and I often wondered why they continued to supply tickets when they knew it wouldn't matter when a writer sat down to his typewriter and decided to perform surgery without using anesthesia.

(Later, most sports departments did away with the practice of taking free tickets. I have no idea how they are able to get the paper in on time without them.)

Let's say I'm in the composing room to begin

putting the section together. A smiling foreman walks over and asks, "How about four for Sunday's Braves–Reds game?"

"You got it," I reply.

A nice, smooth morning follows.

Or, I'm in the composing room to begin putting the section together. A smiling foreman walks over and asks, "How about four for Sunday's Braves–Red game?"

"I've already given them away to my grandfather who is terminally ill and is going to die Monday and his last wish was to see Sunday's Braves–Reds game," I reply.

The National League roundup gets lost. So does Bisher's column. I get a rookie printer with bricks for hands, and I'm eight minutes late getting the section in.

I eventually learned to say, "My grandfather can watch the game on TV. Here's your tickets."

I had a crusty old makeup man from the news side who helped me get the pages in on Saturday nights for the Sunday football section.

His name was Doug Cocking. I loved him. Even though he was small, he was the toughest son of a bitch that ever went eye-to-eye, nose-to-nose with a printer and said, "You lazy bastard, get off your ass and get this page in on time

or I'm going to kick it halfway to Chattanooga."
Sometimes that worked. If it didn't, Doug at least
had tried something.

There was one page to go on a football Saturday night. It was a late page we had held for
Southwest Conference night games. I grew to
hate the Southwest Conference for being in the
Central time zone and playing night games that
ended so perilously close to deadline. The idea
was to put the feature game in the conference
under a main headline and then to follow with
the other SWC games.

A printer they called Boy-Boy was making up
the page. He got the Texas-Baylor game in
under the main headline and then started filling
in the remaining space with TCU–Texas Tech,
Arkansas–Rice, and Texas A&M–SMU. Boy-
Boy locked up the page and said to Doug,
"Want to see this before it goes?"

Cocking took a look at the page and said,
"There's something wrong."

Boy-Boy said, "What in hell is it this time?"
Boy-Boy and R. D. Cocklesmith were brethren in
pain-in-the-buttship.

"You've got the Harvard-Brown game in the
Southwest Conference roundup," Cocking explained.

"What in hell difference does that make?"

Boy-Boy asked, indignantly. Two minutes to go before deadline.

"The difference, you dumb piss-ant," Doug explained, "is that Harvard and Brown are in the Ivy League, and they're already on another page. You've left out TCU–Texas Tech."

Doug pointed at the TCU–Texas Tech type and touched it. Ever so slightly. Maybe the tip of his fingernail hit the dateline that said "Lubbock."

It didn't matter to Boy-Boy. He picked up the tray that held the TCU–Texas Tech type and dumped it.

I could tell Doug intended to do something violent. I wasn't sure what, but his face had contorted, the veins popped out of his neck, his fists were clenched. He had the eyes of Charles Earl Whitman as he climbed the steps to the tower on the University of Texas campus that day and began shooting at anything that moved.

What Doug did was pick up an empty type tray and try to kill Boy-Boy with it. Boy-Boy managed to duck Doug's swing, however, and ran. Doug chased him. They disappeared out the back of the composing room, headed toward Spring Street.

Thirty seconds to go before deadline.

There wasn't time to reset the type Boy-Boy

had dumped. I would hear about it Monday morning for having Harvard and Brown in the Southwest Conference roundup—but I had no other choice.

"Go ahead and take it," I said to a reserve printer the composing-room foreman had fetched me. And there they were on the page for the world to see Sunday morning: the Harvard Horned Frogs and Brown Red Raiders.

The Reverend was another printer. They called him that because he was a religious nut and occasionally went around the composing room handing out pamphlets entitled *Are You Saved?* and *Five Ways to Heaven.* He went to one of those churches where they spoke in tongues.

If you are not familiar with that, it's where a member of the congregation will become so moved—"slain in the spirit," they called it—and begin speaking in a strange language of which he or she had no previous knowledge. The words were supposedly sent to the person directly from God.

The minister, whom God had given the ability to interpret any sort of language that a person slain in the spirit might say, would then pass on the meaning to the congregation.

The tongue-speaker might say, "Ala babble

meno lipbog filadingdong," and the minister would break in and say, "Woe be unto the wicked, for they shall perish," which is what he decided "Ala babble meno lipbog filadingdong" meant.

The Reverend told me a great story once. I had mentioned something to him about my basset hound, Plato, getting his ears in his food and then dribbling wet Purina Dog Chow all over the carpet.

"I gave my wife a dog one time," said the Reverend. "It was just a little ol' feist dog. My wife named him 'Norman,' after her brother. He drank himself to death and went to hell. The Bible says, 'A drunkard shall not enter the kingdom of heaven,' and I tried my best to tell him. . . ."

"So what about the dog?" I said to the Reverend. I was afraid he was about to start barking in tongues or some such thing.

"Little ol' dog was mean. He'd just soon bite you as look at you. He'd go in the garage, and if he couldn't find anything else to chew up, he'd start on the tires to my truck.

"I was going to have to get shed of him, but I decided I would see if the power of God could cure him of his meanness."

I had to hear the rest of this.

"How did you do that, Reverend?"

"I anointed his head with oil."

"You did what?"

"I got hold of him, then poured oil over his head and asked God to cast out the demons that beset him."

"What kind of oil did you use, Reverend?" I asked.

"Any kind will work," he said. "I just went to the kitchen and got some Wesson Oil."

"Did it work?"

"Never had a minute's trouble with that dog again."

The Reverend cost me a deadline once in the name of the Lord Jesus Christ, his savior.

It had been a tough morning. Engraving lost one of my photographs, and I had to remake the page. It looked like hell.

Hyland's Hawks story was missing for a time. We finally found it over next to the obit page. It was about 10:08, and I had a fairly good shot at making the 10:10 deadline. Only the sports front was left. Bisher's column had run slightly short, and the Reverend was spacing out the lines to fill the hole.

Suddenly, he stopped working, he dropped his makeup tools on the floor, and grasped the table that held the page. His head rolled back and his eyes closed and he seemed to be about to have some sort of fit.

"You okay, Reverend?" I asked him.

"Gee-zus is here!" he screamed out.

"Do what?" I asked him.

"Geee-zus is here!" he screamed again.

There were two minutes to go before deadline, and my printer was having a vision.

"Reverend," I said, "Jesus can wait a couple of minutes, can't He?"

At that point, he started speaking in tongues.

A minute to go.

"Reverend," I said, "get hold of yourself."

"Ika dong feldo mana quartzel," he replied.

Thirty seconds.

"Reverend," I begged, "please finish the page. I'll buy you and Jesus both a cup of coffee as soon as you're finished."

"Hilma, botswa, fingo dellabelle extapo," said the Reverend.

I was a minute late.

I found the foreman.

"The Reverend's having a vision," I said to him. "Can you get me another printer?"

He sent over R. D. Cocklesmith, who complained for a good three minutes before he finally finished spacing out Bisher's column and sent the page on its way.

I was five minutes late on the first edition, and when I tried to explain why to the managing editor, he said, "Surely, Jesus has enough sense to stay out of the composing room."

Getting out the Sunday section during football season was an awesome task. I am certain I could learn brain surgery, how to build a computer, and French. I put out the *Atlanta Journal-Constitution* Sunday sports section during two football seasons. Nothing could be as difficult or more complex than that task.

We staffed between eight and ten college games each Saturday. Bisher and *Constitution* sports editor Jesse Outlar would flip-flop on Georgia Tech and Georgia games. At least two other writers would also be at the Tech and Georgia games to write what we called sidebars, since Bisher would never leave the press box and go to the locker room to find out what the coaches and players had to say. He figured he could write better than they could talk. He was right. The sidebars guys would get the quotes. The winning coach would always say, "First, I want to give [the losing team] a lot of credit. They played well and were coached well." Nobody ever said, "But, Coach, you won fifty-eight to zero."

The losing coach would always say, "We got

outplayed and outcoached.'' Nobody ever asked him, ''You got any more startling news?''

Other staffers from both papers would cover Southeastern Conference games, and we usually were wherever Clemson, South Carolina, and Florida State were playing. We'd have everybody with a camera out as well.

But staff coverage of college games was only a part of it. Anybody who has the task of producing a newspaper sports section would like if team sports seasons didn't overlap. Basketball season should begin in January and go until spring-training baseball begins. Baseball should go from April until Labor Day. Football would start after that and go until January 1, when basketball would start again. But that's not what happens anymore. They bounce a basketball almost until the Fourth of July now. I've had a great deal to say about Furman Bisher, sports editor of the *Journal,* but Jesse Outlar, sports editor and columnist for the *Constitution,* certainly had his moments. My favorite line of his was, ''If the National Basketball Association had been in charge of World War Two, Germany and Japan would still be in contention.''

Pro-basketball teams start playing exhibition games in October, then play six months of regular season games to eliminate about four teams, and the rest of them start all over again in the play-offs.

Speaking of basketball, the Atlanta papers on Saturday tried to carry the results of every high school game, boys and girls, played on Friday nights. That's a lot of basketball results. The effort became so difficult for Rex Edmondson, who covered high schools for the *Journal* years before I arrived, he was driven to paraphrase a poem, "Song of the Chattahooche," written by Georgia's greatest poet (There's been more than one. James Dickey is from Atlanta), Sidney Lanier. The poem began something like:

> *Out of the hills of Habersham*
> *Down the valleys of Hall*

And then, with apologies to Mr. Lanier, "blah, blah, blah."

Edmondson typed his new version and tacked it on the bulletin board. It went:

> *Down through the hills of Habersham*
> *Into the valleys of Hall*
> *Every son of a bitch and his sister*
> *Is bouncing a goddamn ball.*

Baseball goes into October, too, when football is in the middle of its season. So, on a Sunday, you've not only got 8 zillion college football games to get into the paper from around the country, but, in my case, I also had to deal with the basketball Hawks, the baseball play-offs, and the World Series. I also had to have advance stories on the Falcons and other Sunday pro-football games, and, to borrow from Rex Edmondson, some son of a bitch or his sister was also throwing a golf tournament, a horse race, a car race, or a tennis match—and some fool would always call around ten-thirty, trying to get the results of some local bowling tournament into the paper.

I would come in at my normal five on Friday mornings and work until twelve-thirty on the Friday afternoon section. After that, I would get the Sunday layouts. The first Sunday edition was called the bulldog. I don't know why. I should try to find out, but it's already been a long book, so let's get on with it.

Each week, when Minter would do the assignment sheet, he would designate one person to produce the bulldog. It was usually somebody he was mad at. Robinson was always getting the bulldog, it seemed.

The bulldog Sunday edition gets on the street late Saturday afternoon. Sections like the comics and Travel and Perspective and Arts and TV

and Fashion that aren't concerned with breaking news are produced in the middle of the
week.

Classified and whatever inserts are to be included in the Sunday paper (There seem to be
more and more of them. Notice your Sunday
paper now weighs more than your car?) are also
produced early.

A lot of people want to get their Sunday papers on Saturday, I suppose so they can figure
out early on what houses are for sale, what editorials will get them mad, or what *Peanuts* has
to say.

That leaves the news section and the sports
section. They undergo a lot of changes during
Saturday night. Sports more than news, of
course, unless there's a big fire, a plane
crashes, or somebody important dies.

There usually would be only two or three
pages in the sports section that wouldn't
change after the bulldog. We usually carried two
pages of outdoor news and a pro-football page
that remained intact throughout all editions.

But the rest of the section would change almost every edition, three of them, as the night
wore on and stories and photographs from afternoon and night games came in.

The pages that would change would have to

be filled with mostly wire feature stories and photographs for the bulldog. The bulldog man would go through the wire every day for timeless material. Then he would send it down to be set in type. Saturday morning after the Saturday daily was in, he would go down to the composing room and fill the section with the advance type, which would be tossed out later for breaking stories.

I would take my page layouts home with me Friday afternoon. I would have a list of every football game in the country and the time they were to be played. I would also have a list of whatever else would be taking place on Saturday. The Hawks were in Poughkeepsie for an exhibition game with the Celtics. It was game three of the World Series. And God Knows What Else.

After dinner, I would go into my bedroom, where I also had a desk. I would lay out each page and check off each game or event until I had a place for it all in the Sunday section.

But it was never that easy. A lot of things could happen. I will list a few of them:

* Bisher would get carried away and write thirty inches when I had estimated he would write only twenty-five. Cut Bisher

and you die. I'd have to figure out a way to get his entire story in.

* Something odd would happen at a Tech game. I had to find room for that, too.
* I would have Alabama-Tennessee on page 8. But Tennessee would pull off an astounding upset, and I would have to move it on to page 1.
* A plane would crash. That happened to me. I was about through with the next-to-last edition when they called me in the composing room to tell me the plane carrying the Marshall University football team was down, and a lot of people were dead. That had to be the lead story in the section, and I had to rush to set the story into the edition I was trying to close.

I lowered the eight-column sports masthead and ordered an eight-column, 60-point headline to cover a crash story that would run across the top of the page, five lines deep, and then jump to another page.

That meant everything else on the page had to be lowered. I jumped more of Bisher's Georgia story and Outlar's Tech story and Minter's piece from the Alabama-Tennessee game, and I cut the feet off the players in the photograph in the middle of the page. Somehow it all fit and, with the exception of footless football players, looked as though I had planned it that way in the first place.

* The World Series would get rained out.
* I would block out a vertical spot for a photo to go with the Georgia sidebars. All photographs from the Georgia game would be horizontal.
* Some pro bowler at the Little Rock Open would bowl a perfect game. Normally, I would put the results of the Little Rock Open bowling tournament in agate type (very small type) under the final results of some car race. But somebody bowling a perfect game is news, so I'd have to find a spot for it.
* A story coming in over the Western Union telex would catch on fire.

They never mentioned any of this in journalism school.

The *Constitution*'s veteran Charlie Roberts was in Baton Rouge one Saturday for the LSU–Ole Miss game. I had it across the top of page 2. It was a night game being played in a Central time zone, which meant I could expect to have Roberts's story about ten minutes before deadline.

I wrote the headline ahead of time. I wrote

"OLE MISS STOPS LSU." The good thing about headlines is the words can be separated by a printer. If Ole Miss won, then fine. If LSU won, all I had to do is tell the printer to move "LSU" where "Ole Miss" had been and vice versa. "LSU STOPS OLE MISS."

Writers covering games that will end near deadline will send a page after the end of each quarter. This is called "running." I had assigned Charlie Roberts to send three quarters of running so that I could have it already set in type before the game ended.

As soon as the game was over, he would then send a "top" to the running on the telex.

NPR [night press rate] Collect, Baton Rouge.

By CHARLIE ROBERTS
Journal-Constitution Staff Writer

BATON ROUGE, LA.—The Louisiana Bayou Bengals, ranked fourth nationally, convinced rival Ole Miss that their ranking is for real with an easy 31–7 romp over the Rebels here Saturday before an aroused gathering of 82,000.

Then there would be a couple of other paragraphs summarizing who scored what.

I had the headline set. I had Roberts's running. I had to close at twelve-fifteen. At twelve, I called the office from the composing room.

"Got Roberts's top yet?" I asked.

"Any minute," said the desk.

Five minutes passed. No top. I called again.

"Nothing yet," I was told.

I don't get the LSU–Ole Miss story and Minter and Bisher will kill me.

Ten after. I called again.

"Still nothing."

Somehow I felt if I went up to the office and stood by the telex machine and prayed hard enough, Roberts's top would come to me.

The minute I got back to the office, I saw the machine had already started.

"Get me the first paragraph off and run it down by hand," I said. I started back to the composing room. I would make it. *Just* make it. But then something caught my eye. It was the Western Union telex machine that was typing out Roberts's top. There was something odd about the machine. There was smoke coming out of it.

I broke for the machine. By the time I made the six steps to it, I saw a flame. A flame! The Western Union machine was on fire, and Charlie Roberts's top was in there!

I never did find out what caused the fire. Some sort of electrical short, I suppose. But I do know that I reached down among the flames, with complete disregard for my personal safety, pulled the paper away, and saved it (not to mention my ass).

With all the other difficulties involved in getting a Sunday football section out, there was also the matter of readers calling in for scores. Calls came by the hundreds on Saturday night.

It was a terrible inconvenience for a desk man, up to his ears in editing stories or writing headlines, to have to answer the phone and hear on the other end, "Hey, buddy, who won the Stanford-Cal game?"

Nobody in Atlanta really cared who won the Stanford-Cal except people who had money on it, which at times seemed to include about everybody in town.

What we could never figure out about the callers was why they often would phone in at four in the afternoon to get a west coast score. Didn't these dummies know about the three-hour time difference between the coasts?

One afternoon a desk man picked up the phone around four in the afternoon, eastern time, and some nitwit asked, "How'd UCLA and Oregon State come out?"

The desk man looked at the clock and answered, "They're warming up," and hung up the phone.

I had another staffer, David Davidson, who became my college editor and was one of the best ever to grace the department. He was from Mississippi. If it didn't happen in the Southeastern Conference, he didn't care much about it.

He was in the middle of writing a game story on deadline. The phone was ringing, and he was the only one available to answer it.

The caller said, "You got a score on Wyoming and Utah State?"

David said, "Wyoming and Utah State? Who gives a shit?" and hung up.

Worse perhaps than the score calls were the calls made in order to settle arguments at bars. Two guys get into the sauce and start arguing over where Y. A. Tittle, the great New York Giants quarterback, went to college.

One says, "We'll by-God call the paper. They'll tell you he went to LSU."

"He went to Texas, you idiot," his friend would say, "And I've got fifty dollars says I'm right."

So there sits somebody like Hyland.

He answers the phone: "Sports."

The guys in the bar always started out the same way:

"Hey, buddy, look here. Where did Y. A. Tittle go to college? LSU or Texas?"

"LSU," Hyland answers correctly.

But that's not enough.

"Tell my friend that," says the caller. "Just a minute. Hey, Arnold, come over here, I got the sports department on the phone!

"Hold up a minute. Here comes Arnold. I want you to tell him just what you told me."

"Hey," says Arnold.

"Hey," says Hyland, thinking of something delicious at this point.

"Where'd Y. A. Tittle go to college? Texas or LSU?"

"Texas," answers Hyland and hangs up the phone.

Who knows how many bar fights were started that way?

The assistant sports editor of the *Atlanta Journal* got one plum a year. He could have his pick of any college-bowl game and go there to cover it. He could also take his wife and get a chance to cheat on his expense account, too, like the beat writers.

They didn't pay us much back then, and as the saying went, "If you don't cheat on your expense account, you're not cheating anybody but yourself."

You could cheat on meals the easiest. You were allowed three a day, and you didn't have to run in a receipt for any expenditure under twenty-five dollars.

Let's say a beat writer was in Manhattan. In Manhattan you had to pay for the bad service. So the beat writer was up late writing his story for the next day's paper, and then he would hit a bar or two over on the East Side (a lot of Atlanta sportswriters fell in love at Maxwell's Plum, but I won't mention any names). So he wouldn't get up until noon, but he would put down breakfast on his expense account anyway—$13.45. They have to bring in the eggs from Jersey, I suppose.

He would grab a hot dog on the street for lunch—$17.50 on the expense account. Then, he would ride the team bus out to Shea Stadium, but put down $19.50 for a cab ride. He'd eat the free dinner they gave the writer in the press box, and that was $24.95.

Beat writers usually drove nicer cars than other members of the staff.

My first year as assistant sports editor, my wife hated trains so we flew to our bowl game in New Orleans. We stayed at the Monteleone and drank at the Carousel Bar in the lobby that actually moved you around in a circle while you were seated. I was more impressed with that than the Dixieland Bank at Preservation Hall.

Legend still has it a writer covering one of the early Super Bowls in New Orleans was sitting at the Carousel Bar in the Monteleone and was approached by a hooker who said to him, "Honey, I'll do anything for $100.

The writer asked, "Anything?"

And the hooker confirmed, "Anything."

So the writer said, "Okay, go to my room and write a column and a sidebar."

Arkansas played Ole Miss in the game. I forgot who won, but I managed to make a couple of hundred extra on the trip. Breakfast is expensive in New Orleans, too.

My second year, I looked long and hard at the bowl lineup. I didn't want to go back to New Orleans. I was leaning toward Pasadena and the Rose Bowl.

One day, I said to Minter, "I think I'm going to take the Rose Bowl this year."

He said, "You're not going to a bowl game this year."

I asked why.

He said, "I'm going to need you in the office."

Nobody ever won an argument with Jim Minter. So I didn't say anything else. I was hurt. And disappointed. And I pouted for a couple of days.

Hyland and I were both divorced by then, and we were sharing an apartment. Skip Caray, the voice of the Atlanta Hawks and son of the legendary Harry Caray, now the voice of the Chicago Cubs and mayor of Rush Street, even moved in for a while after he ran away from home.

I didn't even get the Naugahyde couch and chair in my divorce. Frank got out with his clothes. We rented enough items of furniture to get by.

Christmas was near, and we were both depressed. There is something about looking into a refrigerator and seeing only a few cans of beer and a slice or two of American cheese to make you feel lonely and sorry for yourself and make you think that being married certainly had its good points after all. Christmas season makes it even worse. And then I wasn't even going to get to go out of town on a bowl trip! We did a lot of drinking, me and Frank.

Minter told me to come to the office New Year's Day around five. He said we would work on the next afternoon's edition, a big one with all the bowl coverage, the evening before, and then let another staffer come in the next morning to put together what we had laid out.

I got to the office at six o'clock. Minter wasn't there. On my typewriter, there was a folded note. I opened it. I had to read it twice before I believed it.

It was from Minter. He said he was sorry he couldn't have told me earlier, but the reason he hadn't allowed me to go to a bowl game was that, effective that day, he was the new managing editor of the morning *Constitution.*

"Somebody needs to be there for the transition," he said. "I didn't want you to be off at a bowl game when you would be needed so badly."

Minter to the *Constitution.* DiMaggio to the Red Sox. Halas to the Packers. Truman to the Republicans.

The *Constitution* was our enemy. We had fought them with Minter leading our charge. And now he was one of them?

I called Hyland at the apartment.

"Minter's gone to the *Constitution,*" I announced.

"To do what?" he asked.

"He's the new M.E."

"An era has passed," said Frank.

We talked on. The primary question before us now was, who would be Minter's successor? We decided it would have to be Wilt Browning, the baseball writer.

He was next-eldest to Minter and Bisher. We

all respected his dedication to his beat, and we knew he was a family man and didn't carouse, and that's the sort of person that usually got the jobs where you told everybody else what to do.

I was certain it wasn't going to be Frank. He wouldn't want the job, anyway. Frank loved the road too much. And taken off expense account, he probably couldn't afford the pay cut.

It certainly wouldn't be me, either. I was only twenty-three. I wasn't married anymore, and I had definite carousing tendencies.

Wilt. Had to be.

"I don't think I'll want to keep this job under Wilt," I said to Frank. "He'll probably be there for years. There won't be anyplace for me to go."

"What do you want to do?" Frank asked.

"If Wilt gets the job," I said, "I'm asking for the baseball beat."

Covering major-league baseball did intrigue me. Maxwell's Plum after games at Shea Stadium. Dodger Stadium and Los Angeles. I didn't get the Rose Bowl assignment, so I still hadn't seen California.

The thing about the airplanes did bother me a little. Cover 162 baseball games, and you spend about half your life in an airplane. I mentioned my fears to Frank.

"Nothing to worry about," he said. "In case there's an emergency on board, all you've got to do is bend over, grab your ankles, and tuck your head between your legs."

"And then what?" I asked.

"Then you can kiss your ass good-bye." Just what I needed.

I called Minter, too. He seemed noncommittal on who might succeed him. He said the decision would be Managing Editor Durwood McAllister's and Bisher's.

"But it's probably going to be Wilt, right?" I asked.

"Probably," he said.

Wilt thought he was going to get the job, too, and he wanted it.

"I've seen all the baseball I want to see in this lifetime," he told me.

"Wilt," I said, "I think I'd like to change jobs. Two years in the slot is enough."

"What do you want to do?" he asked.

"I want baseball," I said.

He didn't hesitate.

"It's yours," he said.

Three days after Minter left us, Bisher called me into his office.

"Grizzard," he said, "you're my new executive sports editor."

I was the youngest person on the staff. Skip Caray, who also did a television sportscast on a local station, announced my appointment on his show. And he called to congratulate me, and he mentioned something I hadn't thought of: "Do you realize," he asked me, "you're now Frank's boss?"

I went to our refrigerator and drank what beer was left and pondered it all. Six years out of high school, and I'm running the place.

Me and Frank wouldn't have a problem.

No way.

Would we?

14

Before he moved upstairs as managing editor of the *Constitution,* Jim Minter had hired some new faces to replace some of the old ones. Bill Clark got his overtime pay and was gone. Teague Jackson took a job in golf. Bill Robinson had a misunderstanding with the paper, and he was gone. Wilt Browning gave up the baseball beat and went to work as public-relations director of the Atlanta Falcons, the unchallenged worst franchise in the National Football League. Doing PR for the Falcons was a little like doing PR for the Italian Army during World War II.

Newspaper people were different (euphemism for "weird") from other people I had known in my brief twenty-three years. They just kept falling into my life from someplace in Celestial Central Casting where they create characters whose flaws and frailties and specialties make them almost immediately unforgettable.

So, the replacements:

* * *

—Norman Arey. He had been a boy wonder in the department-store business in North Carolina. In his early twenties, he was already some sort of retailing genius. But he wasn't happy doing that. He wanted to be a sportswriter. He had a wife, a family, and a more-than-comfortable living, but he chucked it all and got a job on the sports staff of a suburban Atlanta daily, the *Marietta Daily Journal,* covering local high school sports.

Not satisfied there, either, he began to call and write Minter at the *Journal* about a job with us. As a matter of fact, Norman either wrote or called Jim every day for six months.

When the openings came, Minter needed another helper with the high school teams, so he hired Norman. I don't know for certain, but I think Minter hired him just so he wouldn't have to deal with Norman's calls and letters anymore.

Norman couldn't write a lick. But he was a determined sort (as evidenced by his never-ending effort to obtain a job on the *Journal* sports staff). And he wanted to learn.

Norman's first assignment for the *Journal* was to cover a Friday night high school football game between two local schools, Chamblee and Druid Hills. I took him aside Friday morning and tried to give him some guidelines.

"Norman," I said, "you are writing for an afternoon paper. By the time people get their *Journal*s Saturday afternoon, most of them who care will already know who won the game you are covering. The *Constitution* and radio and television will have had it.

"So what you have to do is find an angle to the game. You have to talk to the coaches and get some color. It's not enough just to report what happened for an afternoon newspaper."

He nodded as if he understood. And he did in a way. And in any other situation, he might not have written what I still consider to be the worst lead (opening paragraph) of a sports story I ever read.

Here's what happened to poor Norman. Chamblee scored the winning touchdown on the last play of the game. However, the Chamblee head coach, just as the runner crossed the goal line, collapsed on the sideline. He was rushed to a hospital and then pronounced dead on arrival from a heart attack.

I will never forget coming into the office to do the Sunday edition, picking up the Saturday afternoon section, and reading following:

By NORMAN AREY
Atlanta Journal Staff Writer

Chamblee's exciting come-from-behind 21–14 victory over rival Druid Hills Saturday was somewhat marred by the death of its coach.

Somewhat marred?

Norman was an excellent piano player. He played classical, he played jazz, but what he did best was play Jerry Lee Lewis, the Killer.

Norman not only sounded like Jerry Lee when he played and sang "Great Balls of Fire," he could also put in all the Killer's antics, such as playing the piano with his feet and kicking his stool away when he got on a roll.

Norman's wife was Peg. They had met at the University of Georgia, where Norman had transferred from the University of North Carolina.

Norman and Peg were the Fred and Ginger, the Marge and Gower Champion, of the *Journal* sports department. They could dance. Their specialty was the Belly Roll, which came straight out of the fifties from North Carolina. Norman and Peg doing the Belly Roll in the living room of their house was a sight to behold. It was no Lambada, to be sure, but a fairly sexy dance for the time.

Norman quickly picked up the nickname "Crazy Norman." He never did learn to write, but he did develop into one of the great information-gatherers it's been my pleasure to work alongside. Norman could, in fact, get the facts.

The Friday before a Georgia–Georgia Tech football game, we got a tip that Eddie McAshan, the Tech quarterback and the first black football player at the school, had had a falling out with the head coach and had been suspended from the team. He wouldn't be accompanying his teammates on a Friday bus ride to Athens from the Saturday game.

Both Friday home-delivered editions of the

Journal were already gone, but we still had the street-sales blue-streak edition. This was front-page sort of news.

I dispatched Norman to the Tech campus and told him to do whatever was necessary, but to find out if McAshan was not making the trip and, if he wasn't, why.

There were forty minutes before deadline. When Norman arrived at Tech, the coaches and players were boarding the buses to Athens. Norman asked the head coach, Bill Fulcher, where McAshan was.

Fulcher wouldn't comment. Norman asked some of the players. They were afraid to comment. When Fulcher had seated himself in the front of one of the buses, Norman went inside, closed the door, and wouldn't let the head coach out or the driver in until somebody told him about McAshan. Norman got his story.

Norman Arey did something else that changed my life dramatically. There were several of us at the *Journal* who played golf. Teague would get us on the local private courses for free.

I had come from a golf-deprived background. There was no Moreland Country Club. I had picked up the game in college, but I was never very good at it.

I was twenty-two when I quit golf. I was playing in a foursome with Teague and Hyland and Tom McCollister on the seventeenth hole at the historic East Lake Country Club in Atlanta, where the immortal Bobby Jones had learned the game. On the seventeenth, I hooked my tee shot in the water. I calmly put my driver back in my bag, announced I would never play golf again, and left the course.

Later, when Norman had joined the staff, he asked me one day, "Does anybody on the staff play tennis?"

I certainly didn't. I was assistant sports editor of a large newspaper, and I had no idea how you kept score in tennis. There had been no tennis courts in Moreland, either.

Norman asked around and found no other tennis players on the staff. Mr. Persistence finally said to me, "I need somebody to play tennis with. I'll show you how."

I weighed 135 pounds when I graduated from high school. But because I drank a lot of beer, ate a lot of country food my wife prepared for me, and got no physical exercise whatsoever anymore, I had bloomed to 200. I sort of enjoyed being overweight. I'd been skinny all my life. Suddenly, though, I had this big fat face and was up to 42 in the waist. I distinctly remember my mother had to take up my baseball pants my senior year in high school. They were 28 inches in the waist and were too big for me.

I agreed to meet Norman at the DeKalb Tennis Center in Atlanta. I had bought a pair of tennis shoes, a tennis shirt, and some tennis shorts, 42 inches in the waist. I borrowed a racquet.

Norman said, "Hold the racquet like this, and swing it like that."

I played tennis every day for the next sixteen years. I lost forty pounds in less than a year. I went from 42 tennis shorts to 34s. I looked better. I felt better.

It took me about three months to be able to beat Norman. Then, when I beat him one day at last, he never beat me again. Ever. I think he has always secretly hated me for that. I became a fair player. I even won a club tournament or two, and one wonderful year had my name in the rankings book with my partner as the number-13-ranked thirty-five-and-older doubles team in Georgia.

I had to give up the game when I was thirty-nine and awakened one morning to find I could no longer brush my teeth with my right hand because of the pain in my elbow and shoulder, put there by the fact I had played tennis every day for sixteen years. I went back to golf.

Norman basically became inactive as a player after I beat him a couple of hundred straight times. But the late sixties and the early seventies were tennis's boom time, and Norman became the first tennis writer in *Atlanta Journal* history. He did a splendid job.

He started a national ranking service for collegiate tennis teams, and later quit the paper to go to work for Lamar Hunt's World Championship Tennis tour. There will be more on Norman and me and professional tennis tournaments later.

One other thing. Norman suggested he and I quit smoking at a staff New Year's Eve party. It was our eighth or ninth day of nonpuffing. I called Norman at home. Peg answered the phone. Norman wasn't there.

"Is he still smoking?" I asked her.

"We were sitting in the living room last night," she said. "Me and Norman and the kids and the dog." The dog was a large black poodle named Buffy. "Suddenly, Norman got off the couch, stood up on the coffee table, looked toward the sky, and announced to us all, in a very loud voice, 'God wants me to smoke!' Then he went down to the convenience store, bought a carton of cigarettes, and sat up all night smoking."

If God wanted Norman to smoke, it occurred to me, He certainly wanted me to smoke, too. I went to the nearest store, bought myself a carton, and smoked until I was too sleepy to light another cigarette.

What I finally did about Norman's writing was not allow him to write. I simply would send him out on assignment to gather information. He would then give me that information in the form of a memo, and I would have Hyland or another veteran put the information in the form of an article. Nothing wrong with that. Give me somebody who can bring back the information, and I can always find five other people to put it in the English language. Norman's best work came in the form of a diary he convinced a high school football player in the Atlanta area to keep while he was being recruited by various colleges. After recruiting season was over, Norman took the diary, brought it to the office, and we published it.

One anecdote from that diary I'll never forget. The kid had an idea that maybe he would like to be a doctor someday. When he visited Duke, recruiters took him over to the Duke hospital, where doctors allowed him to put on a doctor's outfit and sit in on a hysterectomy. That cured the kid's desire to be a doctor. He went to Georgia and majored in journalism instead.

* * *

—Priit Vesiland: Minter also hired him away from the *Marietta Journal,* and gave him Robinson's old job as outdoor editor. Priit was a handsome young blond fellow who once wrote a story on the outdoor page questioning whether the killing of animals should be considered as a sport.

"Just what I need," said Minter. "An outdoor editor who is antihunting."

Priit was born in Estonia. His father, a college professor, had got his family out of Estonia and into the United States when the Soviets moved in after World War II. Priit was an intelligent, sensitive individual. He had a pretty wife. He expressed ideas and thoughts I'd never heard before. His arguments against racial injustice were a long way from Clark and Hyland discussing Bill Russell versus Wilt Chamberlain.

Every day that I spent in the composing room, the more I became anti-union. Perhaps they had once served a purpose in the country, but the union I had to deal with was, more than anything else, a giant, arrogant pain in the butt that killed incentive and was stubbornly single-minded.

What the union did to Priit Vesiland broke my heart.

Priit had crossed a picket line when there had been a strike at the *Marietta Daily Journal.* In retaliation, union workers there went so far as to call Priit's wife, telling her of a nonexistent affair her husband was supposed to be having with another woman at the newspaper. They also sliced the tires of his car. They even threatened his life.

When Priit left and came to the *Journal,* he thought the harassment was over. Not so. Union members in our composing room heard from their brothers and sisters in Marietta, and thus were determined to make Priit's life miserable.

He had to make up the outdoor pages twice a week. The minute he walked into the composing room, the badgering would start.

"There's that scab!" somebody would shout across the room.

"Get the hell out, scab!" would follow.

His copy would mysteriously get lost. His type would be pied.

"You touched the type, scab," a printer would say.

Priit would deny it. But it wouldn't matter. The type for his page would still be all over the floor, and he would have to wait until it was set again.

They sliced Priit's tires at the *Journal,* too. They made his life miserable. But he still turned out quality work. He wrote a story about the death of an outstanding show horse that was a brilliant piece of writing.

We went fishing once together up on Lake Alatoona, north of Atlanta. We caught a long string of crappie, went back to his house, cleaned them, cooked them, and ate them. Priit told me then he was planning to leave the paper.

"I want to get into photography," he said.

What he wanted to do was get the hell away from the composing room.

Priit left. He wound up as a photographer with the *National Geographic.* I used to get post-cards from him from all over the world.

The new technology eventually killed off the composing-room union. A user-friendly computer could do what a user-unfriendly printer could do, and do it better. Me, I miss glue pots and the sound of manual typewriters in a newspaper office. But I still think of computers as Priit's revenge.

* * *

—Ron Hudspeth: Minter got him out of the West Palm Beach bureau of the *Miami Herald.* He hadn't been on the staff for two weeks when I needed to find him on a Sunday to give him an assignment that had come up unexpectedly. I called his house. His wife answered the phone. I asked for Ron. His wife said he wasn't there.

I asked if she knew when he would be in. She said she didn't. I asked if she would she give him a message. She said she couldn't. "Ron doesn't live here anymore," she told me.

Atlanta became *the* singles mecca in the South in the early seventies. Hyland and I were both divorced and often sought neon, but nobody ever took to it like Hudspeth, the boy from Bell Glade, Florida, on the outskirts of the Everglades.

We came to give him a nickname, too. We called him "the Butterfly." In a bar, he was everywhere. Frank liked to prop on the bar and argue sports. Not Hudspeth. He fired on everything that moved. Oh, those warm spring Friday nights at Harrison's on Peachtree, the singles bar that became an Atlanta legend.

The girl-childs were flocking there. From places like Vidalia and Augusta and Montgomery and Birmingham and Ty Ty and Albany (the Georgian pronunciation is "All-Benny") in the south, to Ringgold and Dalton (from whence would later come Marla Maples and Deborah Norville) to the north. They would wear those sundresses and you couldn't move in the place on Friday's.

"This is living," Hudspeth would say, above the noise of the mating horde.

It was. There basically had been only one woman in my life since I was thirteen. Paula. But she was gone. And, once I had adjusted to bachelor life, this Harrison's on Peachtree was a veritable gold mine. I would have found it, of course, if Ron Hudspeth hadn't come to work at the *Atlanta Journal,* but his divorce gave me a regular running mate.

Running bars alone—even great ones like Harrison's—has its drawbacks, especially if approaching strange women is difficult, as it most certainly was to me, especially before I'd got a few VOs and water inside me. There will always be that fear of rejection in most men. It is called the Buzz-Off-Creep Theory.

She's beautiful. She's alone. But what if I walk over there, say something clever like, "How long have you been in Atlanta?" "What's your sign?" or the ever popular opener, "Do you think wrestling's fake?" and she replies, "Buzz off, creep?"

A friend of mine once said it even better.

"It's not the walk over to talk to a girl or to ask her to dance that's so bad. It's the walk back when she says no that gets you."

But Hudspeth wasn't afraid. He would fire, and if rejected, would go on undaunted to his next target. What made it easy for me was when he would join *two* ladies at a table. As soon as I figured he had broken the ice, I would walk over and introduce myself. I had to take second choice, of course, but the taking of an occasional cull in a city like Atlanta was often quite rewarding.

There was something else Ron and I shared. We both had the same ideas about what should be in a sports section.

Sportswriting was changing all over the country in those days. Sportswriters suddenly weren't all team men anymore. What writers wouldn't think of writing twenty years earlier was exactly what the new breed wanted to write.

Of course, the new breed showed signs of its immaturity. I was sitting between two sports writers following a Georgia-Florida football game in Jacksonville's Gator Bowl.

One of the writers was a kid like me, who wanted to write The Truth, with some poetry tossed in.

The other was from the old school. He'd been there a thousand autumn Saturdays before, and he wanted to finish his report and get to the bar.

It was a classic confrontation of the new and the old breed of sportswriting.

The old writer already had two pages of his story typed. The kid hadn't even completed a first paragraph yet. He would put a sheet of paper in his typewriter, hit a few bars, and then draw the paper out of the typewriter and throw it, with obvious disgust, to the floor.

After this went on for a good 20 minutes and discarded paper was all over the press box floor, the veteran looked over at the frustrated youngster and asked one of the great questions in the history of journalism: "Hey, kid. What don't you just write what happened?"

Writers once covered up for athletes. But no more. Writers once never asked the tough questions of coaches and managers and athletes. Now, you asked them. You confronted them.

During Watergate, we would say, "If Woodward and Bernstein can bring down a president, why can't we stand up in front of a football coach and ask him why he kicked a field goal on fourth and inches?" The rest of the paper used to call us the "Toy Shop." But suddenly, there were issues that were real. Desegregation of southern collegiate teams was one.

Bear Bryant's Alabama team played Southern Cal and had been thrashed by the power running of Sam Cunningham, who was black. Bryant, the story went, saw the light, and began actively recruiting black athletes, who had once either gone to all-black schools or had been recruited on the West Coast or in the Midwest.

This joke must have been told a thousand times:

"The Bear's on the practice field the first day of fall workouts, and a black kid comes up to him and asks if he can try out for the team. The Bear thinks the whole thing might be a hoot. The white kids will surely kill the kid. But they give the ball to the black kid, and he breaks eight tackles and speeds down the sideline for a touchdown.

"Look at that Indian go!" says the Bear.

There's a true story they tell about something called the Sky Writers. In the late sixties, the Southeastern Conference office in Birmingham came up with the idea of chartering a plane that would carry sportswriters from all over the South to the various SEC football camps, just prior to the opening of the season.

The Sky Writers were in Oxford, Mississippi, interviewing Johnny Vaught, head coach of the Ole Miss Rebels. A few blacks had already broken the SEC color barrier by that time. Vaught was asked, "Are you going to begin to recruit blacks at Ole Miss?"

Vaught bristled and answered, "As long as I am head coach at the University of Mississippi, never!"

Reporters dashed for their typewriters. But John Logue of the *Journal* just sat there.

"You aren't going to write what Vaught said?" he was asked.

"That's news?" Logue asked back. "What am I going to write: 'For the fiftieth straight year, Ole Miss is not going to recruit black athletes'?"

When I became executive sports editor at the *Journal,* Frank Hyland and Ron Hudspeth were my point men. Hyland left the Hawks for a time to work the Falcons. He was sitting in a booth in a restaurant in Greenville, South Carolina, where the Falcons held preseason practice, one evening with two other writers and the Falcons head coach, Norman Van Brocklin. I mentioned earlier Van Brocklin had little or no use for sports writers, all of whom he thought were communists.

Hyland was sitting across the table from Van Brocklin. They both had a few drinks, and then Van Brocklin, known as the Dutchman, looks over at Frank and says, "Hyland, you're a whore writer."

Frank recalled, "I wasn't sure what a whore writer was, but I figured it wasn't a compliment. So I said to Van Brocklin, 'I may be a whore writer, but you're a loser.'

"Van Brocklin turned redder than he already was and said, 'I'm not a loser.'

"I said, 'Oh, yeah? Check your record.'"

At that point, Van Brocklin reached across the

table, grabbed Hyland by the tie, and pulled it.

"I was choking," said Hyland.

Van Brocklin then pulled Frank across the table. Nobody landed a serious blow, but Frank's tie was ruined, his sports jacket got ripped, and he didn't get to sit and enjoy the prime rib he had ordered before the scuffle broke out.

Frank called me at home and told me what had happened.

"Write it," I said.

"I will," he replies. "As soon as they send the prime rib I ordered up to my room."

Later, Frank covered the Braves for me. One night in the clubhouse, he asked Hank Aaron a question Aaron didn't appreciate. The future all-time home-run leader happened to be eating from a can of strawberries at the time, and he threw the strawberries in Frank's face.

"It's not everybody," said Frank, "who gets into it with two Hall of Famers in one career."

"What did you think when Bad Henry threw the strawberries in your face?" I asked Frank.

"I had this strange thought that they were pretty good strawberries," he answered.

Hudspeth also covered the Braves and the Falcons. He ripped them both furiously for their continuing shortcomings.

He once asked Van Brocklin a tough question, and the Dutchman took off his coat and said, "Let's stack some furniture," meaning, "Get the furniture out of the way, I'm going to mash this commie's face in."

Hudspeth managed to avoid fisticuffs with the Dutchman, who, as all Atlanta Falcons coaches finally do, got fired. Van Brocklin retired to his farm in Social Circle, Georgia, fifty miles east of Atlanta. After the firing, Ron managed to get an interview with the Dutchman's wife, who had a memorable quote:

"Can my husband be happy on the farm?" Mrs. Van Brocklin asked back. "Let me put it this way—pecan trees don't drop touchdown passes."

There were a couple of other new guys on the staff in addition to Arey, Vesilind, and Hudspeth. Jim Hunter came in from South Carolina and took over auto racing and some college coverage. Minter also decided Hunter could fill in on the Hawks, occasionally.

On Hunter's first day at the paper, Minter told Hyland to take the new guy to the Hawks practice and introduce him to the players and Coach Richie Guerin.

On the way to practice, Hyland asked Hunter, "Do you like beer?"

They never made it to practice, and Hunter was supposed to do a feature on the Hawks the next morning.

No problem. While Hunter was at South Carolina, he had covered a Clemson basketball player who had been a late draft pick for the Hawks. Hunter, upon arriving in the office the next morning, decided to write a story on the kid from Clemson, using material he already had.

But a problem arose on deadline. On a routine call to the Hawks office, Hyland found out that the kid from Clemson was going to get cut that morning. It would be obvious to Minter that his crack basketball writers had not spent much time with the team the day before.

So Hyland called Coach Guerin and pleaded with him to keep the young player on the roster one more day, so that the paper wouldn't have egg on its face, and Hyland and Hunter wouldn't have Minter on their ass.

Guerin agreed. Hunter and Hyland were saved.

Hunter had almost as many contacts in auto racing as Bill Robinson. He also had a history of tarrying in the post-race grape and driving off in pace cars.

The most memorable piece he did on auto racing was from the Darlington Motor Speedway in Darlington, South Carolina. Two guys had driven a camper into the infield with three prostitutes in the back. Right there in the broad daylight of Sunday, Hunter reported that the line from the back of that camper was longer than the line to the ladies' restroom. The infield got so drunk and rowdy before the race was over, police finally built a makeshift jail on the premises to detain those arrested. It was hastily put together, with some strategically placed cement blocks for a foundation, and plywood walls.

The jail had been up about ten minutes and was already bulging at the seams with good ol' boys charged with drunkenness, fighting, solicitation of prostitution, public indecency, and starting a fire without a permit, when the inmates pushed down a wall and a mass escape took place to the ringing cheers of spectators who were all but ignoring the race.

Minter had hired another guy, named Ron Sanders, to work the desk and do an occasional high school story. Hyland and I often disagreed as to which lead was the all-time worst—Norman's "somewhat marred" or Ron Sanders's lead on a high school baseball game involving Atlanta's Bass High. Bass had played Grady, and Grady had won in a rout.

Sander's lead:

When spring comes, it's natural for a boy's thoughts to turn to the ol' fishing hole. So Grady got itself a string loaded with Bass Friday afternoon, winning 9–0 and doing just what came naturally.

"Norman's lead didn't have a single cliché," Frank would argue. "An all-time worst lead must have clichés, contain simplistic allusions, and have no redeeming qualities whatsoever. At least Norman had some realization that the thrill of victory can be tempered by death."

Good argument, but I still go with Norman.

Ron Sanders lasted about three months before it was suggested he find a new profession. Minter called me one day from his office at the *Constitution* several years later and asked me to come see something. He had a letter from Ron Sanders, who, sure enough had found a new profession—the ministry.

In his letter, Ron told Minter he had found the Lord and wanted to make all his previous wrongs right again. He said that when he left the paper, he took with him a dozen new grease pencils, two new reporter's notebooks, and a copy of the *Official Baseball Guide* for 1957. He sent Minter a check for five dollars for the pencils and notebook and returned the 1957 *Official Guide.*

The staff had a name for me, their twenty-three-year-old Grand Imperial Llama Potentate Executive Sports Editor. They called me "Lieutenant Fuzz," after the boyish bungling lieutenant of the Beetle Bailey cartoon strip. I always figured it was Frank who came up with the name. But I couldn't blame him or the staff. They had all served under Jim Minter—George Patton—and now they had me.

As it turned out, I did have some trouble being Frank Hyland's roommate/boss. It wasn't serious trouble. It was just that after I got the job, I became a little more aware of the necessity that I be basically awake in the office in the morning. It would go like this:

We would finish the paper at one or so in the afternoon and all hit Underground Atlanta. Frank, Hudspeth, Hunter, Simmons, Priit, Dr. Whitley, and me. We would start at the Bucket Shop, a sort of Harrison's Beneath the Streets, and we would talk shop, women, and the death of kings. We would, of course, get blitzed. The evening would normally reach its crescendo when Frank would go out onto the streets of Underground Atlanta to do his Charlie Chaplin walk among the tourists.

Frank could walk just the way Chaplin walked. From somewhere, he would also come up with a hat of some sort and an umbrella that he would carry under his arm. He would walk his walk and doff his hat to the ladies, and he was a riot. But as the hour would get later, I would mention to my roommate, Frank, "You've got to be in the office at seven. Let's go home."

Frank was not a man to give up the night easily. "You go ahead," he would say. "I'll be in at seven."

I would get up at five-thirty and shower. I'd call in to Frank in his bedroom at six. "Frank," I'd say, "it's six. You've got an hour."

"I'll be there," he would answer.

Seven, no Frank. Seven-thirty, no Frank. Eight, maybe Frank. One morning, Frank hit the office at eight-fifteen, after about an hour's sleep, and dozed off on the rim. The executive editor, Bill Fields, happened to walk by my desk and ask, "Is Frank Hyland asleep at the rim?"

"He got here at four-thirty and stripped the wire," I lied. "He'll be okay."

I could have dealt with Frank being late occasionally if he had not done something I could never understand.

I would leave him, sound asleep, at six-fifteen. He would be late to the office and, after the first edition was in, I would call him to my desk and give him hell about it.

"I ran out of gas," Frank would say.

"Frank," I would say. "What are you, *crazy?* I left you in bed at six-fifteen. I left you in the Underground at one this morning. I know why you were late. I'm your goddamned roommate. You were late because you just didn't get your ass up."

I finally made the smart move—I resigned as Frank's roommate and got myself another apartment. It was better after that. When Frank said, "There was a wreck on the interstate," at least there was about a one-in-a-thousand shot that was why he was late.

Regardless, Frank was still the best all-around talent who ever worked for me. He could do it all. Report. Write. Edit. Lay out the paper. Write wonderful headlines and photo captions. His best headline came one morning when he sat on the rim quite ill and quite green.

Peahead Walker was a character of the southern sports scene. He coached football in North Carolina and had a million jokes and stories. Peahead was probably the most sought-after sports speaker in the South in the late sixties. But Peahead died. The *Constitution* carried the obit in the morning paper. The headline had said something like, "COLORFUL PEAHEAD WALKER DIES."

We had a Peahead obit, too. We had coded

headlines at the *Journal.* I had ordered what was known as a K-3 on the Peahead story. A K-3 was one line of 36-point type, three columns wide, with an 18-point "kicker" above it.

You've seen kickers on headlines before. They look something like this:

TASTED GOOD   (KICKER)

"MAN BITES DOG"   (Headline)

Everybody on the rim took a shot at the Peahead headline, but none satisfied me. "It needs to say something about Peahead knowing a lot of jokes and stories," I said.

Frank opened his eyes and said, "Give the damn thing to me."

He wrote:

HE'S DEAD

"HAVE YOU HEARD THE ONE ABOUT PEAHEAD?"

No way I could run it, but it sure went down in my Headline Hall of Fame.

Frank could take four wire stories about the same thing, pick out the best of them all, and compose one on his own typewriter that would sing. And he could do it on deadline with that Camel sticking out of his mouth and his head probably hurting more than any of the rest of us could realize.

He loved newspapers. And he loved the game of newspapers. He was the guy you wanted in your foxhole with you. You're five minutes before deadline and the wire offers a bulletin: *Casey Stengel has died.* You wanted Frank with you. He could be stubborn and sarcastic and immovable, but if I had one man to hire to work beside me in the fine art of getting a newspaper out, it would be Frank K. Hyland.

It was different with Hudspeth and me. I was his boss, but we still managed to run the streets together and maintain a fairly professional relationship in the office. And, Lord, the ladies we sported. But how many ideas did we come up with for the section on how many barstools, while the band played "Proud Mary"?

It was during a lull at Harrison's one night, as a matter of fact, that we devised what I still believe was the first attempt by a sports section to have an editorial page.

It was Hudspeth's notion that other writers besides Bisher needed an outlet for more commentary. "We're out there with the teams," he'd say. "We cover them day-to-day. Bisher comes out once a month. We know where the bodies are hidden."

With Hudspeth's help (while the band played "Jeremiah Was a Bullfrog" and "Bridge Over Troubled Water" and other songs from the early seventies I came to hate), we came up with my page 2 concept.

I didn't ask anybody if I could do it. I didn't consult with the managing editor, and I certainly didn't consult with Bisher, who I figured would be steadfastly against any infringement on his bailiwick.

First, I went to advertising layout and asked if they could arrange the ads five days a week so I could get a five-column hole at the top. That was for what I called "Perspective." It would be a piece of staff opinion. *Sports Illustrated* now runs "Point After" on the last page in its weekly magazine. Ron Fimrite remembers Billy Martin, etc., etc. I had the idea first.

Under "Perspective," I wanted room for something I could call "People in Sports"—a compendium to be gleaned from the wires and other sports sections. Under that, I wanted "Reaction"—letters from readers.

I even came up with a complete new headline style for page 2. Kickers that appeared on top of headlines were always set in a smaller-size type than the main head. I turned that around. I came up with something we called "bullet head." The page would look like this:

PERSPECTIVE
Aaron Can Break Ruth's Home Run Record If . . .

PEOPLE IN SPORTS
Papa Bear George Halas Celebrates a Birthday

REACTION
Hudspeth Off-Base on Calling Braves "Losers"

Page 2 took off immediately. Hyland and Hudspeth both wrote "Perspectives." They raised hell.

The letters poured in. The only real problem I had with the page was horses would occasionally show up in "People in Sports." Somebody on the desk would be chosen to compile "People" each morning. I wanted humor. I wanted So-and-so's third baseman's wife was picked up for shoplifting; some college football coach had been fired for having sex with a cheerleader; Howard Cosell had been attacked on the streets of Cleveland by irate Browns' fans, angry at some innocuous statement he had made on *Monday Night Football.*

I got some of that, but at least twice a week I would look at "People in Sports" and there would be an item about a racehorse. I finally issued a memorandum to the staff that read:

For the last time: If it has more than two legs, it has no business in People in Sports.

It took Bisher about a week to realize what had happened. Furman and I weren't getting along anyway. I always wondered if the reason he had seen fit to give me the executive sports editor job was that he figured a kid like me would be easy to run over and he could get back to the complete control he had of the sports department before Minter. But I was determined he wasn't going to push me around. He was my idol at the typewriter. He was my enemy when it came to how the paper looked and what appeared in it.

There was Bisher's early morning call. Furman would get up, read the *Constitution,* and then get mad. He would see something they had before us. (It didn't matter to him that the story had broken at seven o'clock in the evening, on the *Constitution*'s time.) It might be something as small as the Fellowship of Christian Athletes All-American College LaCrosse team, but if it made the morning paper first, it would make Bisher mad. So after he read the *Constitution,* he would call me. No matter how busy I was trying to supervise our first edition, I had to stop and deal with the Bisher call.

"Good God, Grizzard!" he would begin. "The *Constitution* broke the Fellowship of Christian Athletes All-American LaCrosse team. Were we asleep at the switch again?" It was always that "again" that got me.

I would try to explain. We would argue. I would slam the phone down. Bisher would call his travel agent and make plans to fly to London to cover Wimbledon. For Christmas one year, my future second wife gave me a dartboard with Bisher's photograph in the bull's-eye.

I tried to get a lot of feature material on the sports front. We did some off-the-wall things about an ex-Falcon turned bank robber, a hockey team in Macon, Georgia, of all places, called the Macon Whoopees, and a Rattlesnake Roundup in Whigman, Georgia. Meanwhile, Bisher would come into the office around eleven, see the first edition, find a story about some guy who had a lifetime batting average of .233 and played second base for the Pittsburgh Pirates in the late twenties, and he would scream to the heavens.

"We're not running a magazine here, Grizzard! This is a newspaper. A *news*paper. The obit we ran on [whozits with the .233 lifetime average] was a terrible error in news judgment."

Bisher once went somewhere exotic like Morocco, where he rode the Royal Moroccan train and played golf at the Royal Moroccan golf course with the Royal Moroccan king or some such thing. He was gone about three weeks. When he returned, he went back over all the sports sections he missed with his red grease pencil. He circled everything he didn't like. He didn't like a lot more than he liked.

He called me into his office between editions.

"Grizzard," he said, "we just aren't playing the little stuff big enough."

"But, Furman," I said, "if we play the little stuff big, then we won't have any little stuff anymore."

Made sense to me.

Bisher thought a minute and then said, "You're the goddamned executive sports editor, *you* figure it out."

So, soon after page 2's debut, I heard the call from Bisher's office. "Grizzard," he said, "got a minute?"

I walked in. I never took a seat when I went into Bisher's little office. I felt a bit safer standing up for some reason.

"What the hell's going on on page two?" he asked.

"I'm trying to start a sports editorial page," I told him.

"Well," he said, "I thought this was just a onetime thing. Do you mean to say, we're going to have this on page two every day?"

The general manager of the paper himself had come down one day to tell me he thought page 2 was a great addition to the section. The managing editor liked it. The pro teams were raising hell about it. The readers loved it. I was prepared to go to the wall with Bisher about it. But Bisher didn't order it out of the paper. He simply said, "One thing to remember. If nobody's got anything to say, leave it at that. Don't force opinion and commentary."

I would cut "Perspective" to three times a week eventually. Bisher was right. As a matter of fact, he turned out to be right about a lot more things than I gave him credit for at the time. It had to do with age and his perspective.

We did spend too much time on features and not enough on details, such as making certain all the attendance lines were at the bottom of each day's baseball box scores, seeing to it the rosters for the annual Blue-Gray all-star football game in Montgomery, Alabama, were in the paper, and not failing to realize that just because, at our tender ages, we'd never heard of a dearly departed Pittsburgh batting star, a lot of people older than us *had*—and would like to know if he had died. Bisher cared. He wanted the sports section he represented, or that represented him, to be without reproach.

I want to say it again: Bisher was right. As much as I fought him, cursed him, and hated to get that morning call, the old man knew his newspapers. When Earl Mann, who had owned my beloved Crackers during my boyhood days, died in 1990, the Atlanta papers didn't do much with it. I was outraged. A brilliant Bisher column (he's still at it at seventy-two) made me feel better.

The *Atlanta Journal-Constitution* moved out of 10 Forsyth Street in 1972 and into a new six-story building around the corner on Marietta Street. Underground Atlanta, beset by crime, closed. Amtrak took over the nation's passenger trains. The Union was torn down, and what was left of the Georgian was quietly put to sleep. The winos and hobos had to go somewhere else.

The sports department in the new building sat at one end of the newsroom. A waist-high partition was all that separated us from the gatherers of real news from the real world. It was the dawn of the new technology era for newspapers.

They took away our manual typewriters and gave us electric. Hot type was on the way out. Soon the Linotype machines would vanish, and type would be set by some magical, computerized method.

The power that was the composing-room

union was dying. The newsroom, with the help of the new technology, was getting more control of the production process. Soon it wouldn't matter if the printers went out on strike. They couldn't close the paper down anymore. Push a button here and push a button there, and *voilà,* a newspaper.

I didn't like many of the changes. I missed the old building. We had carpet on the floor at 72 Marietta Street. Frank had to find an ashtray to dispose of his Camels. Electric typewriters are too quiet. I missed the jingle and jangle of somebody pecking away at a manual. The phones didn't buzz anymore. The new ones made a sound that reminded me of the coo of a sick pigeon. You couldn't say "copy boy" anymore, because now there were girl copy boys, and the new sensitivity made the word "boy" socially unacceptable.

I couldn't edit with a pencil anymore. I had to use a felt-tipped pen. I had to mark out words carefully in deep black so whatever it was that was setting type now would understand it should skip over those words.

You sat at your electric typewriter, and before you did anything else, you had to type the pound mark (#), followed by the letters *PD* at the beginning of the margin set.

When you had finished whatever it was you

were composing at the electric, it was necessary to type #ET, which signaled Hal it had reached the end of that particular article. Said veteran *Constitution* columnist Celestine Sibley, "Pound *PD* is going to be the *ET* of me."

Professional athletes were forming unions. Hockey had come to Atlanta. Gasoline was short. Nixon was in deep doo-doo. Men were growing sideburns and wearing leisure suits. Lime-green ones. And Babe Ruth's career home-run record of 714 was being challenged by Henry Aaron of the Atlanta Braves.

The hype began at the start of the baseball season in 1972. With a good year, Aaron could break Ruth's record that season. This was big. It was one of the biggest sports stories of all time, and it was happening in my town.

We began the countdown. Each time Aaron hit a home run in '72, we dropped in a little box on the Braves story that noted what number home run it was and how many more Aaron had to hit to get to Ruth's 714.

Aaron hit 713 on the last day of the season in 1973. In five more months, spring training would begin, and Aaron would tie and then break the record when the season began in April.

Management wanted a Henry Aaron special section that would come out before the season began. I began work on it in January. I had to plan it and design it. I basically ceased to deal with the day-to-day operation of the department. All my time was put into the special section and planning for the day Aaron would tie the record and the day he would break it.

What had never occurred to me was that racism would get involved in the process. The more we wrote about Aaron's challenge, the more phone calls we got calling us "nigger lovers." The callers all wanted to point out that Aaron might, included, break the record, but that he had more at-bats than Ruth.

The composing room was all white, all male. The printers referred to Aaron as "Super Nigger," as in, "How many stories you doing on Super Nigger today?"

I began to worry that something might happen to Aaron. What if some nut decided to save the white race's pride and kill him? I ordered an obit written and filed away just in case.

I was determined to make the Aaron special the best piece of newspaper work I had ever done. I ordered stories on his boyhood days in Mobile. I spent hours on the phone tracking down family photos. I dispatched a writer to Mobile to do a piece on the old neighborhood.

Baseball experts said the secret to Aaron's

hitting was his powerful wrists. The writer in Mobile uncovered the fact he had worked in an ice house as a youngster and had to lift heavy blocks of ice. Thus, the powerful wrists.

I ordered a listing of each of the 713 home runs Aaron had hit in the major leagues. I wanted the date of each homer, and who threw the home-run pitch for the opposing team. I could have filled encyclopedias with the amount of information I had compiled on No. 44. I even had Hyland ghostwrite a piece by Aaron himself. The strawberry incident had long since been forgotten.

I got my layout. It was filled with ads. I had been promised copious space. I didn't get it. There wasn't room for even half the material I had gathered. I had to shrink marvelous photographs to make them fit in the space I had been given. I was prepared to give them a Cadillac, but management was willing to settle for a Nash.

But there was still The Record. The Braves opened the season in Cincinnati and sure enough, Aaron tied Ruth's record on opening day. Then the Braves came home to play the Dodgers. The problem I faced was that I had to have everything in place for each game, in case it was the one that gave us number 715. What if Aaron didn't hit it for weeks? I would still have to be ready each night, just in case.

A few weeks earlier, I had hired Chuck Perry, my old assistant at the *Daily News* in Athens. Chuck had become executive editor of the *Daily News* and *Banner-Herald,* but I'd convinced him he needed to try it in the Big Time. Chuck would be my assistant. His first day at work was the day the Braves were to play the Dodgers in their home opener. He came in at seven that morning. We got the edition out, went to lunch around one, and then came back to work on planning for the next day, in case Aaron hit 715.

I had every conceivable angle to the story covered. I even had a staffer go into a men's room each time Aaron came to bat so that if he did hit the homer, Norman could do a sidebar on some unfortunate soul who was standing at the urinal at the moment history was made.

Chuck and I were in the press box in Atlanta Fulton County Stadium at six, a couple of hours before the first pitch. Aaron came to bat in the bottom of the first inning before fifty thousand. Al Downing was pitching for the Dodgers. Aaron hit it out to left. Chuck and I split back to the office.

We worked all night. The writers came in and typed their stories. We went through hundreds of photographs trying to find the ones that best told the story.

A huge spring thunderstorm hit about two in

the morning. The lights went out a couple of times. Around three-thirty, the storm ended. The cleanup people were in the newsroom. The only noise was that of their vacuum cleaners working on the carpet. I was sitting at the copy desk, editing and laying out the pages. Suddenly, I heard a noise. I jumped. Chuck jumped. It sounded like an elephant.

I'm serious here. It sounded like an elephant. Aaron breaks the record, a frightening thunderstorm had hit, and now it's four in the morning and we hear an elephant.

It turned out to be Mike McKenzie, a new staffer I had hired to cover the Hawks. He had finished his sidebar. We thought he had gone home. But he had walked down to the men's room first, and when he came out, he decided to do his elephant impression.

To be honest, it was a damn fine elephant impression.

"Why did you do that?" I asked McKenzie.

"Just felt like it," was his answer.

Our support staff came in at seven. But Chuck and I stayed until the first edition came up and we could see the results of our efforts. We wanted to hold them in our hands. The best story came from a men's restroom. The poor guy standing at the urinal had figured there was no way Aaron would hit the homer his first time at bat.

We left the office at eleven in the morning. Chuck's first day at work had lasted twenty-eight hours.

We went and had a large breakfast.

"What makes us want to work this hard?" Chuck looked up from his country ham and grits and asked me.

"We love it," I said.

* * *

Hudspeth met a girl. He met her in the elevator at the newspaper. She worked for the company that supplied our vending machines. He got on the elevator to go down for coffee, and she was on her way there, too. Hudspeth got a date with her. All those nights on the streets, and he meets a girl on an elevator at the newspaper.

She clipped the Butterfly's wings. All of a sudden, my running mate had been taken away.

That had a lot to do with why I got married for the second time. I was struck down at the newspaper, too.

I was sitting at my desk in the sports department. Tons of kids came in all the time. The tour guide would say, "This is the newsroom. Those

are typewriters. There are the editors. There are
the reporters. . . ."

So I'm sitting at my desk one day, and I hear
a female voice say, "And that is the executive
sports editor, Mr. Grizzard." Only the voice
didn't pronounce my name as I pronounced it.
The voice said "*Griz*-erd," as in "lizard"; not
"Griz-*zard*" as in "yard" and "lard."

I looked up. She was gorgeous. Maybe cute
is a better description. She was short. She had
those eyes. Big, wide eyes. She was smiling as
she spoke to the kids on the tour. Great smile.
Big and wide like her eyes.

Her accent was decidedly southern. It had a
peculiar lilt. Syrupy, but not *too* syrupy. It was a
small-town accent. Small-town accents were
disappearing in the South. Small-town people
were moving to the cities, and suddenly everybody was sounding like Nelson Nowhere on the
television news.

The girl disappeared down the steps with the
kids toward the composing room. Maybe the
Reverend would have a vision for them.

I called the public-relations department,
which handled the tours for the kids. I asked the
name of the girl. It was Kay.

I gave it an hour or two, then walked down to
the fourth floor to PR. Kay was sitting at her desk.

"I need to talk to you," I said to her.

She looked up with those eyes.

"I heard you giving the tour," I went on. "You blew my last name."

"But aren't you Mr. *Griz*-erd?" she asked.

"It's Gri-*zard,*" I said. Then followed it with, "Want to have dinner with me tonight?"

"Sure," she replied.

We went to dinner. We went to her apartment afterward, and she took out her guitar and sang songs to me.

It was over after that. She was from the low country of South Carolina. That was the accent.

She'd gone to college, but it hadn't worked out. There was a boy, and they were going to get married, but that hadn't worked out, either. She thought about becoming a flight attendant. A family friend had a connection at the Atlanta papers, and that's how she had got the tour-guide job. She'd keep it until she could get on with an airline.

Six months later, on a warm April afternoon in 1973, I looked at Big Eyes and she looked at me, and I just got caught up enough in that tender moment to blurt out, "Why don't we get married?"

I didn't think I'd ever find anything to top her, even in Harrison's. She could sing, and she was good to hold and fine to have, so I said what I said, and she said, "Let's do it."

And then she asked, "When?"

And, tempestuous fool that I was, I said, "Why not as soon as possible?"

I called my stepbrother, Ludlow Porch, because I knew he wouldn't tell me I was crazy, and I needed somebody to take care of some details.

"Ludlow," I said, "I've decided to get married again."

"What are you?" he asked. "Crazy?"

"But this is different," I said. "We have a lot in common."

"Oh, does she like to drink and chase women in Harrison's, too?"

"No," I insisted. "We both enjoy the same kind of music, for instance."

"I like Waylon Jennings, too," Ludlow said, "but it's no reason for me to marry him."

When he finally decided I was sober and determined, he asked what he could do to help. I said, "I want to have the wedding at your house, because there's not room for me and her and the preacher in either of our apartments. I also need you to get your wife to arrange for a cake and do some decorating, and I need you to find me a preacher. But be careful. The preacher who married me and my first wife quit the pulpit and went into the used-car business six months later. I blame him for a lot of our problems."

"I'll do what I can," said Ludlow.

"And one other thing," I said. "I want to ride the train to Fort Lauderdale for our honeymoon. Trains are romantic."

"There is still a train that goes from Atlanta to Florida?" he asked.

"No. We'll have to drive to Savannah to catch it. It comes through about two in the morning."

"Let me see if I have this straight," Ludlow said. "You want to get married for the second time, even though you were a complete failure as a husband on your first attempt, and you want to do it as quickly as possible, which I assume is as soon as you can get a license and your blood tests.

"Then, you want my lovely wife to obtain a cake and decorate the house, and then you want me to find a man of the cloth who has no intentions of going into the used-car game, and then you want me to reserve you two tickets on a train that you'll have to drive four hours after the wedding to catch at two o'clock in the morning. Is all that correct?"

"It is."

"Call me in the morning," said Ludlow. "I'll get on it right away."

Two evenings later, I stood with my bride-to-be in Ludlow's house. He was my best man. His wife was maid of honor. Ludlow's six kids just sort of hung out and watched.

And the preacher. Do you remember crooked Indian agents in the old "B" westerns? That's what this guy looked like. He'd sell a Comanche a used car with a bad transmission in a heartbeat. He started the wedding by opening a Bible and uttering, "Well, according to this . . ."

It was quite obvious the man, who was wearing a toupee that looked a lot like a dead cat had been glued to the top of his head, was very inexperienced.

"Where did you find this guy?" I whispered to Ludlow as the preacher fumbled through his Bible looking for some verse he'd forgotten to mark.

"Who do you want on two days' notice?" my stepbrother replied. "Billy Graham?"

The wedding cake was a little dry, but I did think the black crepe paper Ludlow's wife had hung from the ceiling was a nice touch. "Lincoln's funeral probably looked a lot like this," I said to Ludlow.

We arrived at the Amtrak station in Savannah an hour before time. An old black man was sleeping on one of the benches. The only other person inside was the guy behind the ticket window.

"Train's two hours late," he said to me before

I could say anything to him. "Trouble out of New York."

"The train's two hours late," I said to my wife of five hours.

She had voiced some hesitancy to spending our honeymoon night—or early morning—on a train, but I mentioned a Clark Gable movie I'd seen once where he was on a train with some actress I can't remember and they seemed to enjoy it a lot. Besides, I also pointed out what an adventure riding the train would be. I think she muttered, "This is more adventure than I can stand," when I told her the train was two hours late, but I couldn't be sure because it was hard to hear her words over the snores of the old black man sleeping on the bench.

Then things got ugly.

I told the ticket agent my name and that my wife and I had a bedroom sleeper compartment booked to Fort Lauderdale.

He asked me our names.

I told him.

"Nope," he said. "Got no reservations for a sleeper under that name. You'll have to go coach."

I would have screamed, but the old black man seemed to be sleeping so peacefully, and I didn't want to alarm my wife any further.

Imagine us starting out in life in coach where

people who coughed a lot and carried their belongings in paper sacks would be located, and
there would be no way to lie down.

"There obviously is some sort of mistake," I
said to the ticket agent. "I know these reservations were made, and I must advise you also
that that woman standing over there and I were
just married, and if you don't come up with bedroom accommodations for us, we are still going
to get on the train and go up in coach and perform wild sexual acts on one another, which will
get us arrested, I am sure, but it also will disrupt
the entire train and be terrible public relations for
Amtrak when the story hits the papers."

Noticing the ticket agent was a frail man, who
wheezed and was probably one of the ten people in the world I could frighten with physical
violence, I also said, "Not only that, but before
I board the train, I am going to come behind this
window and kick you and punch you and pull out
what is left of your hair and call you and members of your family terrible names. Then I'm
going to spread the word over this entire community that you are a bed-wetting, homosexual
communist. Do you have that clear?"

The ticket agent began making telephone
calls. A few minutes later, he called me back to
the window.

"It's the best I can do, I swear," he said. "There isn't any bedroom space available, but I can get a roomette."

For those unfamiliar with railroad sleeping accommodations, a bedroom will sleep two. A roomette will sleep one. Barely. A roomette is sort of like your closet with an army cot in it. Two small dogs would have trouble carrying out the mating process in a roomette.

Then it hit me. Ludlow. He did this on purpose. He purposely didn't make us any train reservations because the man has a sick sense of humor and decided to play a very cruel practical joke on two crazy kids in love.

I took the roomette because I had no other choice, then I phoned Ludlow and awakened him and said. "This is really funny."

"What's funny?" he asked back as he emerged from his sleep.

"You not making us any train reservations," I said, my voice bristling with anger. "We've wound up with one roomette. One or both of us could get hurt trying to carry out a honeymoon-night function in that small a space."

"You think *that's* funny?" said Ludlow. "Let me tell you what else is funny. Remember the guy with the weird toupee who married you?"

"How could I ever forget him?" I said.

"He was no preacher. He runs the Texaco down the street. I got him to marry you in case you changed your mind about all this during the honeymoon and needed an out."

I never mentioned that part to my new wife, of course. I was so convinced only death would do us apart, I felt Ludlow's idea of doing me what he considered a favor was anything of the kind. We were married now, and there would be no turning back.

You *can* have sex in a roomette on a train hurtling through the Florida night, by the way, but I didn't have the nerve to tell the chiropractor how I actually injured my back.

We drove back to Atlanta a week later. On a Friday night. Fort Lauderdale had been great. We'd phoned our parents. Her dad sent champagne. But the minute I walked through the door of my apartment, where we had decided to live until we could find something larger, the feeling hit me.

I looked at my wife, and she still had those eyes—but why were there suddenly bars on my windows? And what was she doing with those leg irons? And I wondered if maybe I could say, "Listen, baby, I'm going out for a couple of hours. Okay?"

I could go down to Harrison's. I'd keep my ring

on, honest. I'd sit at the bar and have a drink. Alone. I wouldn't think of flirting. Of course I wouldn't. I was married. I'd be back before ten, and we'd make love and then watch an old black-and-white movie and go to sleep, me tight to her back, holding her as we slept.

But I didn't ask. Instead, I just sort of sat around and tried to ignore the feeling. But the son of a bitch wouldn't go away.

It came back every day. It started about noon and peaked at the cocktail hour.

I tried everything. I even found an apartment in the far suburbs and moved us there, miles from Harrison's and nights out on Peachtree Street. We made friends with married couples in our complex and had cookouts. We even got a dog.

I'd make margaritas, and we'd sit on the floor and drink them, and she'd sing "People" and "Leavin' on a Jet Plane" and "Me and Bobby McGee," and I'd join in on "City of New Orleans," a song about a train, and we'd laugh about our honeymoon night.

But that goddamn feeling wouldn't leave me.

Friday night. Stuck in the 'burbs. Cooking out with the Flournoys, who fought constantly.

I still loved her, but there was some hate for her, too. Why had she agreed to marry somebody like me? It was her fault. If she'd turned me down, I'd never have had to go through all this.

When I finally went crazy, I went *hard* and crazy. I gave in and went to Harrison's after work one afternoon. I scored and got home at two in the morning, and she cried because I hadn't called her. I lied, said I'd got into a poker game and had too many drinks and had simply forgotten to call her and promised I wouldn't do it again. But I did, two days later. I walked into Harrison's—with my ring in my coat pocket.

She cried a lot and the Flournoys broke up and our dog turned up pregnant. But at least I had being executive sports editor down. I had the people I wanted, and I went to a meeting of an organization called the Associated Press Sports Editors in New York. A guy from somewhere came up to me and talked about the graphics we were doing in Atlanta, and he said he liked the page 2 concept and wanted to talk more about it, and he said, "I really like what you guys are doing down in Atlanta."

I felt proud. Despite whatever would happen in my second marriage, I knew one thing would never change. I would never leave the *Atlanta Journal* sports department. Maybe when Bisher retired, I'd take over the column and give my replacement hell, but I would always be in that place.

Then Durwood McAllister, managing editor of the *Journal,* asked me to go to lunch with him one day. After he had eaten, he looked at me and said, "You've done a great job in sports, but I think you're ready to move up."

It would take me four years to get over that statement.

15

This was to be my fourth promotion in my young newspaper career. I had been promoted to sports editor of the *Athens Daily News,* to assistant sports editor of the *Atlanta Journal,* and then to executive sports editor of the *Journal.* Now, my managing editor, Durwood McAllister, a nice man everybody called "Mac," wanted me to leave sports and become associate city editor of the paper.

"I want you to do the same thing on the news side you did in sports," Mac announced.

I asked him what he meant by that.

"We've got too much government news and

not enough people news," he said. "I like the way you emphasize people on the sports pages."

Here was his plan: I would move to the news side and work under the present city editor, a rotund individual named Bob Johnson who was always writing me memos telling me what he thought I should do in sports.

"Call me buttinski . . ." his memos would begin, and then he would make his suggestions, all of which I ignored. It wasn't that Bob Johnson was a bad person or anything. I just figured I knew all there was to know about producing a sports section by that time, and if I wasn't going to listen to Bisher, I certainly wasn't going to listen to somebody who spent his days editing stories about dull public-service commission hearings.

After six months as associate city editor, Mac explained, I would have the news side operation down, and I would then become city editor, replacing Bob Johnson. I was not clear on what was going to happen to Bob Johnson at that point, but, to be honest, that wasn't my major concern.

My major concern was that I really wanted no part of the *Journal* news side, which seemed to have the imagination of a piece of Velveeta cheese.

The graphics were terrible. The front page always looked the same—as if all the type, heads, and photos were put into a shotgun and fired at the page. Very rarely was there anything on the front page that resembled any effort to give the reader something he or she could enjoy. Vietnam certainly was front-page news, but it seemed to me the *Journal* ran the same lead headline every day:

"BIG MARINE GUNS BLAST
HEAVY RED BUILDUP"

In fact, I distinctly remember the first edition coming up one day with the headlines transposed. It read:

"HEAVY RED BUILDUP
BIG MARINE GUNS BLAST"

There was one time, however, the news editor, who designed the front and decided what went where, did attempt to put something on the banner that didn't have to do with Vietnam or a new sewer system for some suburban Atlanta county.

Harold Lloyd, the comedian who made 'em howl back in the early days of movies by hanging off buildings, died at age 408 or something. The *Journal* news editor, Carl Newton, who was nearing retirement, was a big Harold Lloyd fan.

Maybe 15 percent of our readership had ever heard of Harold Lloyd. Carl put Harold Lloyd dying as the lead story in the first edition. (It went inside the paper in the second edition.)

We often laughed at the news side in the sports department. Some reporter actually did a series on the sewer system in one of the suburban counties that ran longer than a pregnancy. "Art Carney couldn't talk that long about sewers," Frank Hyland observed.

The sports pages and the news pages looked as though they were from two different newspapers. Our sports pages were tricked up with borders and big photo and type set in different widths. I was convinced that good layout was important. I smoked Marlboros because I liked the way the pack looked. I wanted my pages packaged well, too. In the last several years, newspaper graphics have changed dramatically. *USA Today* prompted practically every paper in the country to go to a large color weather map. And there are few papers left (*The New York Times* being one) that don't have color on the front page as well as modern graphics.

So Mac said, "I want you to do the same thing on the news side you've done in sports." But the problem was, I couldn't. The city editor certainly could assign stories and edit copy as he saw fit. But the city editor had nothing to do with the layout of the pages or where stories were placed. That was the news editor's job.

What I really wanted to be was executive news editor. I wanted control of it *all.* Give me the same control I had on sports, and in fact, I'd do the *exact* same thing on the news side I'd done in sports.

Nope. Associate city editor for six months, then city editor.

I didn't want it. I knew I didn't want it. I had the job I wanted, and I wanted to keep it for a long time. Going to the news side seemed like being transferred to Newark.

But what if I did eventually get to do what needed to be done—redesign the news section? What if it won plaudits? Would I then be able to one day move into a managing editor's job?

Power. Big-time power. And big bucks, too. I was convinced the managing editor made at least thirty thousand dollars a year—all the money on earth.

I took the job. I think the reason I did was because of a flaw in my personality that makes me never want to disappoint anybody. I hadn't wanted to disappoint my mother, which was the primary reason I never stole a hubcap or hung out at the pool hall and always studied hard. I hadn't wanted to leave writing and go to the slot for Minter, either, but I didn't want to disappoint him. And Mac was a nice man. He was impressed by my work. I didn't want to disappoint him, either.

The new associate city editor of the *Atlanta Journal* started work Monday morning at six-thirty. By eight, I knew I had made a horrible mistake.

I wasn't supposed to tell anybody I'd be moving up to city editor in six months, but I think Bob Johnson knew something was up. He didn't exactly welcome me with open arms.

I sat on the city-desk rim. Johnson was at the head of it. Three other assistant city editors were seated around the rim. I made four. Bob Johnson handed me a story from the education reporter. It had something to do with an important Board of Education meeting coming up. I read it. It was boring. I repaired a little grammar and punctuation, but that was about it. The story went into the city-desk box, then a copy person picked it up and sent it down to the composing room.

Bob Johnson handed me another story. It was about some ordinance the city council had passed. Does anybody really read this stuff?

Carl Newton, the news editor, sat at a desk behind me. Charles Salter, the photo editor, who also wrote about fishing on the outdoor page, sat next to him. What will follow soon is the dialogue they had my first day, deciding on a photograph for the front page of the *Atlanta Journal.*

In sports, we chose photos based on several criteria:

* Which photo best tells the story of the article it accompanies?
* Which photo could simply stand on its own? Say you got something off the wire that was unusual, a jockey falling off a horse, a football player turned completely upside down by a hard tackle, a collision in an auto race. The story that accompanied it may not be that important, but the photo was so unusual, it would tell a story of its own.
* What photo would reproduce well? We tried to stay away from anything that would come out fuzzy or in any way difficult to distinguish. Newspaper photographic reproduction has become much better in the past ten years, so this is less important now. But we are talking nearly two decades ago here.
* Was the photo a cliché? Basketball arm-

pits, baseball player slides into second,
football piles of laundry, golfer out of the
sand trap. Clichés all.

It wasn't like that on the news side, however.
The dialogue:

NEWTON: Cholly, get me a two-by-six for the
front.
SALTER: Here's an interesting photograph,
Carl. Look and see what you think.
NEWTON: Dammit, Cholly. I don't have the
time to look.
SALTER: Well, Carl, how about this one? I
think it'll reproduce quite well, and look how
the rays of the sun are pouring down on the
water.
NEWTON: Dammit, Cholly. I don't care what
the damn thing looks like. Just give me a
two-by-six and go fishing.

What would have happened if during World
War II Newton had asked Salter for a two-by-six
and refused to look? Salter might have throw
out the Iwo Jima flag-raising for a picture of a
guy holding a fish.

Newspapers don't call photo captions by that
name. They are called "cutlines." I was a strong

believer in good cutlines. I liked *Newsweek*'s style. Let's say *Newsweek* was carrying a story about Leonid Brezhnev. They might include a photo of the late Soviet premier making a speech to the Politburo. But *Newsweek* would never write a cutline that read, *"Soviet premier Brezhnev makes a speech."* It should be quite obvious to the person looking at the photograph that Brezhnev, with his mouth open behind a podium was, in fact, doing just that. What *Newsweek* would do was identify the person in the photo, follow that with a colon, and then have a line that makes reference to the main thrust of the accompanying article. Maybe:

"BREZHNEV: *Are the Soviets softening?*"

Over in sports, we all awaited the spring cliché photo—the picture of a college coed sitting under a tree on campus enjoying the recent warm weather on the news side.

The cutline would always say: *"Agnes Scott student sits under tree on campus and enjoys the recent warm weather."*

I can see that. You don't have to tell me in a cutline. Give me this:

"SPRING FOR A DAY: *Agnes Scott student greets that lucky old sun.*"

Frank Hyland and I were the overseers of cut-lines in sports. We would cringe if a bad one got past the desk. Take something like Jack Nick-laus hitting out of a trap on the second hole at Augusta National during the Masters.

BAD CUTLINE: *"Jack Nicklaus hits out of sand trap on second hole at Augusta during third round of Masters."*

IMPROVED CUTLINE FOR THE NEXT EDITION: "MR. SANDMAN: *Jack Nicklaus finds his way off the beach and into Masters third-round lead*."

When the Braves actually shocked the world by winning the 1969 Western Division pennant in the National League, Minter and I worked all night putting out the first edition for the next day. He had me write the cutlines for the many photos.

Our main photo on page 1 was a picture of Brave outfielder Rico Carty, who called himself "the Beeg Boy," pouring champagne over the head of Atlanta mayor Ivan Allen, who had been the main force behind getting the Braves moved from Milwaukee to Atlanta.

My cutline said something like:

"BUBBLING OVER: *The Beeg Boy and the mayor celebrate the miracle on Capitol Ave-nue."*

When the paper came up, Minter looked it over and said to me, "You're a great cutline writer."

I hope whoever writes my obituary makes a note of that.

* * *

After the first edition was finished on the *Journal* city desk, the next order of business was to decide what we wanted the only female member to go and fetch us for breakfast. Today, of course, they would look at us and say, "Go get your own goddamned doughnuts." But we're still in the early seventies here, so each morning she dutifully went for doughnuts, sausage biscuits, and even an occasional box of Krystal cheeseburgers, which we came to know affectionately as "gutbombers." After we ate, the first edition would come up, a few changes would be made for the final, I would edit a few more stories about a county commission meeting here and a mayoral press conference there, and I would be on the tennis court by one-thirty.

I tried a couple of things.

I was reading a small wire story in the first edition. It was about a Georgia man who had been found shot dead in front of his estranged girlfriend's house in Atlanta. The man turned out to be a high school classmate of mine. I hadn't seen him since we graduated in 1964.

I called a friend back home to ask if he knew anything about the circumstances. He informed me there was a lot of talk around town about our former classmate going around saying about how he had been involved with the CIA and had been heavily decorated during the Vietnam War. "Nobody is real sure," he said, "if anything of that is true, or if he is lying or suffering from delusions of grandeur."

I assigned a reporter to do the funeral. It turned out to be one amazing story. There was a friend at the funeral who broke up during the service and finally spilled the beans about what had happened.

My classmate hadn't been decorated in Vietnam, and certainly had no connections with the CIA. He had made his stories up apparently to impress the folks back home, and his girlfriend, who had eventually jilted him.

He had decided to try to win her back by having her find him with a bullet wound in her front yard. He would tell her he had been shot by the CIA because, as the old movies used to say, he "knew too much."

The friend would drive. My classmate, upon

nearing the girl's house, would take a small-caliber pistol and put a large paperback novel next to his abdomen. He would then fire a bullet through the novel. He figured the novel would slow the bullet sufficiently so that it would not be a serious enough wound to kill him or inflict real damage. But he would be shot, and his girlfriend would feel sorry for her brave lover and take him back.

He fired the shot. The friend drove to the front of the girl's house, took the paperback away so nothing looked amiss, and my classmate rolled out onto her lawn. That's where he bled to death.

What a story! I lobbied for front-page play.

I said to Mac, "We *need* stories like this. It's what we looked for in sports. If we just throw it inside with no graphics, it will be lost."

I knew that would be what would happen to the story—my first on the city side—if I didn't go directly to Mac. Carl Newton would set it in one column, put a 36-point head on it, and bury it on 8-A.

I managed to get a photo of the dead man from his family. Then I managed to get Mac to allow me to lay it out on the top of page 1. Newton could fill in the bottom.

I blew the picture up to two columns. I set the story in two-column, indented type so I could set it off with a border.

My headline read: "DEATH FOILS A LOVER'S CIA HOAX."

You *have* to read a story under that sort of headline, don't you? You put in "death" and you put in "lover," and you put in "CIA," and it's a cinch.

Minter called down from the *Constitution.* "You have anything to do with page one today?"

I told him the whole story.

"We missed it," he said. "Helluva job."

I thought, Maybe Mac will see now. Maybe he'll go ahead and make me city editor and let me lay out page 1, and this will be fun after all.

But nobody said much about the story at the *Journal.*

One day, President Carter decided to grant amnesty to the draft dodgers who had fled to Canada during Vietnam. And who happened to be in Montreal with the Braves? Hyland.

I didn't ask anybody, I just called Frank at the Queen Elizabeth Hotel in Montreal, woke him up at eight o'clock, and said, "Frank, how about one for old times' sake?"

"What the hell do you want?" he replied. "I didn't get to bed until four."

"Listen to me, Frank, I really need this. Carter has granted amnesty to the draft dodgers in Canada. Go find some and get their reactions. Find out how long they've been away, what they've been doing, and how they feel about having a chance to go home."

I had to promise to buy him a case of Heineken. Four hours later, the Western Union telex fires up in the wire room. It's Frank with a great piece. He found a bar—naturally—where American draft dodgers were celebrating the news. He sent back a remarkable human interest story. I got that piece on page 1, too, and I thought, Am I a great scrambler or what? The news breaks, and I notice the Braves are in Montreal, and I get our guy there to do a firsthand, exclusive piece.

The next day, Bob Johnson says, "Let's go get a cup of coffee."

We get the coffee and sit down in the break room.

"You made a mistake yesterday with the amnesty story," he said.

"What are you talking about?" I asked.

"You should never have gotten Hyland to do

that story. It sent a message to the news staff that you're still hung up on sports and want to use sportswriters to do stories from the real world. It wasn't good for morale."

I sort of gave up after that. Maybe if I hung around ten or fifteen more years, I might wind up with some control over the news side, but I didn't want ten or fifteen more years of somebody telling me I'd made a mistake by improvising and getting a firsthand, human account of a major story. First, I had figured there was no way I'm ever going to get permission to send a news staffer to Montreal. Resources were a little slim in those days. Second, I know Frank's got all day because the Braves are playing a night game and all he would do is sleep until noon anyway. Third, I knew Frank, regardless of how much he would complain about having to get out of bed, went after any story full bore, and fourth, I knew Minter would read the story and ask his desk, "Why in the hell didn't we call Minshew [Wayne, the *Constitution*'s baseball writer] and get him to do it first?"

The competitiveness was still in me.

I lasted six months. There was no way I could ask to go back to sports. The new executive sports editor, Don Boykin, was quite capable.

Kay and I were living in a suburban apartment

complex by then, and she had taken a job working in the resident manager's office. What she got paid was we didn't have to pay any rent.

We didn't have many expenses. There was a car payment. (I had bought a new 1973 Pontiac Grand Prix, blue with white seat covers. The '68 Cutlass, as happened often with my cars, sort of fell apart. The glove box wouldn't shut anymore, I couldn't pick up FM on my radio, and the ashtray was full, so I traded it in.)

I also now had a part-time correspondent job with *Sports Illustrated.* They paid me around eight thousand dollars a year.

So I decided I would become a free-lance writer. I didn't know much about how to become a free-lance writer, but it is one of those occupations you can go into just by saying you are one.

The first time anybody asked me what I did, I answered, "I'm a free-lance writer." That made me a free-lance writer. I didn't mention I hadn't sold anything yet or didn't have an assignment yet, but what difference did that make?

There are a lot of occupations like that. Screenwriters fall into the same category. So do artists, poets, midnight gynecologists (otherwise known as "pickup artists"), environmentalists, adventurers, and political analysts.

I met a guy at a party one night, and he had

a lot to say about a lot of things, and I was curious as to what he did. "Are you in the media?" I asked him.

"No," he said, "I'm a political analyst."

Later, I found out he was unemployed and just went to parties and had a lot to say.

It's sort of like Jesse Jackson. Jesse Jackson is the Reverend Jesse Jackson, but I don't think he has a church. Nor does he go around with a tent, healing people. Jesse Jackson is basically a free-lance "black leader," as in "black leader Jesse Jackson arrived in town today to address," etc., etc.

Who *pays* Jesse Jackson? Somebody must. On Fridays, where does he go to get his check? Who signs it? Who buys his expensive suits? Who pays for the chartered Lear?

So here I am, the free-lance writer.

Mac tried to talk me into staying at the paper. I really didn't get into the fact I saw no future ahead of me. I just said I'd always wanted to be a free-lance writer, and I walked out of the *Atlanta Journal-Constitution* building six years after I had walked in as a new employee.

For about the first three months, being a free-lance writer was a lot of fun. I would get up around ten in the morning, drink coffee, eat breakfast, and read the paper. Around noon, I would ease over to the DeKalb County Tennis Center and play tennis until it got dark.

I found out something interesting during that period. If you don't have a real job, you can save a lot of money. First, I didn't need to buy any more shirts, slacks, ties, or suits. All I ever wore were tennis shoes and tennis shirts. I ate lunch at the tennis center. Hot dog and Coke. Dollar and a quarter. No expensive downtown lunches. I didn't have to drive downtown anymore, so I saved a lot on gasoline money.

I continued to do the *SI* work, but I was yet to break in as a paid free-lance writer. I did buy one of these writers' guides that gives you the name of every magazine on earth and tells you how much they pay for free-lance material. There was an Atlanta Falcons football player who was a big deal in the Fellowship of Christian Athletes. I sent off a letter to some Baptist publication suggesting I do a piece on him. I never heard back, and later I found out some out-of-town group had wanted this player to speak to a high school FCA group, and he had asked the guy who called him if he would get him a hooker while he was in town.

I was putting a lot of spin on my second serve by now, and my backhand volley, which had been very weak, was improving.

Around the fourth month, I sort of got the feeling like you do the fourth or fifth day you're out of school sick. It's fun to start with. You get to sleep late, and your mother feeds you in bed and brings you ginger ale. But then you start missing your friends and what's going on at school. It's amazing how quickly you can get well when you reach that point.

I had stayed in touch with Minter. Finally, after five months as an unpaid free-lance writer, I sort of hinted I might be interested in coming to work for him on the *Constitution.*

We agreed almost completely on what a newspaper should have in it and what it should look like. So Minter hired me and gave me one of the great titles—special-assignments editor. I wasn't sure what I was supposed to do, and neither was he. We would make it up as we went along.

Durwood McAllister, so I heard, believed my leaving the *Journal* had been a ploy cooked up by Minter and me, so he could get me to the *Constitution.* It wasn't. Jim just said to me, "You belong back at the paper. I'll find a way to get you back."

The first job Minter gave me as special as-signments editor was to improve the *Constitution* sports section. The guys over there loved that, especially the executive sports editor, my rival for so many years, Mickey McCarthy. He saw my piddling with his section as an insult, not to mention a signal that I would eventually replace him.

All I really wanted to do was clean up their layout a little, get a little more organization going, and stop veteran Charlie Roberts, a wonderful man, from writing such things as ". . . he chortled with a mock shudder," whatever that meant. Wonderful men can still write some strange things.

There was also a famous Charlie Roberts lead.

Henry Aaron had hit one out against Cincinnati, but outfielder Pete Rose jumped above the fence and caught the ball momentarily. But when he slammed against the fence, the ball came out of his glove and was falling back into the playing field. Rose somehow got back to his feet and leapt and caught the ball before it hit the ground, saving the game.

Charlie wrote, "Pete Rose will tell you the best defense for de fence is defense." It's not "somewhat marred," but it's close.

So I piddled here and there with the sports section, and then Minter sent me to the features section to work on it.

The veteran television writer was about to re-
tire. He had one of the great tricks for getting out
of the office early. Each day, he would wear a
coat and a hat in, and he would hang them on
a rack in the features department.

I could never find this guy, but I'd see his hat
and coat were hanging in the office and I would
figure he was around somewhere. I'd tell myself
I'd catch up with him later, then I'd forget about
whatever it was I wanted to ask him or get him
to do.

What I found out was that he had an extra
coat and hat he kept in his desk. When he
wanted to leave early, he would wait until nobody was watching, then he would put the
dummy coat and hat on the rack, put his other
hat and coat on, and split. I would have done
something about this, but Minter said, "He
doesn't have but three months to go. Might as
well forget about it."

There were two brilliant young writers in the
Constitution features department. One was
Gregory Jaynes, who wrote a marvelous series
on the North Georgia mountains. He later
moved on to *The New York Times.* Art Harris
was on the staff, too. Art was in his early twenties, and he had some sort of condition that
caused all his hair to fall out. Art didn't have *any*

hair on his head, nor did he have any eyebrows. In fact, he looked exactly like Telly Savalas, so everywhere he went, people called him "Kojak." I had the feeling Art was going on to great things in journalism.

I once assigned Art a story on pigeons. "Pigeons?" he asked.

"Pigeons are all over big cities," I said. "Where do they come from? Why do they seem to like cities? Why do they seem to like statutes? What do they eat? Can we eat them?"

Art did a great pigeon story. His best anecdote never got into the paper, however.

Jim Kennedy, heir to the Cox family throne (they owned the papers and Lord knows what else), was fresh out of college and was working at the papers to learn the business. Jim loved hunting, and he had been catching pigeons on the roof of the *Journal-Constitution* building to use in training his hunting dogs. We figured, A) that was illegal and B) even if it wasn't, we ought not to put it in our pigeon story.

Art went on to *The Washington Post.* He is the man who brought down Jimmy Swaggart in *Penthouse* and the one who also got a lot of the goods on Jim and Tammy Faye Bakker. He remains a hero of mine.

I was also involved in two special series we

did at the *Constitution.* The first, written by political editor Bill Shipp, was called "City in Crisis." Atlanta's politics had been almost completely taken over by blacks. But the downtown white power structure had all the money—so there was a stalemate between the two groups.

Minter assigned me to do the graphics. The series was to start in the Sunday combined edition, which was put out by the *Journal* staff. I had to get special dispensation from Executive Editor Bill Fields to let me put the series on the top of page 1, design it as I wanted, and then to give word to the *Journal* not to touch it. He did.

We also did a series entitled "The Welfare Mess." Good series. I went down to Georgia's southern coast to McIntosh County, which had the state's lowest per capita income, to see how they were dealing with welfare. I sent back a story about a man I found living under an I-95 river bridge with his dog. The county welfare caseworker had told me she had tried to get the man to accept welfare, but he wouldn't.

I parked my car and climbed down under the bridge. The man said he didn't need any welfare because he had the bridge to keep the rain off, and he had a boat from which he could catch fish to keep him in food. I offered him five bucks. He wouldn't take it. I offered him half a pack of

Marlboros. He took it. I went back to my room at the posh Cloisters, the five-diamond resort on Georgia's exclusive Sea Island, and wrote about the man, his dog, and what it was like to live under a bridge.

A devastating tornado hit Atlanta while I was at the *Constitution.* I handled the coverage and did the layouts, including a picture page.

The Vietnam War ended when I was at the *Constitution.* I put out that section, too.

But I was getting antsy again. Mostly, what I did was sit in Minter's office and talk to him. He complained, "Not many of 'em around here have any idea of what I'm talking about."

I got a little bored and frustrated. I didn't know where all this was leading to. Then I got an assignment about an Atlanta sports artist, Wayland Moore, from *Sports Illustrated.* I got the writing bug again. Six months after rejoining the *Constitution,* in the spring of 1975, I was a freelance writer again.

I also hooked up again with Norman Arey, who had left the newspaper to work for Lamar Hunt's fledgling World Championship of Tennis. Norman traveled to each tournament all over the country and had a myriad of duties under his title as public-relations director.

I traveled with him to a couple of tournaments.

Norman had gone bald at this point and had a five-hundred-dollar hairpiece. I was at a tournament in Philadelphia with him. Sunday night, we took the train to Richmond for the next week's tournament. We both lingered in the lounge car too long and took ourselves a couple of naps. When I awakened, Norman's five-hundred-dollar rug had fallen from his head. The lounge car attendant was sweeping it and the other trash away when I stopped him and saved Norman's five-hundred-dollar hair.

Norman even got me a couple of jobs. A professional women's tournament was coming to Atlanta's Omni, and the promoter hired Norman to handle PR. Norman then hired me to do the public address for the tournament, five nights for three hundred dollars. The third night, I finally got the name of a new Czech women's player down right. *Nah-Vrah-Tee-Lo-Vah.*

Then Norman called one day and said he had us a week's work at a local Atlanta public-relations firm, and it would pay us each five hundred dollars. Norman had left the WCT by then because he was never at home with his family and Peg. I knew very little about public-relations work, but there were few things I wouldn't have done then for five hundred big ones.

Here was the deal:

The PR firm, Ball, Cohn & Weyman, had two

new clients. One was a new Legends of Tennis tournament, featuring aging players like Ken Roswell and Rod Laver, that was coming to Atlanta.

The other client was Atlanta's Six Flags Over Georgia, which had just constructed a giant parachute-jump ride it wanted to promote. Norman took the Legends job because he had all the right tennis experience. I got the parachute-jump ride.

What we were supposed to do, Norman and I, was to call media outlets all over the South to seek a little publicity. So I started calling newspaper cronies. I'd give them my pitch, and they would listen, and then they would all ask the same question: "What the hell are you doing pushing some dumb carnival ride for a PR firm?"

I said I was in it for the money. They all said to me, "You belong back at the newspaper."

No way that was going to happen. I had already quit twice.

Monday: I don't get a single confirmed plan for a parachute-jump story.

Tuesday: I have a great idea. Why don't I try to get a job with the *New York Times* Atlanta bureau, covering Deep South sports? The *Times* had just sent a man to the West Coast to cover sports out there. It seemed perfect.

The trouble was, I didn't know anybody with

The New York Times. I made a couple of no-luck calls on the parachute jump, and then I remembered Jack Semmes.

I had attended a seminar for sports editors at the American Press Institution at Columbia University in New York City. I met Semmes there. He was a fellow southerner and was deputy sports editor of the Associated Press, headquartered in New York.

Jack and I became close friends. He later left New York to become dean of the journalism school at Auburn University. He would know somebody on *The New York Times.* So I called him and asked if he could get me in the front door.

"Let me make a few calls," he said.

Tuesday afternoon: To hell with the parachute jump and the five hundred dollars. I wasn't born to be a hack. Jack Semmes called me back. He told me if I really wanted the *Times,* he would help me. But he also said I could move to New York and get on the desk of the AP sports department. And then he said, "There are two sports editor's jobs open, too—the *Philadelphia Daily News* needs a guy, and so does the Chicago *Sun Times.*"

"I really want to write, Jack," I said. "I'm not moving to New York to sit on a desk, I hate

Philadelphia, and I've never been to Chicago, but I hear the weather's bad."

He said he'd get back to me on the *Times.* I snuck out of the PR office and went and played tennis.

Wednesday morning: I am sitting at my desk at the PR office, thinking. Chicago. That might be pretty exciting. The Cubs and the White Sox, the Bears and Bulls and Black Hawks and Notre Dame and the Fighting Illini. What's a little cold weather? And how cold could it be, anyway?

Chicago had a proud newspaper heritage, that was a plus. Ben Hecht and *The Front Page.* There were three newspapers there. One company owned two, the *Chicago Daily News* and the *Sun-Times,* but there was a battle with the *Chicago Tribune.* Maybe I could convince them to let me run the sports department *and* write on occasion. It was too late to go back to the *Journal* or the *Constitution,* and I just had a feeling the *Times* thing would never work out.

I picked up the phone at Ball, Cohn & Weyman, and called the Chicago *Sun-Times.* I asked for the managing editor's office. It's ten-thirty Wednesday morning.

I told the managing editor's secretary I was calling about the vacant sports editor's job. The managing editor, Ralph Otwell, came on the line.

I told him who I was, and I told him my background. He asked if I knew Reg Murphy, the former *Constitution* editor of kidnapping fame. I said I did. He said he and Murphy had been Neiman Fellows together at Harvard. Ralph Otwell took my number and said he'd be back to me in an hour or so.

I never really asked him, but I think he called Reg Murphy to ask about me. I assume Reg gave me a good recommendation because Ralph Otwell called me back from Chicago. "Can you be here Friday for lunch and an interview?" he asked. "We'll put you up in our suite at the Executive Inn."

"See you Friday," I said.

I walked out of my office and told the first guy I came to—I can't remember if it was Ball, Cohn, or Weyman—thanks, but I'd had enough of the PR game, and that they didn't owe me any money. I figured they were going to pay for the phone call to Chicago, and that would make us even.

I talked to Kay about Chicago. She seemed excited. I think she thought if she could get me out of Atlanta, I might become a better husband.

How to get to Chicago without flying? I was heavy into another nonflying stage at this point. I wasn't going to ride a bus to an interview with the Chicago *Sun-Times,* however, and it seemed too far to drive. I decided to take the train.

There was only one way to do that. I would have to drive to Birmingham and catch Amtrak's Miami-to-Chicago Floridian. It was a three-hour drive to Birmingham. I boarded the train at three in the afternoon on Thursday. I arrived in Chicago's Union Station at eight the next morning, on a pleasant October morning, 1975.

I took a cab to the Executive Inn, took a shower, ate some breakfast, then went and bought a copy of the morning *Sun-Times* to look over the sports section.

It was a mess. The layout was terrible. The headlines and cutlines were awful. This was the Big Time?

But I also thought, This will be a piece of cake. Give me a layout pad and half a day, and I can make this thing look 100 percent better.

I went to see Ralph Otwell at the *Sun-Times,* across the street and the Chicago River on Wacker Drive. He was an older, soft-spoken man who smoked a pipe. He seemed quite harmless. "I want you to also meet and talk with our editor, Jim Hoge," he said.

What editor? At the *Journal-Constitution,* the managing editor did the hiring and firing. All the editor was in charge of was the editorial pages.

The three of us, Jim Hoge, Ralph Otwell, and I, went to lunch. Hoge scared the hell out of me. A strikingly handsome man, he was just off a cover of *GQ.* He had severely punishing eyes that were hard to meet. He was no-nonsense.

"Do you know our sports section?" he asked.

"I saw a copy this morning."

"What would you do to improve it?"

"The layout is terrible."

"Why?"

"The stories should square off vertically. There's too much clamor on the pages. It doesn't look like there's been any thought into what to play where. You don't play your photographs large enough, and the headlines and cutlines show little or no imagination."

"What do you think of the writing?"

"Poor. I didn't understand a word of what Bill Gleason [columnist] had to say. And where did you get this guy Lacey J. Banks, who covers the Bulls? His story personified 'Offense' and 'Defense' and then he made up a dialogue between them. What in the hell happened in the game?"

Hoge never flinched. He offered no defense for the section, nor did he say he agreed with anything I had said. Ralph Otwell lighted his pipe. I was covered in sweat.

We went back to Hoge's office at the *Sun-Times.* I had brought along some examples of my layouts. Some he liked. I had brought along the special section I had done of Henry Aaron. He didn't like that.

"You mentioned clamor," he said. "Look how clamored this is."

I tried to explain that I'd done the best with the space I had been given. He did not seem impressed.

"We'll get back to you," Jim Hoge said to me.

I got back on the train at nine that evening and arrived in Birmingham at three Saturday afternoon. I went to Harrison's and met Hudspeth. I got home at one. Kay was worried. "Why didn't you call?" she asked me. I didn't know the answer to that one.

I made up my mind that if Jim Hoge offered me the job, I would take it. I would move to Chicago, Illinois, and out of the state of Georgia for the first time in twenty-two years. I was twenty-eight at the time. I had been born in Georgia, spent a few years out of the state with my father, being transferred to various army bases. Then I spent eleven years growing up in Moreland, Georgia, four years at the University of Georgia, and then seven working in Atlanta.

I loved Georgia. I took up for Georgia. I had a

Georgia public school education, I had a Georgia accent, and it burned me when someone from the North would run down the South, and Georgia in particular. I hated it when New Yorkers would ask, upon hearing me speak, "Where are you from? Texas?"

"No," I'd say. "Georgia."

And then they would say, with a laugh, "Well, shut yo' mouth, you-all."

That wasn't funny. In the first place, nobody had said "Shut yo' mouth" in the South in a hundred years, and Yankees were always screwing up "you-all."

"You-all" was never used in the singular sense. If I were addressing one person, I would never ask "Would 'you-all' like something to drink?" I would just use "you." And if I were addressing two or more persons, I wouldn't say, "Would you-all like something to drink?" I would use the contraction, "y'all."

There was a lot of other stuff. Yankees called Cokes "pop." Why? Because it was supposed to go "pop" when the top came off? It doesn't go "pop." It goes "whoosh." What you say, to be *proper,* is, "I'll have a Co-Coler."

Coca-Cola's home is in Atlanta, and if we wanted to say "Co-Coler," we could. I wasn't going to tell a New Yorker he had to say "hot dawg" instead of "hot doo-ug."

I was raised on southern food. My dress was traditional (they call it "preppie" now). Yankees tend to dress funny. They wear black socks and sandals with their shorts, for one thing. You can pick out a Yankee tourist in Panama City, Florida, in a heartbeat.

I always felt Georgians and southerners were looked down upon. Hey, I wanted to say, we've got paved roads now, too, and indoor plumbing.

And there were the racist things. If you were from the South, you were automatically expected to say "nigger" about every other word.

I really had no racial agenda at that point in my life. To be honest, I had been so involved in the newspaper business, Vietnam had sailed by me, too, with the exception of losing one fraternity brother and a high school classmate, neither of whom I was particularly close to. I simply figured black people should be able to eat in any restaurant or stay in any hotel they pleased. It was fine with me black students shared classrooms with me as a student at Georgia.

I had only worked with two blacks in the newspaper business. Minter had a part-time stringer named Alfred Johnson who covered Atlanta University (Morris Brown, Morehouse, and Clark College) sports. He was paid on a per-game basis and had another job with the Atlanta boys' club. I sort of liked Alfred, but I admit it didn't go any further than that.

In my last summer as executive sports editor, Mac had hired a black reporter named Chet Fuller, who came with impressive credentials out of college. Mac didn't have an opening for him on the news staff at that point. One wouldn't come open until September. But the paper occasionally hired journalism students for summer internships. Mac gave me Chet Fuller, who would be my summer intern and then move to the news side.

Chet Fuller was talented and had tremendous potential as a writer. He also had a great sense of humor. We were sitting on the rim one day, and Kent Mitchell, who had replaced Priit Vesiland as outdoor editor, asked Chet where he lived. Chet told him. Kent said, "I don't live far from there."

Chet said, "There goes the neighborhood."

Chet went on to write a critically acclaimed book, to become an editorial-page columnist, and is now an assistant managing editor at the Atlanta newspapers.

Ten days after my interview in Chicago, Jim Hoge called me in Atlanta and offered me the job as executive sports editor of the *Sun-Times.* It would pay $28,000 annually.

I accepted. Kay and I immediately drove to Chicago and found a top floor, two-bedroom apartment in a four-story building for $425 a month. Apartments in Atlanta of the same sort would have gone for maybe $250. But I was making $28,000 a year, remember?

The apartment was on Chicago near the North Side, on Arlington Place, just off busy Clark Street, eight blocks south of Wrigley Field, where the Cubs played their home games, all in the daytime. In 1975, nobody would have thought of putting lights up at Wrigley Field.

We were close to Lincoln Avenue, the only street in Chicago that runs diagonally. The Biograph Theatre, where John Dillinger was fingered by the Woman in Red and shot down by the G-men, was still in operation, showing nostalgia movies. There were clubs on Lincoln Avenue where you could walk in with your guitar and get up and sing. Bette Midler had been discovered in one of those places on Lincoln Avenue.

We were close to Lincoln Park and the Lincoln Park Zoo. We were only a few blocks from Lake Michigan and the Oak Street Beach.

I had given away all of my dog Chauncey's puppies. I found a good home for her, too. No dogs in our new apartment.

I was to report to the *Sun-Times* on November 8, 1975, a Monday. On Saturday, a beautiful, bright autumn day in Atlanta, we left Casa Loma apartments and headed north on highway 41 toward Cartersville, Georgia, where we could pick up I-75 North. The last traffic light between Atlanta and Chicago in 1975 was in Cartersville, Georgia, just before you hit the interstate. The route was 75 to Chattanooga, 24 to Nashville, 65 to Gary, Indiana, and into Chicago on the Dan Ryan Expressway.

I started having my doubts at that last traffic light in Cartersville. Was I doing the right thing here? Whom did I know in Chicago? Nobody. What if I were a flop? What would I do then? Come back to Atlanta and beg Minter to hire me for the third time? What if I absolutely hated Chicago? What if the people were rude to me because I was from the South? Where could I get a sliced pork-pig barbecue sandwich and good fried chicken? What about the crime? I used to watch *The Untouchables* all the time on television. Was that an accurate depiction of Chicago street life?

Hoge seemed tough. But was he also mean? Could I work for him? What about the sports staff? Hoge had told me it was my section, and I could do what I wanted to do. There would be shake-ups. There would be assignment changes. Would the staff resent my age and the changes I would make and the fact I was from the South?

Where would I find a great bar like Harrison's? What if I went in there and didn't meet anybody? Nothing worse than sitting in a bar and not knowing anybody. Would I miss my friends Hyland and Hudspeth and the other men I had sported with?

Chattanooga. I've been quiet for an hour.

"What are you thinking about?" asked my wife.

"Nothing," I said. A lie. I was thinking about a million things.

Nashville. What if something happened between Kay and me? What if I wound up alone and divorced in Chicago with no Harrison's to fall back on?

Louisville. My stomach hurt.

Gary, Indiana. God, what an ugly place.

Chicago and the Dan Ryan Expressway. Six lanes on each side, trains running down the middle. It's raining. I'm looking for the Fullerton Avenue exit, but it's dark and it's raining and I can't see a thing and people are whizzing past me at seventy miles an hour bumper-to-bumper.

We find the Fullerton exit. We find our new apartment. We're both too tired to unload anything. I bring up a six-pack I'd had iced down in the car. I drank it and went to sleep. I had my first Chicago nightmare that very first night. I dreamed I was on the Dan Ryan Expressway and all the other cars were being driven by the Grim Reaper and there were no exits, and I had to drive on and on in total exhaustion and I'm halfway to Des Moines when I finally wake up.

Nightmare No. 1. Others, many others, would follow.

16

First day. November 10, 1975. It's still relatively warm in Chicago. The high is in the 60s that day.

I have on a blue blazer, khaki slacks, white shirt, red tie, and a pair of Bass Weejuns. I look like I'm going through fraternity rush at the University of Georgia.

I leave the car for Kay. I took the Clark Street bus. It lets me off near the *Sun-Times* office, which is just a few steps from the rival *Tribune.*

The sports department is on the fourth floor. The first time I had seen it, my feathers had drooped. There was no clearly marked separation between the sports department and the news side—just five rows of desks sitting quite close together, three abreast. My desk was next to the sports rim, which looked exactly like the one at the *Journal.* I had always wanted my own office at the *Journal,* but there was only one in the sports department, which was separated from the news side by a waist-high partition, and Bisher had occupied it.

I take the elevator to the fourth floor and stopped and tell Jim Hoge's secretary I had arrived.

"He'll be with you in a minute," she said.

I waited *thirty* minutes. Finally, Hoge walked out, dressed impeccably as always, and stuck out his hand. He smiled and said, "Welcome."

He had called a meeting of the sports department to introduce me as the new executive sports editor. The old sports editor (Jim Mullen) believe it or not, was going to stay on until he retired in six months—and would keep the title. Hoge had decided to replace him as the department head, but to let him stay on until his retire-

ment and cover the Chicago Bears football
team.

Here was my staff:

Bill Gleason: Columnist.
Tom Fitzpatrick: Columnist
Jerome Holtzman: Baseball writer
Joe Goddard: Baseball writer
Bob Pille: College writer
Joe Agrella: Horse racing (turf) writer
Dave Van Dyke: General assignment, tennis
Lenny Ziehm: Desk and golf
Marvin Weinstein: Desk, auto racing, and
Guild steward
Joe LaPointe: Desk and general assign-
ment
Eddie Gold: Desk, hockey writer
Dave Manthey: High schools
Don Edwards: Desk, some layout
Harold Newchurch: Clerk, racing results, and
handicapper
Bob Langer: Photographer
Emil Stubits: Makeup editor, assigned to the
composing room
Seymour Shub: My assistant
Lacey J. Banks: Basketball and once-a-
week columnist

Let's go over them again in more detail:

—Gleason: Veteran, mid-forties, maybe. Irishman with a temper. Loud, always gesturing with his hands. Cigar always in his mouth. He had asked the paper for more filing cabinets years earlier, but he had been refused. He vowed to pile every piece of mail that came to him on his desk until he got the new space. I couldn't see him over the ten-year-old mountain of paper. I knew he was in the office and at his desk only by the blue smoke from his cigar that rose over the pile.

He was from the South Side of Chicago, and South Siders were a proud group. He didn't like anything about the North Side, particularly the Cubs. He preferred the South Side White Sox. He often wrote in parables. I read Gleason for three years, and I'm not certain I ever had any idea what he was trying to say. I often wondered if it was just me, or whether the readers were puzzled, too.

—Fitzpatrick: Also Irish. They called him "Fitz." I would say late thirties. He had won a Pulitzer Prize by running with the gangs the night of the Democratic party riots in 1968 and had filed report after report back as the night wore on. He had a book published that gave examples of his work that night. Brilliant.

Fitz drank. All newspaper people drank, but Fitz drank a lot, and sort of hung it up after his Pulitzer. You couldn't fire a Pulitzer Prize winner, so he'd been sent to the sports department to write a sports column. He was supposed to write five days a week. He wrote one occasionally.

He would come into the office, smelling of a few eye-openers.

"Got a column today, Fitz?" I would ask.

"Not today," he would say.

"But, Fitz," I would reply, "you're supposed to write one five days a week."

"I know," he would say, and sort of look at me with a half-smile.

I complained about him to Hoge, who chewed him out about a thousand times, but nothing helped. As I said, you don't fire a Pulitzer Prize winner.

—Holtzman: A dark, severe man in his late fifties. He was the dean of American baseball writers. He had written a book, *No Cheering in the Press Box.*

He never smiled, but he had the keys to Cooperstown. No major leaguer ever got into the Hall of Fame if Holtzman didn't want him there. He had tremendous sources. He was writing about the fact there would one day be a baseball players' union and possibly a baseball players' strike *long* before anybody else got on the story.

Despite all this, he was a terrible writer. He wouldn't talk to anybody and get quotes. Used all the clichés, like circuit-clout, hot corner, keystone. Impossible to deal with.

—Goddard: He was in his late twenties and eager. He liked the idea of fresh blood taking over. Worked his tail off for me.

—Pille: Good guy. Had a lot of tremendous Woody Haynes stories.

—Agrella: I never met him. He was always at the track.

—Van Dyke: Young, energetic.

—Ziehm: Young, too. Did some of the layout work for me.

—Weinstein: I never saw him smile.

—LaPointe: Another kid who wanted to learn. Give me twelve Joe LaPointes and I'm happy. He wanted to be a hockey writer.

—Gold: Covered home Black Hawks hockey games. We didn't spend the money to cover the team on the road. Quiet man in his late thirties. He had that Mr. Peepers look. His older brother had been a doorman in an old Chicago theater, and would slip his little brother in for performances. He had heard Henny Youngman countless times, and knew at least a thousand Henny Youngman jokes. He was a nervous sort of guy, and when he would be typing close to deadline, I could hear him reciting Henny Youngman jokes to himself: "Hear about the shoe store that burned down? Not a sole was saved."

—Manthey: Late twenties. Devoted to the high school beat. Always covered the International, Chicago's big dog show. We used to talk a lot about dogs. Dave Manthey was a keeper.

—Edwards: Desk, some layout work. Quiet. Never gave me any trouble. Always had a couple of pops before he came to work. Fine with me.

—Newchurch: Young black man. Friendly, always cooperative. He took down the racing results and the following day's charts. We carried a couple of handicapping boxes on the racing page. One was "Tack Towne." For months, I thought Tack Towne was a real person. Harold did Tack Towne.

—Stubits: It was hard to tell how old Emil was. I'd guess late forties. He was a nervous man, too. The composing room will do that to you.

—Bob Langer: The best newspaper photographer I'd seen since Browny Stephens. *Sports Illustrated* had tried to hire him for years.

—Shub: He was near retirement age, too. They called him "Sandy." He was a Jewish guy from Skokie. I would have never made it without him. He had basically been running the department for the old sports editor. He handled the expense accounts, made out the week's work schedule, argued with Weinstein, the Guild steward, and usually put out the day's first edition, the Green, which hit the street around four in the afternoon for commuters going back out to the suburbs.

He had arthritis. At times, I don't see how he held a pencil. His hands shook. But he worked harder than anybody. I was constantly amazed at his energy.

—Banks: Black man in his late twenties. Hoge had hired him from Kansas City and had given him the Bulls beat. The *Sun-Times* had put in an affirmative-action policy, and Lacey was a beneficiary of it.

The *Sun-Times* had a large black readership, and the Bulls had a large black following, yet there were no black sports columnists in any major newspapers. Lacey was given a once-a-week column, with his picture, and the *Sun-Times* even took out a front-page ad on the cover of the industry's Bible, *Editor and Publisher,* to publicize his column.

He was also a lay Baptist minister. He had a strong, resonant voice. Lacey J. Banks would be my second Chicago nightmare.

Hoge called the meeting in a conference room at the *Sun-Times.* Each member of the

staff was there, with the exception of Joe
Agrella. He was somewhere writing about hay-
eaters.

Hoge introduced me. He gave them my background. Then he turned it over to me.

I stood up before the troops, stared into the
empty eyes before me. I was nervous and un-
steady. The sweat began to pour out. I said that
I was happy to be at the *Sun-Times,* that I
wanted to improve it and make it a big-league
section as I knew it could be, and a few other
clichés. Then I asked if anybody had any questions. Nobody did.

Then I gave them a few thoughts about what
I might do—improve the graphics, work on better writing, do more in-depth and offbeat features. Save for my words, God, was it quiet in
that room.

After that, I named a few of the sports sections that really impressed me around the country: the *Los Angeles Times,* the *Boston Globe,*
the *Philadelphia Inquirer,* the *Louisville Courier-
Journal.* I asked, "Can anybody here add to that
list or make a comment?"

Nothing. I was inside the Tomb of the Un-
known Sportswriter.

Hoge saw the trouble I was in and saved me.
"Well, if nobody has anything else, let's go back
to work," he said.

The schedule went like this:

Seymour Shub and a few others reported to work around ten in the morning on weekdays. Shub would get the layouts for the next day's paper and begin work on the Green edition. During baseball season, we always tried to get a Cubs final for the commuters if they were playing a home game.

Those working nights reported in the late afternoon and then produced three other morning editions. What was easier about Chicago was that it was in the Central time zone. East Coast games were mostly over by nine-thirty, and West Coast results were in a couple of hours later. There wasn't nearly the panic we had in the Atlanta composing room to get in games finishing near deadline.

What I also liked was that the *Sun-Times* was a tabloid. It made laying out the paper easier, because it didn't take as many elements to finish a page.

Surprisingly, I would have none of the problems in the *Sun-Times* composing room that I had had in Atlanta. Not only did the pages come together more quickly, but the printers were more cooperative and more willing to work as well. It was the newsroom union, or Guild, that would cause me the most headaches in Chicago. The only labor problem involving the *Jour-*

nal had been the Bill Clark case. But members of the Chicago Newspaper Guild, which included members of the *Sun-Times* sports staff, were fiercely union. There was not one second's extra work without overtime.

It was a completely new experience for me, one nobody spoke with me about or explained to me before I came to work. I was naive and ill-prepared for a problem that arose my first week at the paper, one I would have to deal with, in some fashion, during my entire career in Chicago.

The first time I put out the green edition, I did something that would play a major role in what was about to happen. I got the edition in on time. I was experimenting with cleaner-looking, vertical layouts. I had reduced the size of the sports logo, which seemed to be about the size of Kansas when I got there.

The back page of the *Sun-Times* was the front page of sports. You read the section from the back toward the middle, which took a bit of getting used to. But what I liked about dealing with the tabloid open-page front (or back, if you want to get technical) is that, in many ways, it was designed like a magazine cover.

I thought the sports front had been much too cluttered, so I began reducing the number of articles that started there. I wanted one major headline, a large photo, and then other smaller heads, teasing to stories inside.

You know the tabloids at the grocery stores that feature headlines screaming, "NAZI AS- TRONAUTS RETURN TO EARTH?" That's what I wanted, as far as packaging went. I wasn't about to put a head out there that read, "NEW CUBS MANAGER FROM MARS," but I would go with a huge Langer action photo, and a big headline screaming, "CUBS SWEEP REDS." Done neatly, a tabloid page can get much more immediate attention from a reader than a broadsheet with seven or eight smaller elements on a page. That made things easier in the composing room, as well. Pages came to- gether much faster than they had in Atlanta where the papers were broadsheets, wider and longer pages than tabloids.

When I returned to the rim after the Green closed, I did what I always did when I had worked the slot. I found myself a large waste- basket. Then I cleared off every piece of paper that was still on the rim, so it would be neat for the person who was putting out the next edition. There would be leftover copy, leftover local copy, rejected headlines, full ashtrays, rejected photos that didn't make the first edition. I would do sort of a sweep with my forearm and dump it all into the wastebasket.

The trouble started the first week. Shub had put out the Green. Lenny Ziehm had come in to work the night desk. When the Green arrived on my desk, I looked through it and came upon the once-a-week Lacey Banks column.

It was something about a couple of news-boys. There were religious references. I'm think-ing, They're letting this sort of thing in the paper? It had little or nothing to do with sports. The writing was cumbersome. I didn't get the point of the column.

I sat down with Shub and Ziehm to plan the rest of the night. "Take that Banks column out of the paper," I said.

I could see shock fall over the faces of both Shub and Ziehm.

"Are you sure?" asked Shub.

"We aren't supposed to touch Lacey's col-umn," said Ziehm.

Not supposed to touch it? Since when did a beat writer get to write a once-a-week column the executive sports editor couldn't touch?

"Shouldn't you ask Hoge or Otwell first?" Shub continued.

"Just throw the column out," I said. "It stinks."

I was at my desk the following morning. Lacey J. Banks walked over and said he wanted a word with me. I said, "Sure." He wanted to know why his column hadn't been in the morning edition.

"I didn't like it," I said.

He asked why.

I said it really didn't have anything to do with sports, I didn't want my writers expressing their religious beliefs on the sports page, and that I hadn't understood the point of the column.

"Why wasn't I told the column wasn't going to be in last night?" Lacey went on.

I said I didn't have time to track him down last night.

He walked away. I thought nothing more of our conversation.

The next morning when I returned to work there was a pink memo slip in my mail slot. It was from Lacey J. Banks.

What the memo said was he thought I had killed the column because of a racial motive. He said nobody ever killed a column by Gleason or Fitzpatrick, who were white. He said the column made perfect sense. He demanded it be placed in the next day's editions.

I'm thinking, *What?*

Racially motivated? I hadn't cared if Lacey

Banks were orange, the column still stank and had no business in a major-league sports section.

I wondered if the fact I was from Atlanta had anything to do with this. I figured it had. It was a neat story: White racist from South kills black man's column.

I decided I would explain to Lacey how wrong that was. But before I could get a chance to, Hoge brought me in a copy of a local black-owned newspaper. A columnist had written a piece about the column being killed. Lacey Banks was quoted as saying he thought I was racist.

Hoge said, "We've got to handle this."

"How?" I asked.

"If we allow him to get away with this, then it will send a message to the staff that you're weak."

"Was I right to kill the column?" I asked him.

"I read it in the Green. You were right," he said.

I called Lacey and told him to meet me in Hoge's office. Hoge said he had had no business spouting off about his supervisor for public consumption. Lacey said the Lord had shown him the way, and under Guild guidelines he could do it.

I told Lacey nothing I had done was racially motivated. I also told him that his column was suspended. I also said I wasn't pleased with his coverage of the Bulls, either, and that I would be working closely with him to try to show him exactly what it was I wanted from him.

Needless to say, he didn't take any of what I said very well. He said he still felt he was a victim of racism.

I told him he had no other choice than to accept my dicta. He got up and said he would pray about it and get back to us.

That was fourteen years ago. I've often thought about Lacey and our problems and just how they came about in the first place. In retrospect:

The first mistake was made by handing over a major-league beat and a once-a-week column to a person with very little experience and expertise in the first place. But the *Sun-Times* had wanted to send a message to its black readers that it believed in affirmative action. Giving Lacey that big of a stick gave him the false message that he was an accomplished journalist and that he was above any sort of internship or heavy editing. He actually believed his writing was superior when, in my estimation as head of the department, it was terrible.

The paper had done Lacey J. Banks an injustice by throwing him into the deep water. Had he been brought along much more slowly, he might have become an excellent writer.

But then we get into 1975. The idea was that, because of the wrongs done to blacks previously, in order to give a black man his due, perhaps he shouldn't have to live up to the standards set for white people by other white people.

Meanwhile, I was a twenty-eight-year-old kid just off the turnip truck from Atlanta who had never had to supervise a full-time black staffer, who had never had to deal with a staff that was organized, and who was rather bullheaded himself about what was good and what wasn't.

Lacey continued to sulk about the column. He asked me over and over, "When am I going to get it back?"

The truth was, I didn't think he would ever get the column back, because I didn't think he felt he needed any of the guidance I could give him. Again, in retrospect, I made up my mind early that Lacey was a hopeless case.

The explosion came one morning when I was working on the Green. The big story of the day was a possible merger between the National Basketball Association and the new American

Basketball Association. There were meetings going on in Louisville, and the AP had picked up a story by a *Courier-Journal* writer giving in-depth details of what was transpiring. I figured if anybody knew what was going on in basketball, it had to be somebody from Kentucky.

Lacey came in and wrote his own story about the possible merger. It was one page. It basically was a rewrite from what the morning *Trib-une* had carried.

I ignored it. The wire piece was far superior, so I put the wire story in the paper. When I came back from the composing room, I did my normal cleanup job. I forearmed all the waste on the rim into the wastebasket.

Lacey saw the first edition.

"Why didn't you use my story?" he asked in-dignantly.

"The wire piece was better," I said.

"Where *is* my story?"

"What do you mean?"

"I mean I want my copy back."

"It's in the wastebasket," I told him.

The glue pot hit the fan.

Lacey went back to the black-owned newspa-per and made charges of racism against me, the *Sun-Times,* and anybody else he could think of.

Hoge called Lacey into his office again. I was

present. Hoge did the talking. In my mind, he gave Lacey every chance.

"Were you misquoted in the article?" Hoge asked Lacey.

"No," he answered.

"Are you willing to rescind any of the charges?"

"No."

Hoge didn't hesitate.

"Then I have no choice," he said to Lacey. "Clean out your desk."

There should have been a way to get around what eventually happened. I kept thinking to myself during the entire episode, Certainly, nobody would think I would ride in here from Atlanta and immediately tangle with Lacey Banks just because he was black.

If Lacey had been brought along slower. If maybe I had, in fact, worked with him a little more. If Lacey hadn't been so quick to charge racism, if he had shown me a willingness to learn. My only excuse is he certainly wasn't the only problem at the *Sun-Times* sports department. I was up to my butt in alligators almost every day.

The Chicago Newspaper Guild filed suit against the paper, charging that Lacey had been dismissed unfairly. The issue would go before a federal labor arbitrator. Before it did, however, I found out what I had expected all along—that racist feelings knew few geographical bounds.

I got unsigned memos from members of the news staff saying ridiculous and horrible things like, "I'm glad somebody finally got rid of that nigger."

It was an old and unpleasant story. Some felt Lacey J. Banks had been promoted to the lofty heights as pro-basketball writer and columnist simply because he was black, not because he had any special talents for the job. But that was irrelevant to me. I came to make the layout look better and put some zing into the words we wrote. That was all I cared about.

Before the hearings began, I hired a replacement for Lacey, Thom Greer from the Cleveland *Plain Dealer.* He was black. Nobody said to me, "You *must* hire a black replacement," but I knew the message I would send if I didn't—he got rid of the nigger so he could hire a white guy.

In this case, however, I must insist that Thom Greer, had he been plaid, was eminently qualified to take over the basketball beat. He was an excellent writer and reporter. He was a man of great dignity and humor. He was also a terrible poker player—we had a weekly game at my apartment that included him and an occasional

other member of the staff who didn't hate me—
as was I.

The Lacey Banks thing got big. Then bigger.

Another Chicago weekly did something. A
man on a radio station who did commentaries
on Chicago media doings defended me. Said I
was "guilty by geography."

One cold morning, I stepped off the Clark
Street bus and there were black people demon-
strating in Lacey's behalf in front of the *Sun-
Times.*

"WHITE RACIST GO BACK TO ATLANTA,"
said one of their signs.

The thought occurred to me there: I could turn
right around, grab a cab, go back home and
pack, catch a plane (yes, a plane), and be back
in Atlanta and at Harrison's by eight in the evening.

I went on in, however. Luckily, none of the
demonstrators had any idea what the White
Racist from Atlanta looked like, so I managed to
pass by them without notice.

I went through weeks of discussions and
practice-testifying with the paper's attorneys.
Both the *Daily News* and the *Sun-Times* were
owned by the Marshall Field Company, of department-store fame.

As we were entering the room for the first of

the hearings in front of the federal arbitrator, I asked one of the Field lawyers, "Do we have a chance to win?"

He said, "Let me put it this way—we have a white sports editor from Atlanta and the wealthy Marshall Field Company against a black man in front of a federal arbitrator. No, we don't have a chance. We just have to do it for show."

So Lacey Banks and his lawyers and representatives of the Chicago Newspaper Guild were on one side of the room, and newspaper management, me, and our lawyers were on the other. To tell the truth, I felt very lonely in there. I had very little in common with either side, as a matter of fact, and the only other experience I had had in a courtroom as a witness was during the Bill Clark thing back in Atlanta. There, I was a small player. Here, I was The Villain.

They put me on the stand for cross-examination. I still recall some of it:

"Mr. Grizzard," began the Guild lawyer. "Did you not tell Mr. Banks religion had no place on the sports pages of the *Sun-Times?*"

"Yes."

"Mr. Grizzard, is it not true that you once worked for *Sports Illustrated?*"

"I was their Atlanta correspondent."

"In your opinion, as a professional journalist,

what is your feeling about the quality of *Sports Illustrated?* Do you think the magazine exhibits standards that are of a high quality?"

"I think it may be one of the best-edited publications in the world."

"You do. Well, then, Mr. Grizzard, are you aware that *Sports Illustrated* recently did a series of articles on religion in sports, written by Mr. Frank Deford?"

I knew where he was going by now, of course. I had said *SI* was a great magazine, and *SI* had done articles on religion in sports written by the brilliant Frank Deford.

What the lawyer would say to me next was, "If a publication of such high quality—and you have testified you agree with that assessment of the publication—sees a relationship between sports and religion, why then would you say to Mr. Banks when he wrote about religion that it had no place on your sports pages?"

This is where the truth sort of got lost in a courtroom. Okay, so *Sports Illustrated* had written about religion in sports. But Frank Deford writing about the religious philosophies of professional athletes in *Sports Illustrated* was a far cry from Lacey J. Banks doing a give-Jesus-Christ-the-football sort of thing in his sophomoric once-a-week column. The link between the two was so frail, it didn't apply. Not in the real world. But in court, before the ears of the federal arbitrator who didn't know one thing about *Sports Illustrated* or newspaper sports sections, the damage had been done.

I did stop the proceedings one day under direct examination by our lawyers. He asked what my reaction was when Mr. Banks had first charged me with being racist.

I said, "I was bumfuzzled."

The Guild attorney said, "Excuse me. What did the witness say?"

The arbitrator said, "Please repeat your answer."

"I said, 'I was bumfuzzled.'"

"I don't think I am familiar with this term, bumfuzzled," said the Guild attorney.

"Nor am I," said the arbitrator.

I'm sure my attorney wasn't either, but he wisely didn't say anything.

My mother used to say "bumfuzzled" a lot when I was growing up, as in, "It completely bumfuzzles me how you can mess up one bathroom in such a short time," or, "I'm bumfuzzled that you won't eat pickled okra."

The court recorder chimed in, "I'm not certain how to spell the word."

I said, "Like it sounds. B-u-m, 'bum,' f-u-z-

z-l-e-d, 'fuzzled.' Bumfuzzled. It means confused or surprised."

Again, I felt terribly out-of-place. I'm in Chi-
cago-by-God-Illinois getting raked over the
coals by a bunch of northerners who don't even
understand a perfectly good word like "bumfuzzled."

The hearings continued. Lacey testified about
the story he turned in concerning the NBA-ABA
merger, the one I had rejected for a wire story
I thought was more complete.

"How long did you work on this manuscript?"
the Guild lawyer asked him.

"Until midnight," Lacey answered.

"And when you saw the first edition and realized your manuscript had been replaced by another off the wire, what did you do?"

"I asked Mr. Grizzard why he hadn't used my
story."

"And what did he say?"

"He said he thought the one he had received
on the wire was better."

"That's all he said?"

"Yes."

"He didn't sit down with you and explain why
the wire manuscript was better than your own?"

"No."

"What did you do then?"

"I asked him where the piece was."

"You wanted to know what had happened to the manuscript you had submitted, am I correct?"

"Yes."

"Why did you want this manuscript returned to you?"

"I had worked hard on it. I wanted to compare it to the article Mr. Grizzard had chosen."

"The one he chose to run in the newspaper rather than the one you had delivered him."

"Yes."

"Did Mr. Grizzard return the manuscript to you?"

"No, he did not."

"Why didn't he?"

"He didn't have it anymore."

"What did he say he had done with it?"

"He said he had tossed it in the wastebasket."

"The wastebasket?"

"Yes, sir."

"Let me see if I have this straight, Mr. Banks. You worked until nearly midnight on your manuscript. You submitted it to Mr. Grizzard for the following day's first edition. And he not only cast yours aside for a story off the wire—a nonexclusive story, when yours was exclusive—but he

also never gave you any sort of detailed excuse
for why he didn't run your manuscript."

"Yes, sir."

"And then when you asked him for your manuscript back, he said that he had discarded it
into the waste can?"

"Yes."

I tried to explain when my lawyer questioned
me about the incident. I said that Lacey's article
was not exclusive, it was basically a rewrite of
the morning *Tribune.* I also said that if he had
stayed up until midnight working on it, he must
not have started until eleven forty-five. But that
is making an assumption, which they won't listen to in court.

I also pointed out that I always threw *all* leftover materials on the rim into the wastebasket
to clear it for work on the next edition, and that's
the way I had learned to do it when I first started
in the business, because if you didn't get all that
paper off the rim by the time the night was over,
the entire sports department would disappear
under tons of it.

I could tell the arbitrator was not impressed,
and I knew what he was thinking. He was thinking about Abe Lincoln. Remember how Abe Lincoln used to sit up late at night and read from
the dim light of a candle? He could see Lacey

doing this, staring down at his typewriter as the flicks of candlelight danced across the blank page before him. He probably saw a log cabin where this was taking place, too. And here was this black man, struggling over each word of his manuscript. And what happened the next morning? The cruel Simon Legree took this precious manuscript and callously dumped it into a cauldron of waste.

It was the word "manuscript" that helped Banks's case, too. "Manuscript" as in "book"—as in 1,696 typed pages. "Manuscript" is not an operable word in the newspaper business. It's "story," "article," "piece," or, in this case, "one-page, eight-paragraph rewrite of the rival paper's piece."

Then they nailed me again. We had a special Saturday section. People were milling around in the hearing room, waiting to begin. I noticed another black man in the room I had not seen at previous sessions. And he looked familiar to me.

I kept watching him. I'd seen that face before. Then it hit me upside the head like a slashing foul ball into the seats.

It was Alfred Johnson, who had been Minter's stringer for Atlanta University sports teams at the *Journal.* I had forgotten about Alfred Johnson. I had forgotten the circumstances involved the last time I had seen him.

I nudged my lawyer.

"We've got big trouble," I said.

"What's the matter?"

"Just wait. You're going to kill me."

The three Atlanta University schools—Clark, Brown, and Morehouse—were in an all-black conference that was holding its annual conference tournament in Montgomery. It was the first time the tournament had come around when I was executive sports editor of the *Journal.*

Hudspeth was covering pro football at the time, but it was March, and he was available for another assignment, so I had dispatched him to Montgomery, where the Southeastern Conference Indoor Track Meet was taking place. I had mentioned to him that if any of the Atlanta University teams made a move in the basketball tournament, I needed him to be available to cover a game or two.

Alfred came into the office of the old 10 Forsyth Street sports department and walked over to my desk. He said he wanted to get some expense money so he could go to Montgomery and cover the basketball tournament. The budget was so tight in those days that when I dispatched a reporter to cover a night basketball game at Auburn University, a two-lane, 110 mile drive, the paper wouldn't pop for an eighteen-dollar hotel room. You had to drive back that night.

"Have you ever covered the tournament out of town before?" I asked Alfred.

He said he hadn't.

"Have you ever received advance expenses from the paper to cover an out-of-town event before?" I asked him further.

He said he hadn't.

I tried to explain to Alfred he was not an employee of the paper. He was a "stringer." We had stringers all over. They never got advance expenses for anything.

And then Alfred said it. He said, "If I were white, you'd give me the money."

I'm twenty-three years old.

"That's ridiculous," I said to Alfred.

"No, it's not ridiculous, either," he said to me.

"Alfred," I went on, "I don't have time to argue with you about this. Hudspeth's in Montgomery, and if we need somebody to cover the tournament, he's already over there. The paper's not going to let me send anybody else."

Alfred then launched into an attack on me and the newspaper as racists. He got ugly about it. He cursed me. He said, "You better watch yourself when you go out of this building."

"Are you threatening me, Alfred?" I asked.

He cussed me again.

I said, "You'll have to leave the building."

He said, "I'm not going anywhere."

I said, "Alfred, I can't have this. You will have to leave the building, and leave your building pass with security."

"You're firing me?" he asked.

"I am," I said.

He started cursing me again. I went and got Durwood McAllister, the managing editor. He called security. Security escorted Alfred out of the building. It took me about a day to find another Atlanta University stringer, also black, who turned out to be much more conscientious and capable than Alfred.

I hadn't thought about Alfred Johnson in five years, but here he was across the room from me in Chicago, and now I could see the Guild's next move.

Grizzard takes over as executive sports editor of the *Atlanta Journal.* He gets rid of the black guy.

Grizzard takes over as executive sports editor of the Chicago *Sun-Times.* He gets rid of the black guy.

My lawyer buried his face in his hands as Alfred began his testimony, which went something like, "I was one of the top black journalists in

Atlanta, and this white racist gave me the gate."

Our side would bring in Jim Minter to Chicago to give a deposition refuting Alfred's claims of his lofty position, but it wouldn't do any good.

My lawyer said to me, "How could you forget something as important as this incident with Alfred Johnson?"

I didn't have an answer for him.

Somebody had put the Guild onto Alfred Johnson. I never found out who. Perhaps someone who worked for me in Atlanta. My mother had once said to me, "Not everybody is going to think you are as cute and love you like I do." She sure was right.

The arbitrator had a lot to say about the "manuscript callously thrown into a wastebasket" and said I was "racially insensitive." He ordered Lacey reinstated with all his back pay.

But the arbitrator did not have the authority to order that Lacey be put back on the Bulls beat, nor that he be given his column back. The First Amendment protects a newspaper from being ordered what it must print. It also protects newspapers from being told by the government what they can't print.

Lacey J. Banks came back to the *Sun-Times* sports department after several months' absence. By that time, Thom Greer had established himself as a top pro-basketball writer and an integral, important part of the staff.

I put Lacey on the desk. After I left, I heard they let him cover a women's pro-basketball league that eventually flopped, and somebody said he covered some soccer occasionally. I also hear that he was still doing his preaching and often tried to convert wayward staffers.

Sad. Everybody involved shared the fault. It's not a fair world.

I mentioned other problems beside Lacey J. Banks. Count 'em.

* Fitz wouldn't write a column.
* Gleason would go crazy on me and write columns about "Prince Peter (Rozelle), King of All the Footballs." I killed a few of his efforts, too. He used to rant and rave at me and throw his hands about and say, "But, Lewis, you don't understand. I'm circulation."
* Holtzman wouldn't put any quotes in his baseball stories.

I did learn something about being a cocky, twenty-eight-year-old sports editor from Holtzman, however.

I called him into my office one day and began

to tell him how baseball writers should be writing in the late seventies.

I mentioned the need for quotes, and then I said, "And you use too many clichés."

"Clichés?" he asked me.

"Yes," I said. "You are still using worn-out baseball clichés like 'hot corner' for third base and 'circuit clout' and 'roundtripper' for home run."

Holtzman looked puzzled. Finally he said, "Lewis, you don't understand. Those are *my* clichés."

I hadn't thought of that. Here was the dean of American baseball writers, and he probably did come up with those terms. And if a man invented a term, no matter how long he used it, it really couldn't be called a cliché, could it?

I didn't bother with Holtzman's writing much after that.

* One night, we were trying to get out the Sunday edition, and Emil came out of the composing room complaining he couldn't breathe. I didn't know what to do. I didn't know if I should take care of him and forget about getting the paper in on time, or put Emil somewhere until I could finish up the job in the composing room. What if he

died? I compromised. I got Emil a chair
and I said, "I'll keep an eye on you while
I get the paper in."

As soon as the edition closed, Emil
started breathing a lot better again.

* Marvin Weinstein, the Guild steward,
showed no quarter when it came to Guild
rules. If a reporter was in the middle of a
sentence in the middle of a story and his
shift was over, Marvin would order him to
leave the office.

* I hired a new assistant, John Clendenen,
to take over the night desk. After the green
edition, we would hold a nightly meeting
that involved me, Shub, and Clendenen.
John didn't like Marvin. If Clendenen had
somebody working on a piece and Marvin
came over and said, "Leave the office,
your shift is over," Clendenen couldn't understand it and would tell Marvin he was
an idiot. They would argue, then Marvin
would file grievances—and I suddenly
began keeping a large jar of Maalox in my
desk.

* Bob Pille, the college writer, did something
I detested. He covered a Notre Dame–
South Carolina football game in Columbia,
South Carolina, and he made reference to

Sherman's burning of Columbia in his story.

Why did every northern writer have to mention Sherman or the Civil War when he covered a ball game in the South?

I wrote Pille a memo and told him what I thought of his reference, and pointed out that Sherman didn't burn Columbia, anyway. His siege ended in Savannah.

Pille wrote me a subsequent memo, pointing out Sherman had, indeed, burned Columbia. He even had exact dates and a quote or two from a history book.

I wrote him a third memo and said, "I still maintain references to the Civil War when one is covering sporting events in the South is a cliché, but I do stand corrected about Sherman's burning of Columbia, the capital of the great state of South Carolina. Realize, however, I am a product of the Georgia public school system, where we were taught when the little bearded bastard of a firebug got to Savannah, they hung him."

* The Guys with the Mops: Damndest thing. Every Friday night at six o'clock, three guys with mops would walk into the *Sun-*

Times newsroom. All work of a journalistic nature came to a halt. The Guys with the Mops would go around to each desk and put the accompanying chair on top of the desk. Then they would mop the floors. You couldn't remain in the newsroom while they were mopping. There was no place to work, and even if there was, it was tough to work while a guy was mopping underneath you.

I always forgot about the Guys with the Mops. Shortly before six o'clock each Friday, I would start laying out the first Sunday edition. I would have my layouts on my desk, my pencils, my glue pot, the copy, and just as I would begin, here they would come, the Guys with the Mops. I would have to pick up all my work and move down to a table in the employee cafeteria while the Guys with the Mops brought a major news operation to a complete halt.

* Sandy Shub and Beat the Champs: I meant it earlier when I said I loved Sandy Shub. He was such a gentle little man, and he helped me put out a zillion brushfires. But Sandy Shub had another job at the *Sun-Times,* besides handling work

schedules, expense accounts, and keeping me sane. Each year, the *Sun-Times* sponsored a bowling tournament called Beat the Champs. I went through three Beat the Champs. I still couldn't tell you exactly how the darn thing worked. But I do know this: Half of Chicago entered. Bowling, an indoor sport, is big in Chicago. And everybody who entered got his or her name and his or her score set in small agate type in the *Sun-Times* sports section. And everybody who entered then called the *Sun-Times* to ask if his or her name and score was going to be in the paper that day.

Beat the Champs, I swear, lasted longer than the NBA season. And Beat the Champs ate space. It ate it without conscience. It ate space like a lion devouring a lamb. Inches and inches of names and bowling scores, running day after day in my sports section.

Bob Langer brings in a great photo. Can't run it, though. Beat the Champs.

Beat the Champs finally ended when finalists were chosen and they rolled off against some pros. They put the thing on television, and Sandy would proudly state, "We've raised over a million dollars for charity with Beat the Champs."

I hated Beat the Champs. I hated it more than I did when somebody put a horse in "People in Sports" back in Atlanta. I hated it more than I hated communism and loud rock music and cabdrivers who spoke no English, who were in the front seat of every cab I ever took in Chicago.

I eventually began to hate Chicago itself. Oh, there were some moments. I got to meet the famous mayor Richard Daley at the press lounge at Comiskey Park one night. He was very fat.

I found a great place to play tennis, Mid-Town Racquet Club. It had sixteen indoor courts. I joined an early-bird league and played five mornings a week, between seven and nine. That helped keep me sane. I made a new friend at the tennis center, Tim Jarvis.

We were a pair. He was an ex-hippie, liberal social worker, who openly admitted he had used drugs during his hippie days. I was a conservative, southern patriot, who had been close to marijuana only once in his life. I had seen *The Gene Krupa Story,* starring Sal Mineo as the legendary drummer, at the Alamo Theatre in the county seat back home.

We did both have beards, however, and we both enjoyed tennis. The pro introduced us. When Tim heard my name, he said, "Are you the guy who got rid of Lacey Banks at the *Sun-Times?*"

I admitted I was, not certain what would come next.

"I'm glad," said Tim. "He was awful."

I also met a neighbor in the apartment building, Johnny Reyes, a free-lance photographer who was originally from Colombia and knew everybody I knew, including Lacey. He was from Colombia, as in Juan Valdez, the coffee picker, not as in South Carolina, which Sherman burned.

Johnny was always inviting Kay and me over for dinner or drinks. He had a thick accent, and often I had a difficult time figuring out what he was trying to say. I would listen to Johnny, and then when he finished speaking, I had two responses. I would either laugh, say, "You're absolutely right," or "I know exactly what you mean," which I rarely did.

Two weeks after we had moved to Chicago, Kay had gone to visit her family and her brother at his home in Virginia for Thanksgiving. I stayed in Chicago. Thanksgiving night, Georgia and Georgia Tech were to play their annual football game on national television. I planned all day for the event. I bought a couple of six-packs of beer, built a fire, and awaited the game.

Georgia led 42–0 at the half.

Johnny called. I think he said, "Hey, man, come on over. I got some chicks and some food, man."

I thanked him but told him I wanted to stay in my own apartment and watch the football game. Georgia won 42–26. Johnny called again. I said I would be right over.

There were some strange people in Johnny's apartment. I suddenly felt terribly homesick. Back in Atlanta, the bulldog faithful were celebrating. I'm seven hundred miles away with some people who didn't speak English, were puffing away on odd-looking cigarettes, and listening to music I couldn't identify.

"Come try my dressing," said Johnny.

I was hungry. The dressing was good. I ate two helpings. I awakened on Johnny's couch the next morning.

"Hey, man," he said laughing at me. "I put pot in the dressing. You sleep good, no?"

I never ate with Johnny again.

But one more problem—Chicago itself:

Winter came that Thanksgiving weekend. I

had found a neighborhood bar, John Barleycorn's. I went there on Saturday night, sat alone at the bar, and had a few beers. It hadn't been snowing when I walked into John Barleycorn's around seven.

When I decided to leave and walk home at around ten, there was more snow on the ground than I had ever seen before. Maybe five inches. Later, that would be nothing, but I'd been in Chicago only two weeks.

I was wearing my Bass Weejuns. It was eight blocks home. The next morning, my Weejuns had turned white. The two things I had vowed never to do, no matter how much it snowed in Chicago or how cold it got, was wear a pair of rubber overshoes or get me one of those Russian-looking hats with all the fur.

The only individuals I had known in the South who wore rubber overshoes were sissies and nerds, or guys who hung around the science lab a lot and grew up to be billionaire computer-company CEOs. I didn't like those Russian-looking hats because my father used to talk a lot about how one day we would have to fight the Russians to keep us safe from the peril of communists, and how we should have just kept everybody over there when World War II ended and gone ahead and fought them then.

As it got deeper into winter, however, and I

had ruined my third or fourth pair of shoes, I bought a pair of rubber overshoes. But allow me to save some face from the embarrassment of finally giving in to something I had vowed never to do—I never did get one of those Russian hats.

The weather was more than enough to tell me I was in the wrong place. I had never lived anywhere where a television announcer would warn, "Do not go outside with any part of your skin exposed. Frostbite warning."

The lake would freeze. Everybody's pipes would freeze. Streets froze. People walking on streets froze. Cars froze. Dogs and cats froze, and I guess the birds had the good sense to go find a condo somewhere in Florida.

I saw it snow in May. That's not natural. I was down by the lake one June evening, and a temperature sign at a bank read 38 degrees. That's not natural, either. I heard a line that I thought was funny, as well as quite descriptive: "There are only two seasons in Chicago—winter and Fourth of July."

They put up ropes and lines along the street in the Loop so you could hang on and not be swept across the ice and into the Chicago River by a blizzard wind. I had never been in a blizzard until I lived in Chicago. Being in a blizzard is like standing in a wind tunnel, getting pelted by ice cubes going three hundred miles an hour.

April was the cruelest month. One morning an April day would dawn, and you would exclaim, "The long gray nightmare is over." It would reach 67 degrees, and you would put your rubber overshoes away. The next day, it would snow seventeen inches.

I mentioned earlier how I never got a cab-driver in Chicago who spoke English. I never got on a city bus when there wasn't some sort of crazy on board, either. There was a man who rode to work on the same bus as I did who used to talk to his hands, like they do in New York subways.

He would open his hands, look at them, and say, "Good morning, hands." Then he would break into a diatribe involving everything from freeing Castro's slaves to there will never be another Cubs' shortstop as good as Ernie Banks.

A man dressed as Abe Lincoln would ride my bus occasionally. He not only dressed like Lincoln, top hat and the works, he even looked a lot like Lincoln. He was tall and gangly, and had a beard.

He never said very much. The bus driver would always say, "Good morning, Abe," and Abe would tip his hat to the bus driver.

That's nothing. One morning a man with a live chicken on his head tried to get aboard number 151. The bus stopped, and a few people got on in front of the man with the live chicken on his head. When he tried to board the bus, the driver said, "You can't bring that chicken on here."

"I'm a taxpayer," said Chicken Man.

"I don't care," said the bus driver. "No animals on the bus."

A rather heated argument ensued.

The man with the live chicken on his head said, "I'll pay an extra fare for my chicken."

The bus driver closed the door and drove away.

Later, I thought, why didn't I get off the bus and interview the man with the live chicken on his head? I should have, because, now, it would be nice to be able to sit here and explain about the chicken. But I was late that morning, and if I didn't get to work pretty soon, Sandy would fill up three quarters of the sports section with Beat the Champs names and scores, and there wouldn't be room for the U.S. Open golf story. Maybe the guy just liked chickens.

Food was a continuing problem for me in Chicago, too. In Chicago, barbecue was ribs, and that was it. You could find plenty of barbecued ribs in Chicago, but what you couldn't find was a barbecued pork sandwich (described, else-where, as a "barbecue pork-pig sandwich"), and I dearly love barbecued pork sandwiches, which I grew up on at the world-famous Spray-berry's Barbecue in Newnan, Georgia.

You go into a restaurant in Chicago looking for maybe some country fried steak, mashed potatoes, green beans, and other southern de-lectables, and what you might get was Salisbury steak, a baked potato, and green beans that had been steamed. I don't like steamed vegeta-bles. I like green beans that have been simmer-ing for about a week with a large piece of ham thrown in for flavoring.

There were many ethnic restaurants in my rather ethnic neighborhood, but once you've eaten one portion of boiled yak, that's about it for the rest of your life.

Kay tried. She would still fry an occasional chicken or cook a pork roast, and she did man-age to find some grits for breakfast, but where were the home-grown tomatoes, the speckled-heart butter beans, and the fried okra? And the cornbread mix she found was too sweet. I hate sweet cornbread. Not as much as I hated Beat the Champs, but close.

Okay, the hot dogs were good at a little joint up on Clark Street near my apartment. Yankees,

I must admit, know something about hot dogs, even though they pronounce them as they do. I learned to eat nothing but sharp mustard on my hot dogs while I lived in Chicago, a practice I have continued even until today. What's good about northern hot dogs is they are all beef and they are much smaller than the plump dogs they serve down South. I prefer smaller dogs because they are easier to eat, and the smaller the dog, with apologies to Ralph Nader, the fewer rodent hairs I'm getting.

Speaking of grits, I invited my friend Tim Jarvis and his wife over to a Sunday morning breakfast once. Kay had found some country ham someplace, and she was planning scrambled eggs, cheese grits, and homemade biscuits.

Tim and his wife arrived at our apartment. He walked into the kitchen and saw Kay's biscuits, just before they were to go in the oven. He took a long look at them and said, "So those are grits."

The boy needed a lot of work.

Kay began picking up pieces of the midwestern, dull-as-dishwater accent, which concerned me greatly. Her initial appeal to me had been the lovely lilt of her South Carolina low-country manner of speech.

I first noticed the change when she said good-bye to me on the phone one day. Most southerners get off the phone by saying, "Bye," which sounds more like "Bi" with an extremely hard *i.*

Chicagoans said, "Bye-Bye," with the emphasis on the second "bye." It was sort of like, "Bai-Bai."

I said to her, "Don't start sounding like these people. We've got to maintain some of our heritage."

Perhaps that was the first fissure in our Chicago relationship. Gradually, it got bigger.

How to Convince Your Wife to Leave You in Ten Easy Lessons:
1. Get lost in your work (See PAULA).
2. Get up before she does and go play tennis, then go to work and don't come home until you're too tired to do anything but lie on your couch and ask her to bring you beer.
3. Share no interests with her.
4. Have only your own friends. Don't pay any attention to hers.
5. Expect dinner. Don't ask for it, expect it.
6. Take out the stress you feel from work on her.

7. If she thinks she has the talent to sing and wants to go up to Lincoln Avenue pubs with her guitar, laugh at her for being so naive as to think she could be discovered like Bette Midler.
8. If she wants to take a cultural tour of the city, say, "I ain't going to no art gallery."
9. If she wants to get romantic and build a fire in the fireplace, say, "If you want a fire, build it yourself. Who do I look like, Daniel Boone?"
10. Lose her trust.

I did them all. All ten. I lost her trust in Atlanta with my fooling around at Harrison's, and then I added to the problem with the other nine when we got to Chicago.

She left me.

That was fifteen years ago. I remember every vivid detail:

It was early May. I caught a train from Chicago to Dallas. I went to Dallas to attempt to hire a young sportswriter named Randy Harvey from the Dallas *Times-Herald,* one of the country's top new talents.

I offered the job to Randy, and he took it. I boarded the train Saturday afternoon and arrived back in Chicago Sunday afternoon. I caught a cab home.

Kay had supper ready.

"Why don't we go to a movie after you eat?" she said.

I couldn't. Hoge, two weeks earlier, had given each department head another newspaper to study. We were to report the next day on what we had learned from the paper we had studied and comment on what we thought was good or bad about it and what we could learn from it to make the *Sun-Times* better. I had *The New York Times.*

Unfortunately, I hadn't worked on my report. Sunday night after dinner was my last chance.

I finished eating. I spread out *The New York Times* on our kitchen table and went to work.

We had a balcony off our living room. Kay walked outside and was gone a long time. I could tell she was upset, but I still had to do my report.

I tried to make up for it Monday. In the afternoon, after the department-head meeting, I called her at home. I suggested I bring home a couple of steaks and some champagne and we could spend a romantic evening together.

It's odd what the mind records indelibly. I was sitting at my desk in the sports department. I had the phone to my left ear talking to my wife. I had bought a paperback copy of E. L. Doctorow's *Ragtime.* I was staring at the cover as we talked.

"Don't bother with the steaks or the champagne," Kay said.

"You've already planned dinner?"

"Let me ask you a question: What did you do for dinner before you married me?"

"I ate a lot of frozen fish sticks," I said.

"You might want to stop by the Jewel and get some," she said.

I asked, "Why?"

She said, "Because I won't be here when you get home. I'm leaving you."

She hung up. I kept staring at *Ragtime.*

Give her a couple of days and she'll get over it and be back, I thought. How many husbands have thought that when their wives first left them?

But Hudspeth had spoken a truth once. He had said, "Women will forgive and forgive and forgive. But once they turn on you, it's over."

And it was.

I spent the next eleven months living alone in Chicago. I tried everything to get Kay to come back home. I called her, I begged her, I promised to change. I hurt. God, how I hurt.

I've still got a mess at the newspaper, I'm uncomfortable with where I live, winter is coming, there's no Harrison's. And my wife has left me. I spend long hours and much money talking to friends long-distance back in Atlanta. I called my stepbrother one lonely Friday night.

Late Saturday afternoon, I got a call from him. He and his wife were on the outskirts of Chicago and wanted to know how to get to my apartment.

"I've never heard you so down," he said when he arrived. "I was afraid not to come."

That helped. Until he left.

I'd never felt as alone in my life. This wasn't my town. These weren't my people.

I kept hoping a miracle would happen, and Kay would come back. It was often that I asked myself, though, *Do* I really love this woman that much? If she came back, would I change like I said I would, or would I go back to my old ways?

And what if this had happened in Atlanta? I had my pals in Atlanta, my support group. I would have Harrison's on Friday night as a means of filling the void.

I could never answer any of that. And it didn't matter. That was Atlanta, this was Chicago.

I did a lot of eating alone. Drinking alone is bad, but eating alone is worse. You're alone and sober. I stopped going to bed. I would lie on the couch watching television until I went to sleep. Falling asleep on a couch in a living room is preferable to a man filled with the demons of loneliness and regret, lying in a bed meant for two in the dark and the quiet.

The drinking. It's not supposed to be an answer, but it helped. I would sit at John Barleycorn's some nights. Or I would walk to the 2350 where they had two Eddie Arnold country songs on the jukebox and Gladys Knight's "Midnight Train to Georgia." I listened to that a lot.

I tried Division Street, Butch McGuire's. The Bombay Bicycle Club. I never scored. There was no Hudspeth around to lay the groundwork for me.

And the old feast-or-famine rule was working against me. That goes like this: If you are married or have a steady girlfriend, you'll run into more good-looking eligible women than you could handle in a lifetime. You're loose, you've got something at home to go back to, and they are everywhere. But get down and out. Get with absolutely nothing. Be desperate. You haven't got a chance. Famine. Dog days. The locusts have come, and the earth is dark and without form. I couldn't catch a break.

One day, I saw a lovely blonde walking through the newsroom. Despite my classic male fear of rejection, I got on the elevator with her and rode down to the lobby. On the way down, I introduced myself. She introduced herself. She was with somebody's PR firm. She seemed receptive. I asked her for a date. She accepted.

She came to my apartment by cab. I cooked us steaks. I served us a bottle of wine. Afterward, we sat on the floor in front of a fire Daniel Boone could, in fact, have built.

I'm not really certain what happened, but this woman had just completed one of the *est* things, and she was trying to learn to be assertive. We got into a large argument about something, and the next thing I knew we were screaming at each other and I was calling her a cab.

I turned thirty in Chicago. I gave myself a birthday party. I invited Tim and his wife and Sid Cato, another tennis friend, and Johnny Reyes and another guy named Carl, who also lived in the building. Carl was single, and was always bringing home lovely women.

Tim gave me a houseplant. Sid gave me some tennis balls. Johnny Reyes gave me an album of genuine Colombian music. Carl brought me a girl.

Her name was Lorraine. She was sexy.

"This is Lorraine," said Carl. "She's yours for the night."

Lorraine left the next morning. She gave me her telephone number, but it turned out to be bogus. I called Carl. He said he'd heard Lorraine had moved to the West Coast.

I dated a girl at *Playboy.* Not a Playboy girl. A girl who worked at *Playboy.* She used to make fun of how skinny my arms were.

I rode the train home for a long weekend and met a girl in Atlanta.

She came to see me a few times, and even brought me barbecue sandwiches. When she realized I was looking forward to the sandwiches more than I was looking forward to her, she stopped coming.

Kay got her own apartment and a job. I called her an average of four times a day to beg her to come home. I began to neglect my job.

Clendenen, my assistant, scolded me. "You've got to get off the phone and pay more attention to what's going on around here," he said.

I ignored him.

Kay finally leveled with me:

"Remember that weekend you went to Dallas?"

"I remember."

"I never felt as lonely in my life. All you did was work. You never had time for me. On Saturday, I went to down to the Oak Street Beach. A man came up to me and asked if he could sit next to me. *Me*. I told him I was married.

"He asked me where my husband was. I said he was out of town on business. He said, 'If I were married to somebody like you, I wouldn't leave town and leave you out here all alone.'

"Nothing happened, but I did realize I was somebody, too. There were people who thought I was attractive and had talent.

"When you ignored me that Sunday night and went to work after being gone for three days, I walked out on the balcony and made up my mind to leave you."

"Is there somebody else in your life now?" I asked her.

"Yes," she said.

"And you are never coming back?"

"Never," she said.

Sid Cato talked me out of suicide. He told me something I'd never known about him, something he had never talked about before.

Sid had a wife and kids. He was devoted to them. The family went driving one Sunday afternoon. Vandals had taken down a stop sign at a country intersection. There was nothing to tell Sid he was coming to an intersection.

He drove into it. A truck hit his car broadside. His wife was killed. One of his two children was killed. "I'll never get over that," he said to me. "My grief and my guilt were enormous. I thought about killing myself, too. You never get over loses in your life, but you can get better with time."

I probably wouldn't have killed myself anyway, but Sid did give me some hope.

And Tim Jarvis helped. Despite our different backgrounds, we became close. He and his Puerto Rican wife, Paula, worked together counseling Hispanic families. Tim was the most intelligent, sensitive man I'd ever known. I would talk. He would listen.

We had the tennis, and he was a regular in my poker games. Tim had a VW beetle, like my old '66. When I first began playing tennis at Mid-Town, I had to ride the bus. Imagine how I looked at six-fifteen in the morning, standing there in a snowstorm with two tennis racquets under my arms.

After I met Tim, five mornings a week he would pick me up in the VW and drive us to the tennis center. Tim was the least demanding friend I'd ever had. Except for one episode for which I will never forgive him.

One bitterly cold morning, he called around five-thirty and told me his car wouldn't start. We both took the bus to tennis. Afterward, he said, "Let's take the bus back to my apartment. I need you to help me push my car into a garage so it will warm up and I can get it started again."

Sounded easy. It wasn't. In the first place, the

garage was three blocks away from where Tim's car was parked. In the second place, there was snow all over the street, which made pushing his VW like pushing a tank. In the third place, I hadn't bought my rubber overshoes yet, and there I was pushing a Pershing tank down a snowy street in Chicago in subfreezing weather in a pair of loafers. It took us an hour to get Tim's car into the garage. I had snow all over me. I had snow internally. I ruined another pair of shoes.

I asked Tim, "How long have you lived in Chicago?"

He said, "All my life."

I decided Tim wasn't as smart as I thought he was.

I thought, If I could just get the hell out of Chicago and get back to Atlanta . . .

But I didn't see a way out. I'd only been in Chicago just over a year. To leave would send a message that I couldn't cut it. To leave would be a defeat. And what would I do back in Atlanta? Work in a convenience store?

To make matters worse, Jimmy Carter was about to be elected president of the United States. When Carter had first run for governor of Georgia, the *Athens Daily News* had endorsed him. He lost the election, but came back to win later.

When Carter brought his Illinois campaign to

Chicago, he met with Hoge and other editors at the *Sun-Times.* Hoge invited me to sit in. I had known Carter slightly when he was governor. He remembered me. And, incredibly, his Illinois campaign manager was a former minister at the Moreland Methodist Church where I grew up. More incredibly, he had performed the marriage ceremony of my mother and stepfather at the church when I was ten.

All that made me more homesick. The South suddenly was *hot.* The national media was discussing southern language, southern politics, southern food. "Good ol' boy" was a new catchphrase of the time.

After the meeting with Hoge, I asked him what he had thought of the governor.

"I've never seen a candidate more well-versed on the issues," he said.

I felt a good measure of pride.

Tim and I watched the election returns together in November 1976. He was for Carter, too. He was for Carter because he was a liberal Democrat. I was for Carter because he talked the way I did. When the networks declared him the winner over Gerald Ford that night, I got teary.

Give me some credit, though. I did take a few positive steps. I got reinvolved with the paper.

Randy Harvey turned out to be brilliant. I assigned him what we called "take-out pieces," longer stories profiling athletes or looking into issues that were beginning to crop up in sports—drug use, high salaries, etc. I assigned him the best piece he wrote at the *Sun-Times.*

I was stripping the wire one afternoon and came upon a short that announced the death of tennis star Jimmy Connor's father in Belleville, Illinois, downstate, across the river from St. Louis.

I knew about Jimmy Connors and his mother and his grandmother who had trained him, but I'd never read a word about his dad. I sent Randy to find out more.

Mr. Connors had been a toll collector on the Martin Luther King Bridge over the Mississippi. Randy found a bar he frequented. The patrons said he would come there to watch Jimmy play. They said even after a Wimbledon or a U.S. Open, he would never hear from his son or estranged wife. That was the kind of story and writing I wanted, and Randy could deliver.

I had also convinced Hoge to allow me to hire another columnist. Fitz was fizzled, and Gleason was still in the left-field bleachers. I thought a new columnist, one who bit hard and could also write humor, would give us an edge on the

Tribune, which had a larger staff and many more resources than we did, but in my mind lacked the sort of sports columnist I thought Chicago readers would like, a Bisher or a Jim Murray.

I interviewed Dave Kindred from Louisville. His wife didn't want to live in Chicago. I couldn't pay him. I finally hired Tom Callahan from Cincinnati. He wrote well. I liked his ideas. He said to me, "I want to play the Palace."

He lasted a week. I edited a few lines of a couple of his columns, and he resigned and said, "This isn't the Palace, it's the Orpheum Circuit," and went back to Cincinnati.

I hired Ron Rappaport, who was covering baseball for the *L.A. Times.* He wasn't exactly another Murray, but he worked at his craft and was easy to deal with. That meant a lot.

But I never did construct a feeling on the staff like the one that had been so evident in Atlanta. The camaraderie was never there. Maybe it was the Guild that did that. The relationship between management and staff, in so many ways, was adversarial. The new people I brought in were with me, but most of the older ones weren't. It was as Dodgers manager Tommy Lasorda said once: "Half the guys on the team love me. Half hate me. It's my job to keep the two apart."

The rap on me from the anti-Grizzards was

that I played favorites. And I did. I gave the plum assignments to the people who would cooper-ate. I ignored the ones who wouldn't. That's one way I hung on to at least some of my sanity.

I decided to take another step I thought was positive. I decided to move out of the apartment where Kay and I had lived together as man and wife. We were still only separated, but I knew divorce was inevitable. Sid encouraged me to move. It would be a major part of my healing process, he promised.

So I found a new place, an apartment a few blocks south on North Cleveland Avenue. It was an old brownstone. The owner and his wife lived downstairs. They had rented me a one-bedroom apartment on the second floor.

It was late fall 1976. The movers came in the morning. They left to take a final load to the new apartment. I decided to go back through and see if anything might have been left behind. One more walk through, then I would leave this place and, hopefully, the anguish associated with it. I felt as positive as I had felt in a long while.

The last place I checked was the closet of the bedroom Kay and I shared. There was nothing left hanging, and there was nothing on the floor.

Then I looked at the shelf on top.

I saw the white furry hat.

On Christmas Eve 1975, I still hadn't done my shopping for Kay's gifts. I planned to go to Marshall Field around five. I've never been an early Christmas shopper.

But I hadn't got out of the office until after seven, and I hit Marshall Field in a mad rush. I forget what else I bought my wife for Christmas that year except the furry white hat.

She would need such a hat for winter. And it looked like her, somehow. When she opened it and put it on, she looked so pretty, those big eyes and that big smile underneath the furry white hat.

When she first left me, I used to think about her in that hat and curse myself for what I had done and hadn't done that had caused her to leave me. And there I stood. The apartment was empty, except for me and the white furry hat. I picked it up. I looked at it, felt it, and then brought it to my face and smelled it. It smelled like her.

I dropped to the floor and banged my fists against it. I cursed the Fates that had put me on my knees on that floor. When I finally arose, I put the hat back where I had found it. I didn't want to carry it with me, to haunt me further.

But I think I knew at that moment. I think I knew I had to get out of Chicago to save my life.

Or die there from either the cold or the grief or the depression or because of another Gleason column or another night of the Guys with the Mops or another year of Beat the Champs.

* * *

The winter of 1977 was awful, I forget the exact statistics, but there was one siege in January, soon after I had moved into my new apartment, where it didn't get above zero for something like a week. The heat went out in my apartment. My landlord moved me downstairs with him and his wife. I couldn't get to work. The three of us sat there for a week, huddled around the heat vent.

My landlord and his wife were from Philadelphia. One day, he said, "This is crazy living like this. We ought to move to Florida."

I covered the Masters golf tournament in Augusta, Georgia, the first week in April in 1977. I had forgotten springtime in the South, the dogwoods and the azaleas and the girls in halter tops in the gallery on the sixteenth hole at Augusta National.

On Sunday of the final round, I was standing on sixteen. It was a wonderful late-spring southern day.

I had begun to fly a little again by then. The

time off I had to go back home was precious, and I had decided it was foolish to waste half of it riding a train. I learned something about flying, too. If I went to O'Hare two hours before takeoff and drank six double screwdrivers, I wasn't nearly as nervous on a flight. (I had previously been afraid to drink on a flight because of how hard I had prayed it wouldn't crash. I was afraid if I sinned and had a drink, it would make God mad and He would crash the plane. Later, however, I realized if I had asked God what I should do to stop feeling terror on a plane, in all His infinite wisdom He would have said, "Have a couple of drinks.")

I had a 12:15 A.M. flight back to Chicago Monday morning. I had asked about the weather when I called home. They said it was cold, and snow was expected.

On sixteen, I made my final decision. I was going to leave Chicago and come back to Atlanta. I didn't know how long it would take me, or what I would do when I came back, but it didn't matter anymore. Me and Chicago were through.

I went to work Monday around noon. Hoge dropped by and said, "Let's have lunch."

We went to the Wrigley Building restaurant. Hoge had the lamb. I had a cheeseburger.

Hoge told me he wanted me to think about taking over the job of night managing editor when the man who held the job currently retired in a few months. "I see you as a future managing editor," he said to me. "But you need some years getting ready."

I had heard something like this before.

This was familiar. I didn't want to stay in Chicago under any circumstances, much less move from sports. But I felt that tug about not disappointing somebody. Hoge had been great to work for. He wasn't that popular with others. They resented his looks and his glibness, I suppose. They made fun of his clothes. It was the first time I had ever heard the word "preppie." Jim was from a wealthy background. They resented that, too. They had a nickname for him— "Attila the Hoge."

But I respected him immensely. He knew the newspaper business, and he loved it as I did. He supported me in the Banks saga and in every other instance when I needed support.

I didn't commit to Hoge, and I certainly didn't tell him I was going South as soon as possible. But I knew I didn't want to be night managing editor of the Chicago *Sun-Times.* I had tried the news side once and had hated it. Plus, I knew what being night managing editor really in-

volved. It involved coming to work at six in the
evening and crawling out in a blizzard at two in
the morning, and if there was anything wrong
with the paper the next morning, it was my fault.

I went back to the office and sat there and
contemplated my next move. Should I call
Minter in Atlanta and see if there was any possibility the papers might take me back? I was so
desperate to go home, I'd volunteer to be garden editor if nothing else was available.

I believe in God. Here's one of the reasons
why:

"Lewis," said Harold Newchurch, who answered the phones, "line two."

Another miracle.

It was James G. Minter, Jr., in Atlanta. Was
this spooky or what?

"It took you a long time to find a new columnist, didn't it?" he asked me.

"I interviewed every suhbitch in the country,"
I said.

"I'm looking for a number-two sports columnist behind Outlar. Anybody impress you I could
afford?"

They didn't pay well at the *Sun-Times.* The
Atlanta scale was below that.

It hit me. Just like that, it hit me.

"I think I know a guy," I said.

"Who?" Minter asked.

"Me," I said.

"You?"

"Jim, I gotta get my ass out of here. They want me to be night editor, Kay isn't coming back, the weather is killing me, and I've got to get out of here."

I was begging now.

"But you've never written a column," Minter said.

"I know that," I answered him. "But I've read practically everybody in the country now, and I might not be as good as the best, but I think I've got enough sense to know at least what to write about. I could improve."

"I couldn't pay you anything," Minter said.

"That's not the point," I said.

"You serious?"

"Dead."

"Write me three columns and send them to me."

I worked all night. I wrote one column about a college football player in California who was dying of cancer. I wrote what I thought was a funny piece about athletes' overuse of the phrase, "You know." I wrote one about a sports bar in Chicago that turned away a seven-foot basketball player with the Bulls because he didn't have an ID. "Didn't have nothin' to do with the fact he was black," the bar owner had been quoted as saying.

I mailed the three columns to Minter in Atlanta.

Three days later, he called me back. It had seemed like three years.

As I have said before, he was a man of few words. The same man who had sat down beside me that day in the press box at Georgia's Foley Field in 1968 and had asked, "Want to come to work for us?" said perhaps the most beautiful words I've ever heard.

I picked up the phone and said, "Hello." He didn't say, "This is Jim in Atlanta." All he said was, "I believe you can write. I can pay you twenty-two-thousand dollars a year."

I was making thirty-four thousand dollars at the *Sun-Times.*

Exactly twelve days later, April 21, 1977, I boarded a Delta flight to Atlanta. I had got Hudspeth to get me an apartment back at Mi Casa. I had told Hoge, "I just can't live in this place anymore."

I had said good-bye to my staff. I'd said, "Some of you, it has been a pleasure to work with. Others of you, it has not been. And one of you has been an incredible pain in the ass."

With that, Lacey J. Banks got out of his chair, walked over to me, and stuck out his hand. I shook it.

I would never have anything to do with the production of a newspaper section again, I would never manage again. A decade after Wade Saye had taught me layout and after all those mornings and late nights in composing rooms, after all that editing, sweating over graphics, waiting anxiously for a new edition to arrive, that part of my career was over.

I would never strip another wire. I would never put my hands on another tear rule or glue pot. I would never write another headline or cutline.

Hoge offered to let me stay on as a writing sports editor. But I declined. Nothing could have made me stay. I had never even applied for an Illinois driver's license, and my watch remained on Eastern time during my entire Chicago experience.

My first column as the number-two sports columnist for the *Atlanta Constitution* appeared on the front sports page, Monday morning, April 22, 1977.

I had already mailed it to Minter from Chicago. It was about the years in Chicago. It went on about how happy I was to get home. I wrote, "From now on, if it doesn't have a red clay motif,

I'm not interested." I ended it with the conversation I had with a Delta Airlines reservations agent when I called to get my ticket home.

"Will this be round-trip or one-way?" she had asked.

I had allowed a delicious pause, and then I said, "One-way."

Epilogue

My Mother died in October 1989.

Glenn Vaughn has retired as publisher of the Columbus, Georgia, newspapers. He tells me he has lost thirty pounds and has quit smoking.

The *Athens Daily News* lives on.

Gerald Rutberg is a successful attorney in Orlando.

Chuck Perry is editor of Longstreet Press, an Atlanta book publisher. He remarried. He and his lovely wife have a baby girl.

Paula has two boys by her second marriage.

My divorce from Kay was final in the fall of 1977. She is still in Chicago and is a member of a band. She has never remarried.

Tim Jarvis divorced and moved to Atlanta a year after I moved back.

Jim Hoge is publisher of the New York *Daily News.* At this writing, he is in a fight with one of the last powerful newspaper unions to keep it alive.

Lacey J. Banks is still a member of the Chicago *Sun-Times* sports staff.

Jim Minter became editor of both the *Atlanta Journal* and the *Atlanta Constitution.* He was kicked upstairs as senior editor when the papers hired Bill Kovach of *The New York Times.* Minter took retirement and bought a suburban Atlanta daily.

Kovach lasted two years. He was replaced by Ron Martin of *USA Today.* The paper's circulation has been growing rapidly under Martin.

The *Journal* and *Constitution* sports departments have been combined. The section regularly wins the award for Best Sports Section among major dailies.

Bisher is still at it. Minter and I often say to each other, "Bisher was right a lot more times than he was wrong."

Frank Hyland still works in the sports department. He just turned fifty.

Norman Arey is currently co-writing a gossip column for the Atlanta papers. He writes a lot better now.

Ron Hudspeth is single after three divorces. He left the newspapers and publishes *The Hudspeth Report,* which is all about Atlanta nightlife.

Harrison's closed. The clientele got too old.

I wrote a sports column for the *Constitution* for eight months. Then I began writing a humor column for the news side. This is my thirteenth year.

I married for the third time in 1980. It lasted three years. My third wife wrote a book about me titled "How to Tame a Wild Bore." She remarried and moved to Montana.

I live in a house in Atlanta with two Black Labs—Catfish and Cornbread.

This is my thirteenth book.

I'm forty-four.

ABOUT THE AUTHOR

LEWIS GRIZZARD returned to Atlanta in 1977 to write a sports column for *The Atlanta Constitution*, and it attracted a great deal of attention. Even people who didn't normally read the sports pages found themselves looking for it to see what everyone was talking about.

But after about a year, sports could not contain his interest. He realized that there were only so many questions you could ask a six-foot-five, 250-pound naked man in a locker room—that he could answer.

So Grizzard began writing about what went on in the stands, what happened to him on the way to the game, or what Atlantans did instead of going to the game.

His editors wanted to confine him to sports, but they couldn't deny the way the city had taken to the new columnist. His column was regular fodder for discussion on television and radio programs, and readers responded with truckloads of mail. Grizzard understood how to *connect* with readers.

The column was moved from the Sports section to the City/State page, and he was turned loose. He wrote about any- and everything— even sports.

Readers loved the way he spoke his mind. Instead of apologizing for the South, he stood up for it. He poked fun at overpaid athletes and pompous politicians, regardless of their skin color. And then, he'd bring a lump in the throat with a touching eulogy for a friend, or a nostalgic longing for the vanishing small-town life of his youth.

Syndicates came calling, wanting to spread the Grizzard column across the country. Twelve years and 450 newspapers later, he has established himself as one of the most distinctive and popular newspaper columnists in the history of the genre.